Mary McFerren
1347 Lafayette
Denver, Colo.

D1592978

THE TECHNIQUE
of the
FILM CUTTING ROOM

THE LIBRARY
OF COMMUNICATION TECHNIQUES

THE TECHNIQUE OF THE

FILM CUTTING
ROOM

by

ERNEST WALTER

FOCAL PRESS
London and New York

© FOCAL PRESS LIMITED 1969

SBN 240 50657 X

*All Rights Reserved. No part of this publication may be reproduced,
stored in a retrieval system, or transmitted, in any form or by any
means, electronic, mechanical, photocopying, recording or otherwise,
without the prior permission of the Copyright owner.*

*Printed and bound in Great Britain by
W. & J. Mackay & Co Ltd, Chatham*

CONTENTS

INTRODUCTION

THE role of the film editor is a mystery to most people who are not directly involved in film production. Indeed, it is seldom fully understood by those other film production departments who *are* directly involved. They often think that the editor puts his scissors through the film just as the director shouts "cut!" at the end of a shot and there are some who think that a film is photographed in short pieces, just as it appears in the final print. All this, of course, is very untrue.

Film editing, in modern film production, is usually quite a complicated affair. Although following original basic principles, cutting room techniques have changed during recent years with the advent of more complex camera systems and sophisticated methods of sound reproduction. We, who have been involved in film editing for a long period of time, have grown up with change and have adjusted gradually to the new mechanics. Yet, strangely enough, some of the most modern techniques are merely variations of old systems, using up-to-date materials. The young person now entering the film-editing field is involved with both old and new methods perhaps without realizing it.

The work performed by the film editor and his assistants is basically divided into two functions, the *artistic* assembly of film and the *physical* problems of handling it. One is impossible without the other.

Artistic film assembly is a matter of relating the editor's talent to the quality and variety of coverage provided by the film director. The amount of film coverage is obviously of the utmost importance. It has been said that the film editor is as good as the material at his disposal. This is often true, although an experienced editor can sometimes create minor miracles from somewhat indifferent film material.

Physical film handling problems vary considerably. A 20-second television commercial, for example, may often present as many problems in film cutting, as will a half-hour or hour filmed television series. Imagine then, an editor dealing with a multi-million dollar feature production,—the very *bulk* of the film to be handled is formidable. Unless there is some system of routine and control in the feature film cutting room there will only be chaos and frustration. The editor will be constantly chasing pieces of film which he may never find.

In such circumstances, he must be freed from problems of film sorting and filing—the physical role—in order to concentrate on his main function—the artistic role.

In this book, we examine cutting room routines and techniques necessary to allow the film editor to concentrate on this artistic and very rewarding task. Editorial equipment is examined in detail. Although basically the same over many years, some changes have been brought about to cope with new photographic and sound reproducing systems. Large screen images and multiple channel release prints are now the rule rather than the exception.

Here you will not necessarily learn how to put the film together in the artistic sense. But you can see the essential background tasks performed by the assistant editors. Such tasks ensure that the daily screening of new film is properly organized and that film is prepared without delay for assembly by the editor.

The young film student, the newly appointed assistant editor and the film editor himself, may be surprised at the extent of involvement the editorial department has with making a film.

Assembly of film does not only concern picture elements. Sound effects, music and dialogue tracks are other most vital components. Therefore the roles of sound effects, music and dialogue editors are also examined.

Since the editor is very much concerned with the mechanics of certain special photographic effects and trick work these processes are also followed and related to the editing department.

The emphasis is essentially on the major feature film cutting room, where many weeks of shooting are followed by more weeks, maybe months of post-production work. A course is traced from the first day of shooting, through to the initial assembly of film. It then passes on to the post-production period of music recording, sound effects shooting, and track building, right through to final sound mixing and the release print. The very necessary routines which are called for at each stage are thoroughly covered. Students and assistants can see here how important and how very necessary are the daily routines of the cutting room, whatever the nature of the production.

Those of us who have been doing this work for many years are

14

well aware that we learn something new each day. There is always a problem which has never been faced before. Established routines and procedure enable these problems to be dealt with more confidently, more readily.

When I was persuaded into a film editing career more than twenty-five years ago, the person responsible for my introduction to this aspect of the industry did so with some reluctance since he felt at that time that the future of film technicians could in no way be guaranteed. Today, perhaps, I am in the same position as he was then—encouraging young people to enter this field of the film industry.

I have no hesitation in doing so. To them I say—Be persuaded. Be involved. It is one of the most satisfying and rewarding tasks; with an exciting future.

I am indebted to Metro-Goldwyn-Mayer British Studios Ltd and Technicolor Ltd for permission to reproduce their documents.

1

THE INDUSTRY AND THE EDITOR

THROUGHOUT the history of the motion picture industry, the quality of its products has steadily improved. Today's polished and near-perfect results bear hardly any comparison to the grainy, soot-and-whitewash image of yesteryear. Screen proportions have changed. Film is available in many different gauges ranging from 8 mm to 65 and 70 mm. And the introduction of the anamorphic lens has led to the projection of enormous screen images, using modern negative emulsions which are of very high quality.

Those early and primitive efforts did not have the added complication of a sound track and the early film-maker often did everything himself—photography, chemical processing, editing, titling, even to the extent of eventually becoming the projectionist.

Perhaps the greatest change in those times was the introduction of synchronized sound and picture, although the sound was obviously crude, and maintaining synchronization was very hopeful and approximate. Artists who had been important names in the days of the silent film now found it impossible to carry on in the new medium and a different breed of actors and actresses took their place. The technicians, too, were pioneering a new field and each year brought further advancements with their attendant complications.

The excellent productions we see, result from the technical achievements of a vast number of people, artists and technicians alike, who have spent many years in perfecting their methods. Together with the great technical improvement outlined above, multiple sound reproducers which spread the sound throughout the auditorium with great effect have helped quite considerably toward better audience participation.

The techniques necessary to achieve such fine results have, naturally, become more complex.

Production techniques

With the early efforts in professional film-making the motion picture camera was loaded to capacity with film stock, and cranked away on the scene being played until the film in the camera ran out. At this point, the proceedings would be halted for re-loading and then the film would continue as before.

Later developments moved away from this crude style. The effect realized by changing from one camera angle to another when photographing a scene was startling, and the dramatic use of the close-up, revolutionary. The limited film capacity of the camera was no longer important. Scenes were now more dramatically developed by being deliberately broken down into shorter camera "set-ups" by the director and, unlike the stage play with its constant flow of action and dialogue from the same viewing position, this deliberate breaking down of sequences into punctuated camera angles created a new dimension of pictorial interpretation. The *change* of camera angle became very important, as indeed did *maintaining* the camera angle, until any change became most effective. Lines of dialogue often became more startling and dramatic when played "off-screen", i.e.: when the speaker is not on the screen but the listeners' reactions are visible.

Breaking down scenes into shorter sections has given the film director much greater control over artist performance. He is now able to spend a reasonable amount of time in photographing these relatively short sections of film repeatedly until he feels that the best results have been achieved.

Today, with this technique as standard practice, the top class film director not only coaxes the best performance from his artists but also uses his camera to the greatest effect. He can carefully and economically choose the most effective angles for each section of the scene being photographed.

But the director cannot cover a scene by simply starting at the beginning and, every time he wants to move closer to an artist for an important line of dialogue or reaction, stopping the camera, changing the angle and starting again. A scene cannot be built up in the camera. It must be carefully pre-planned so that each camera angle will cover key sections of the scene as visualized by the director in its final form, but without wasteful and expensive overcovering. It would be easy, for example, to photograph each scene in its entirety on every angle—long shot, medium shot, overshoulder shots and individual close shots. Apart from being expensive in time, it would be too much to expect artists to give "peak" performances on each set-up.

Film coverage

The wise director also avoids undercovering a scene, and never attempts to "cut the picture in the camera" that is, to shoot only the amount of film for each scene that he feels will be necessary in final version. It is unfortunate that there are directors who profess to cut in the camera, even today. This ties the hands of the film editor in such a way that, usually, only one version is possible, and perhaps a very bad one at that. The great directors never do this, particularly those who have come to film directing from the school of the cutting room. They know that one of the least expensive commodities related to the total budget in film making is film itself, and that the great thing to aim for is complete flexibility in the assembly of the film material. The great film directors never find it necessary to give the film editor hard and fast instructions on how to assemble a sequence. They know, in their own minds, that they have recorded on film a sufficient amount of material to enable the sequences to be put together as they have visualized them. They are usually very happy to allow the editor to put the film together in his own way without any specific instruction. An editor will often achieve results which are quite superior to the pre-planned patterns of the director.

When the director is aiming for peak performance from the artists involved in each scene, he will also have to know when to accept faults in performance. He must be fully covered on those angles which are more essential to the scene with good material. A mediocre performance on one section of a long shot, for example, may not be worth spending more valuable time in perfecting, since for this part of the action the editor will probably want to use a closer angled shot.

The editor's job

From the many pieces of film, covering or rather more than covering each scene or sequence a selection must be made to give the most smooth and effective result. The most effective result is often a matter of discussion and argument and, the best pattern a question of skilful assembly of the pieces. This is the work of the film editor.

To select and reject, and to smoothly assemble many hundreds of pieces of film into a story sequence of a pictorial image alone would be complicated enough. But the editor must also deal with the accompanying sound track, and this too has several stages of preparation.

Apart from the sequence being "broken down" into individual angles, it is often also shot out of continuity. It is more economical, for example, to shoot consecutively all scenes using the same set. Then the set can be dismantled or otherwise disposed of to conserve space and materials. Likewise any work on exterior locations is more economical if photographed while the film unit is geared to outside work. Again, it may be necessary to concentrate exclusively on work involving an expensive artist so that his or her part may be completed within the contract period.

Clearly, the film editor is often confronted with a huge and complicated jigsaw puzzle. Moreover, the pieces are not all contained in one neat little carton ready for assembly. They are delivered into the hands of the editor over a period of many weeks, depending upon the size of the production, each set of pieces representing a tiny area of the final picture. There is, however, the great advantage with film assembly in that the pieces can be dovetailed together in many different ways. Each variation brings about a subtle change in the appearance and impact of the completed puzzle.

Liaison with production team

The film editor has a close working relationship with all key people in the production team.

During the shooting period there are constant assessments of film quality with editor, producer and director examining the material in detail. When shooting is completed, there is an even closer relationship between these three as the film is shaped into its final form.

The producer is usually the originator of the film in several senses. He may have found the story and prepared a script, perhaps with the assistance of a screenwriter. He supervises the drawing up of a budget, choses the main artists and engages the key technicians, including the editor. He plans the production schedule and keeps a watchful eye on day to day progress, and is always responsible to those providing the financial backing.

The production manager breaks down the script into smaller sections to find which artists, sets or special props are needed for each scene. He estimates the shooting time and produces a schedule detailing everything and everyone needed for each day's work.

20

Also his concern are the hire of technicians (other than key men) labour, equipment, and co-ordinating the screening of daily rushes, shipment of film to distant locations.

He is involved with the editor during the post-production period co-ordinating further sound effect work, music recording and final sound mixing.

The film director is involved at all the early stages and of course is in command of the whole shooting operation. Forming a mental picture of the film in finished form, he must interpret each scene accordingly, breaking them down shot by shot. He plans every move made by the artists and selects the camera angles. Naturally when the film arrives at the editing stage the director's ideas have a considerable bearing on how the editor must cut the film. They therefore work in very close contact when finalizing the film.

The director of photography is responsible for lighting and shooting the film. He captures the mood and atmosphere of the scene on film and decides on the composition for each shot. Naturally the final quality of the photographic image is largely determined by his combination of lighting, exposure, and handling of colour. He and the editor check daily the quality of the print provided by the processing laboratory. If it is colour, the colours may be biased in one direction or another. As sequences are assembled, further colour and density changes might be apparent and it may be necessary to choose a "key" shot, to which all other shots in the scene should be regraded.

The sound engineer with his crew, tries to provide a high quality sound recording following the action of each scene as it takes place, regardless of the conditions under which he must work. He provides either permanent recordings to be used in the final sound versions or temporary ones to be used as a guide at all editing stages until a replacement high quality track can be dubbed onto the film.

The art director who takes care of set designs and plans certain effects may need to make further research in certain areas. Perhaps he will need film from newsreel companies, war museums and film libraries, to assist him. Where additional shots are called for on one of his sets, after main shooting has finished, it may not be necessary to keep a large set standing. By referring to existing film it may be apparent that only a small section of the set need be retained to obtain the required shot. In these later operations he has the assistance of the editor.

The continuity girl who notes actor's positions, prop and other details from scene to scene often needs to refer to the editor's existing film when it becomes necessary to go back on an earlier sequence to make extra shots. The action and positioning of artists must be consistent. Although she may have made very careful notes at the time of the original shooting, such an extra shot may only be successfully cut in at one particular point of the original scene and very careful matching of artist's positions and moves will be essential.

2

FORMS AND USES OF FILM MATERIALS

IN professional film making the picture image and the sound track, although simultaneously and synchronously made, are recorded by separate machines operated by separate crews. The picture camera and the sound recorder (very often both are referred to as "cameras" by their crews) are electronically interlocked when a dialogue or sound scene is to be shot, to ensure that they start up and run together at synchronized speed when the order to start shooting is given. But, since they are each recording something of a totally different nature, the film stock used by each is also different.

Film gauges: lengths and times

The most commonly used film gauges in professional motion picture production are 16 mm and 35 mm, and for the large productions needing an enormous projected image the 65 mm gauge. Although there are proportional differences between the perforation size and spacing on films of different gauges the principles of using one particular gauge will apply equally to the others.

To the editor, who has to work with film to the exactness of one frame, the precise length of a piece of film is of great importance. He must have a firm idea of how much film shows for how long and to what effect.

The editor frequently needs to make use of precise timings, and footages, so it is important for him to know the exact length/time relationships of the particular film he is handling. In the case of 35 mm film, there are 16 picture frames per foot of film. At standard filming speed, $1\frac{1}{2}$ ft. of film represents 1 sec. of time. So 24 picture frames equal 1 sec. of screen time. The standard filming speed of 24 frames per second indicates a consumption rate of

90 ft. per min. Constant references are made in the cutting room to perforations (each frame is within the area of four perforations on 35 mm) and to the standard sound track speed of 24 f.p.s. (frames per second).

Picture negative

The material used in the film camera is a photographic negative film of very high quality which, after development, produces an image in negative form. Monochrome stock is manufactured in a range of emulsion speeds. Colour film, however, offers only a limited choice. Different types of emulsion coating are available for trick work and special effects photography.

After development the camera negative is printed in contact with a positive film giving a positive image working print suitable for projection and editing. As the original negative forms the basis for all further copies, and damage to it would be irreparable, it is handled as little as possible after the first working print has been produced. The negative is stored at the film processing laboratory under conditions of controlled temperature.

Picture positive

This is available in the same sizes as the negative stock (with the exception of 65 mm negative, which is printed on to 70 mm positive to accommodate magnetic sound tracks), in monochrome and colour. But the emulsion coating is designed to print a positive image, usually from a negative. This positive film is a more robust

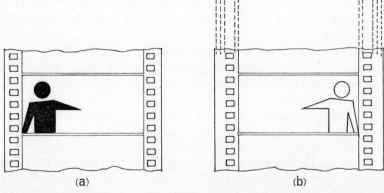

(a)   (b)

Film materials. (a) 65 mm negative is printed on to positive 70 mm film (b) to allow for the six sound tracks which will be eventually coated on to the print. (See page 231).

24

film than the negative and can withstand the wear and tear of cutting room equipment and projectors.

The film editor, in most cases, works with the positive print and, although he and his crew will always handle these prints with respect and care, in the event of accidental damage a replacement print, or "reprint", can always be made from the original negative.

Production which involves speed of operation if the final result is to be of any use (as in the case of newsreel work, and television presentation of current events) may well call for the immediate selection and editing of the original negative as time cannot be spared for the printing and development of positive work prints. This calls for a slightly different technique and skill on the part of the editorial staff, and certainly requires the very careful handling of film.

Sound materials

Sound recordings which find their way into the cutting room can either be the *magnetic* type or the *photographic* type of recording film stock.

Magnetic film is normally used in the earlier stages of major film production and not until the latter stages when distribution prints are being made is the photographic sound process brought in. Magnetic sound recording is an instantaneous operation.

Photographic sound is optically produced on to negative sound film and requires the process of development and positive printing common to all neg/pos photographic methods.

Each method requires its own recording machine and its very different recording system.

Unlike the picture film, magnetic sound recording tape does not necessarily depend upon a sprocket drive for transport through the machine. It might well be a very high quality recording apparatus using conventional recording tape. Particularly when a film unit is on a distant and difficult exterior location, such a machine will be easy to carry and independent of a main electricity supply. Spools of tape are light in weight and give a long recording time. But the machine can be synchronized with the picture camera.

Where weight and portability are less important, however, particularly when working in the film studio, a machine with a sprocketed driving mechanism will be used. The recording mechanism is 35 mm (or 16 mm) magnetic coated film perforated in exactly the same way as the picture negative. Synchronizing picture camera and sound recorder is then simple and more positive.

Whichever type of magnetic recording stock is being used, no processing is involved and they are all capable of being played back immediately. Thus, the sound recordist has a certain advantage over his colleague who operates the motion picture camera. As with the master picture negative, the sound recorder produces a "master" sound track which is used to produce a transfer working "print" for use by the editor. It is always carefully kept so that further repeat transfer "prints" can be made as required. Since the editor is working with picture and sound on separate pieces of film while assembling his working print, the sound "print" on magnetic film is made on to perforated film stock, whether or not the original master recording was made on unperforated tape.

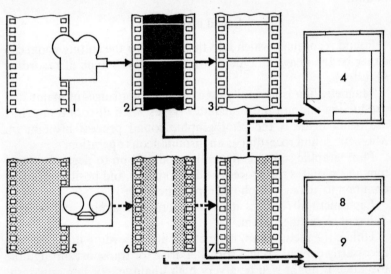

Original shooting, sequence of operations. (1) Exposed picture negative. (2) Developed negative. (3) Positive print, delivered to (4) Cutting room. (5) Magnetic master sound recording, producing an "a" and "b" side master (6). Transcribed on to (7) editor's cutting transfer. (8) Picture negative vault. (9) Sound master storage vault.

To summarize, the production unit produces an original master picture negative, an original master sound recording. From each of these, working prints are made to be used by the editor for cutting the various sequences. Both picture negative and sound master are always carefully stored away in another building and away from the danger of fire and water.

Magnetic sound film

Various forms and sizes of magnetic sound film, both perforated and non-perforated, are in current use in film production. All forms, however, consist of an oxidized emulsion coated on to a cellulose acetate, polyester or P.V.C. base, the emulsion being sensitized to accept the transmitted impulses of sound through a recording head which is in contact with the emulsion as it travels through the recording machine. Apart from being capable of immediate play-back, it can be demagnetized when the recordings carried on it are no longer required, and then used again. This great benefit can also be a great danger. The recordings on magnetic stock must not be "wiped" off accidentally.

In its unperforated form the $\frac{1}{4}$ in. wide tape is familiar to all users of domestic tape recorders. Some professional machines use it also, particularly those mentioned earlier, designed for portability but making recordings synchronized with the camera.

This tape is, however, also made in greater widths for machines that can record multiple stereophonic tracks, such as three track and six track.

If the tape recorder is used for original production recordings, however, the editor is invariably provided with the standard per-forated sound magnetic film when his working transfer "prints" are made.

In its 35 mm *perforated* form, magnetic sound film is almost universally applied to all forms of production. It is used during the initial shooting period, throughout the editing phase and for both music and sound effects recordings until the final master sound track is prepared.

There are several types of perforated magnetic stock and it is well for editing crews to know the most common ones and why there are such variations.

35 mm magnetic full coat

Here the perforated film is coated with oxidized emulsion across its full width. The width of the film area in contact with the standard magnetic sound recording head (and also the reproducing head) is about $\frac{1}{4}$ in., and the recording is positioned on the film just clear of one of the perforated sides. A master recording does not need to be physically cut and when the end of the roll is reached, it is simply turned over and re-positioned in the "feed" section of the

27

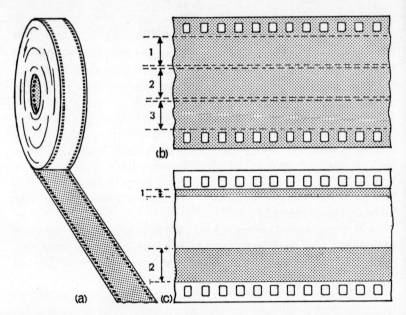

Fully coated magnetic sound track and single track stripe compared. (a) 35 mm magnetic full coat. (b) Positions of right, centre and left tracks on triple recordings. (c) Single stripe magnetic sound film with (I) the balance stripe and (2) the recording stripe.

recorder. Another series of recordings can then be made down the opposite edge of the same film, doubling the capacity. These rolls would be referred to as "A" and "B" recordings and any required transfer prints could be located within the roll accordingly. For the same purpose of economy, but only in certain parts of the film producing world, 35 mm full coat magnetic film is sliced down the centre of the roll to produce two separate rolls, each 17·5 mm wide. American sound editors, in particular, use this film when they are compiling reels of sound effects but it does mean that, not only their editing equipment, but also the projection and sound recording equipment, has to be adapted to take this particular size film.

The same 35 mm full coat film is used where stereo or multiple track recordings are required. This film is wide enough to accommodate three standard magnetic sound heads side by side, simultaneously transmitting their various signals on to the film.

35 mm magnetic striped film

Where multiple recordings are not contemplated, or "A" and "B" recordings will not be needed, the 35 mm film need not be

28

coated across its full width. The single standard magnetic sound head only occupies a small portion of the width of the film. This film is more suitable for the editor's cutting print transfer since it is more economic to manufacture.

The stripe (the oxidized emulsion coating) is just a little wider than the standard sound head in the normal recording position. Although the coating on sound film is extremely thin, even this is enough to prevent perfect level contact with the front surface of the recording head. If the coating is at even the slightest inclination to the head, the quality of sound recording will suffer. So to maintain level and even contact with the recording head all the time, a very narrow "balancing stripe" is coated on to the opposite edge of the film. This passes over a levelling plate in the recording machine.

Photographic (optical) sound film

This, nowadays, is only used at a later stage in the production, never for original recordings. But the editorial staff will eventually have to meet this kind of material and understand it.

The sound is photo-recorded on to sound negative film, in a pattern of varying area from a light which fluctuates by the action of an oscillating mirror that reflects the light beam through a narrow slit. The mirror oscillation is governed by the changes in value of the sound impulses. The film negative requires photographic development before the necessary positive print can be made. It is used in normal circumstances as the means of provid-

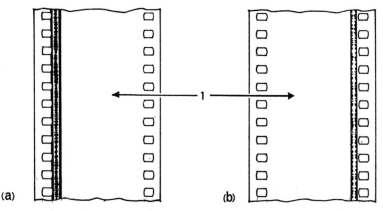

Sections of 35 mm photographic (optical) sound film. (a) Positive print. (b) Negative, both viewed from the emulsion side (I).

29

ing the final combined sound and picture distribution prints in conjunction with the picture negative. For feature film work, photographic sound negative stock is 35 mm gauge with standard perforations, although the area of the sound track itself takes the form of a very narrow band.

Advantages of magnetic film

The transition from exclusive use of photographic sound film during the making of a film to the more recent adoption of various types of magnetic tape caused some initial problems in the film cutting room. Editors and assistants for many years had been able to observe, visually, the fluctuations of the optically produced sound. And, after long experience they could actually "see" the shapes of words being formed in the peaks and valleys of the sound impulses. They were then faced with a new kind of sound track which was completely invisible. Before, cuts were made clear of the ends of words by holding the film up to the light and putting the scissors through after the peaks of the sound modulation had finished. This was impossible with magnetic track so a new means of searching for this clear area had now to be found. Equipment was developed to deal with this problem but, for a long time, most people still felt as though they were working in the dark and longed to be able to "see" those sounds. But the new material offered so many advantages and compensations, most of all in speed of preparation and quality of sound, that they soon learned to handle it with confidence. Gone were the days when assistants had the dreary chore of going through roll after roll of visible photographic sound track, carefully blacking out any spot or blemish and painstakingly filling the clear line which sometimes appeared alongside the most carefully made splice. If left untreated, this would sound like a pistol shot when coming through the reproducing machines. Waiting overnight for the film laboratory to provide a replacement print from a sound negative is now, happily, a thing of the past. Just how important this factor is will be seen later when the stage of final sound recording is reached.

There are dangers and pitfalls with magnetic film: the danger of accidental degaussing (wiping the signal off) has already been discussed. But provided that elementary precautions are taken and equipment frequently checked to ensure that no unwanted magnetism is present, it is a much easier and more pleasant system to work with.

Film processing laboratory

All photographic film, be it for the reproduction of picture or sound is sent to the film processing laboratory day by day during the period of actual shooting from wherever the unit is located. The editor's work is also very much involved with the laboratory.

The choice of film laboratory depends on many circumstances. In feature film production in the United States of America, it may well be that the producing company have their own processing plant, sometimes situated within the confines of the studio itself. In other cases, there may be a financial link between the producing company and film processing corporation, which predetermines the use of one specific film laboratory on a particular production. All films being produced by one company may be processed and release printed by one film laboratory.

The choice of laboratory having been made, and the decision taken to photograph the subject in monochrome or colour, there must be some individual contact between the laboratory on the one hand, and the cameraman and film editor on the other. The cameraman is constantly concerned that he is correctly exposing the negative, and also equally concerned that the technicians at the laboratory are interpreting his visual ideas with their style of printing and, certainly in the early days of an unusual and difficult project, he will want to maintain a very close liaison with the laboratory.

As all orders and instructions for the future handling of film will almost certainly come from the editing department, perhaps the most important liaison to establish is that between the laboratory and the film editor. This association, and the aim to achieve the best possible final result, continues between these departments until the production is completely finished and prints for exhibition are being manufactured as routine.

Laboratory liaison

With any laboratory, many productions are handled concurrently—all wanting their priorities, and all demanding special attention and treatment. Someone in the processing plant is needed to deal with this situation. In order to keep matters reasonably sane, and to give the very personal attention which each production must have, it is established practice that the film laboratory appoint a person who is responsible for looking after the particular requirements of one production. Although there are film graders and printers, developers, negative assemblers, and many other technicians handling the film material down in the bowels of the processing plant (very often throughout the night) the direct contact between the film producing unit and the sometimes distant film laboratory is this one important man. He is called the laboratory production superintendent. Otherwise known as the "lab. contact man", he shepherds a film through its early stages and with the cameraman, ensures that the "mood" of the photography is being correctly interpreted by negative development and correctly graded positive printing. He provides the editor with the fastest possible service in all his requirements during the shooting period. He must also gear his skilled staff, when the time comes for special optical trick work such as dissolves and fades, so that all is ready for the final sorting and cutting of negative when the completion stages are reached.

It is most likely that this man has been previously employed at all levels in the processing plant and is familiar with the key processes involved. He may not have specialized in such work as optical shots and special photographic effects, but must be sufficiently well informed about them. His experience, no doubt, covers handling negative for printing, grading the negative for correct density and colour and supervising film development.

He supervises the production on behalf of the laboratory from the time that shooting starts until the time comes for the screening of the very first combined sound and picture print—the *answer print*.

Each evening, after the completion of shooting, the camera assistant who is responsible for the unloading and shipment of film prepares all the day's undeveloped negative film by wrapping the various rolls and packing them into tins. With each tin he includes the *picture negative report* giving details of the footages of the various shots contained in that roll. He also indicates very clearly the "take" numbers which are to be positive printed in accordance with the requirements of the film director. The reports indicate the type of film emulsion being used, as a guide to negative development. Also any special features of the photography which may call for unusual treatment at the laboratory and where the positive prints, when made, are to be delivered.

Processing

The undeveloped film is delivered to the film laboratory, usually collected at regular times by their despatch service, and the pro-

32

cedures of developing the negative, cleaning it, breaking it down so that only the required "takes" are printed, goes on throughout the night. By early morning, the necessary printed material is ready for the first check screening in the laboratory projection room, and is seen by the "contact" man.

The "grading" of positive prints, both for density of the subject, and colour value where colour stock is being used, is carried out by the grading technician who has assessed the quality of the negative before it is passed on to the printing machine. By his experience, and knowing the progressive lighting range of the printing machine at his disposal, he marks down on his report the strength of printing light and combination of colour filters which, in his opinion, will give a correctly balanced print. This is not entirely a matter of guesswork, based on experience. Tests usually have to be made first from a few frames of negative from the end of each take. Several of these short sections are printed at varying intensities of printer light and combinations of colour filters, so that the grading technician can make a visual choice when he sees these. Even so, aims differ, and although he may have done the initial grading with great care, it may not be exactly what the director of photography had in mind. He may ask for minor adjustments when he eventually sees the prints, particularly early in the production before the "mood" has been set and before everyone understands the objectives.

Checking the positive print

At the beginning of each day, the production superintendent screens the results of the night's work at the laboratory. From this (and a phone call from the cameraman if an unusual or difficult scene has been shot) he knows what type of work to expect and he can make his judgment accordingly. If satisfied that the prints are reasonably closely following the cameraman's requirements, he has them sent immediately to the editor of the production. If, on the other hand, he is not satisfied with the quality of print density or colour balance he sends the negative back to the printing room and has new prints made incorporating his suggested adjustments. If this is done he informs the editor of the production concerned, giving reason for the delay and the approximate time of the availability of the new print. It is most likely that such reprinting would happen near the beginning of a production. After a few days when everyone is geared to their task, it is the exception rather than the rule.

When this situation arises, the contact man gives the earliest possible report on the condition of the negative, regardless of whether he intends to make positive reprints. This is particularly important if the artists are about to finish or the sets be taken down.

Once the prints have been checked and approved at the laboratory these go without delay to the editor. The negative, which remains at the laboratory must be filed very systematically and clearly so that any section can be located at very short notice. Eventually it will all be brought out and sorted into sequence, ready to be cut together in exactly the same way as the editor has cut the working prints.

The film laboratory will probably be involved in much other work during the course of the production, apart from simply processing the original picture negative photographed in the motion picture camera and making prints. Special departments within their organization will deal with special trick effects, all requiring specific film emulsions and specialized camera work which is carried out in the laboratory.

Throughout the course of events and until the final product has been approved, the laboratory production superintendent watches with great care all the processes involved to ensure that the best possible results are achieved.

3

THE FILM CUTTING ROOM

THE cutting room is the editor's workshop. All handling, editing, filming and storage of the positive film in production takes place here. The actual size of the room or rooms in use and the number of staff required to handle a film are largely determined by the size of the production itself. Adequate cutting room facilities must be provided so that all material can be sensibly tabulated and not allowed to accumulate in an atmosphere of confusion.

Whatever the size and nature of the film to be handled, however, there must be a few basic items of furnishing and apparatus to enable the editor and staff to work with a minimum of delay. Time is the most expensive commodity in film making and each day added to the production schedule, for whatever reason, adds greatly to the overall cost. The production unit is expected to work efficiently and speedily and, although not necessarily under the same sort of pressure, the editorial unit must also work with the same efficiency.

Basic requirements

Several simple mechanical actions form the basis of film handling in the cutting room, however unelaborate it may be. For these tasks, the cutting room is fitted out with certain items of equipment—the everyday tools of the editor.

The most practical way of handling any material of great length is by winding from one spool on to another. At all stages of editing the film must be wound back and forth many times during the day. Benches are therefore equipped with a winding and re-winding mechanism.

Even the simplest film sequence requires the handling of separate picture and sound film rolls. As they must be synchronized with each other, side by side, there must be some means of maintaining synchronization of both rolls of film as they are wound. For this, there is a film synchronizer.

The editor has to examine all the film in his room, viewing and re-viewing, as he decides the pictorial shape of each sequence. He must have some means of quickly and easily doing this without the complications of intricate film-threading. So there is a viewing machine.

The editor, working on his first assemblies examines the film, and selecting or rejecting various pieces of film, he gradually builds up the sequence. Therefore, apart from having some means of physically cutting through the film, he needs bins or containers fitted with racks and pegs, or pins on which to hang the separate pieces of film. The sound track too requires editing. As most sound tracks are recorded invisibly on magnetic film, he requires some means of listening to the sounds and "searching" for individual words.

Film which has been cut into sections must be joined together and some means of fast and accurate splicing is necessary. Unused sections of film, and film as yet uncut, is stored and filed with some easy reference for locating the pieces. Labelled film tins or boxes, storage shelves and film racks are required for this.

The large amount of paperwork which accumulates; negative reports, sound reports, laboratory reports, continuity reports, and so on, will rapidly get out of hand unless a system, with clips and hooks mounted in strategic positions in the room is instituted.

The whole organization of the room and equipment needs to be one of calm order if the general air of efficiency is to be maintained as large masses of film begin to accumulate.

Cutting room design

It is doubtful if the ideal cutting room has yet been designed although most editors with years of work in completely unsuitable rooms have very firm ideas on how it should be laid out. Unfortunately, particularly in the older studios, the cutting room dates back to the days when the product and techniques were less complicated and equipment less sophisticated. Space is limited and no matter how good the intentions of the editorial staff, the efficient handling of film is quite difficult.

Where new rooms and buildings have been erected, editorial requirements are not always fully understood and many rooms have been constructed with very little thought of the type of work which will be performed in them. It is not necessarily a question of

36

size and shape alone. Those editors lucky enough to see the morning or afternoon sun are very grateful for some means of blacking it out when they are working on dimly lit night sequences, but very often the humble blind has been omitted at the time of construction. At the same time, good lights, strategically placed in and around the benches, are essential for film examination. Too large a room can be a nuisance unless, for example, everyone is to have their own telephone at their side. It also encourages producing companies to crowd several editors into the same area, all listening to each other's sound tracks and tripping over each other's film. Too small a room can be equally uncomfortable. The ideal room has sufficient space for the editor to sit with his viewing machine alongside his bench and with film racks on which to arrange the film that he is currently examining. He makes constant reference to the script and continuity reports so he also needs a small table set at a comfortable height. As he receives telephone calls throughout the day the phone should be within easy reach.

There should be at least one other cutting bench, and possibly a further viewing machine, so that the senior assistant can deal with film as it is received each day and also take some of the routine chores away from the editor, when necessary.

Assuming the film production to be one of reasonable size, there

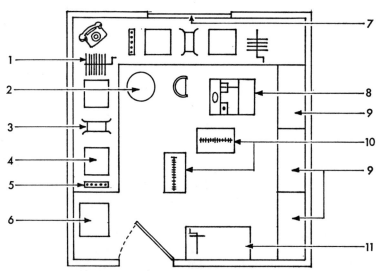

Typical film cutting room layout. (1) 4-spool winder. (2) Film bin. (3) Synchronizer. (4) Bench cut-outs with suspended cotton bags. (5) Film horse. (6) Film waste bin. (7) Window. (8) Viewing machine. (9) Storage shelves. (10) Trims bin. (11) Rewind table.

will be another, perhaps more simple bench, so that a junior assistant can rewind film, sort rolls for cutting and filing, and deal with the daily routine procedures of documentation, splicing and film coding. Film coding should ideally be performed in a separate room. But it may be necessary to have space for a coding machine in the same room. Film coding, the methods and machines, and the reason for it will be discussed later (pages 99–103).

There should be adequate space around the walls of the cutting room for cupboards and storage shelves, where unused film, trims (pieces of film removed from shots that have been used) and unused takes, can be placed in tins, labelled for quick reference and be within easy reach.

Bins with racks and pegs should be of reasonable capacity so that a considerable quantity of film can be hung up in lengths, peg by peg, before they become overfull and film scratched as a result.

Wax pencils in white and varying colours, paper clips, note books, rubber bands, labels and rolls of tape are among the more humble items which are required.

Dust free conditions

All floor and bench surfaces should be made of a material which is neither rough nor dirt-accumulating. Film being wound across the surface of a bench is bound to come into contact with it occasionally and the smoother and cleaner it is the better. The film is certain to meet the floor, too, once in a while. No matter how careful you are when handling large quantities, there are occasions when it seems to come alive and fly out of your grasp. Sometimes bins become overfull and spill their contents on to the floor. So a smooth clean floor will cause less damage. Static electricity builds up surprisingly in film when it is being wound and handled, and can attract dust wherever it may be. It gathers in the layers of a film roll and the abrasive action can cause much damage, especially when the film is new and soft.

General cleanliness and careful treatment of the film by all who work with it is essential at all times, even though only positive working prints are likely to be handled. As more and more work is done, sequences built and re-built, changed and cut again, physical damage done to the film will cause much distress when viewings take place in the projection room. It is extremely difficult to judge quality and effect of scenes when there is such evidence of careless handling and brutal scratching.

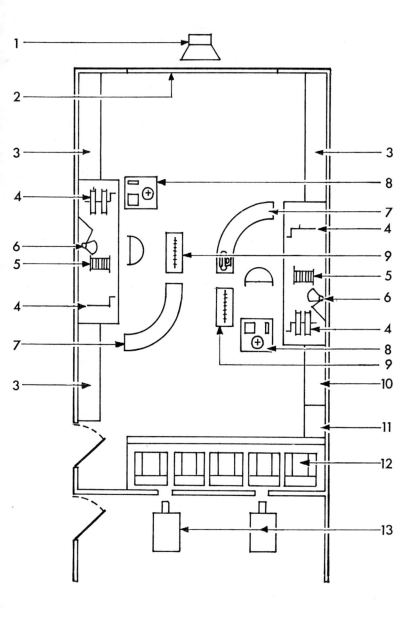

Layout for cutting/projection room. (1) Sound speaker. (2) Screen. (3) Storage shelves. (4) Winders. (5) Synchronizer. (6) Bench light. (7) Table with shelves. (8) Viewing machine. (9) Trims bin. (10) Cupboard. (11) Waste bin. (12) Viewing chairs. (13) Forward/reverse "cold light" projectors. Items duplicated for editor and assistant.

Perhaps the perfect cutting room is one which many of us will never see, but there are those who have been lucky enough to find it. The space is quite adequate for three people, all with excellent benches and each with room for a viewing machine and film bins. Walls are surrounded by shelves, racks and cupboard space. Swivel chairs are mounted on rollers and benches of the correct height, so that you do not have to sit at the viewing machine and then stand up at the bench; it is only a simple matter of shunting back and forth on the chair between the two. The editor and assistants each have a table, curved at their side and to the rear, with shelves and drawers for script, reports, pencils and notes. But the most attractive aspect of all is that the cutting room is also the projection room. A screen at one end and a small booth installed at the other, with "cold-light" (page 39) projection machines capable of forward and reverse running available at all times to the editorial crew. Obviously such facilities could not be expected on any but the large scale and costly feature films. But its time saving and efficiency of operation in the post-production period of such a film can be enormous.

The cutting room should, if possible not be too distant from the projection room. And, when within the studio it should not be too far from shooting stages where the film unit is working.

Film viewing machines

The purpose of an editing (or viewing) machine is to enable the film editor to view sections of the film he is working on at the correct speed and if he wishes, in combination with a sound track.

The machine does not do the job of editing for him. It is merely a tool. Editing machines project the film image on to a small screen, and play back the sound recorded on a separate strip of film. These strips of film may be any length, and unlike a projector, they do not need to be long enough to thread up on to spools. Thus the short lengths that an editor deals with much of the time can be easily viewed and run forward and reversed as many times as he likes with or without the accompanying sound track.

Several makes of machine are manufactured and editors usually have a preference for the machine with which they are most familiar. This does not mean that it is necessarily better than other types available. But it is easier to use a piece of equipment which is familiar. It requires an effort to force oneself to try something new after many years and, in any case, the opportunity does not often arise. New equipment of this type appears on the market rather rarely. Preference for one machine or another seem to vary from country to country rather than between individual editors.

Although there may be many small variations between similar types of machine they fall, basically, into two main categories; the horizontal viewing table and the upright viewing machine. Editors accustomed to working with one type may look with horror at the other, and wonder how on earth they could possibly go through one day with it, even less an entire production. Each has its own merits, however, and it would be wrong to reject either, without considering the advantages and disadvantages of each and to try them out should the opportunity ever arise.

Horizontal table

This type of viewing and editing machine is rather large and bulky but is capable of many sophisticated operations. The picture image is thrown, via a revolving prism, on to a fairly large screen mounted to the rear of the table. It is usually necessary to darken the room when viewing. Very large reels of 35 mm film can be accommodated, and run through on this machine, picture and sound reels being run either separately or in synchronization. The film travels from "feed" plates mounted on the left of the table, through a sprocketed drive to the prism and sound reproducing head in the centre, then to the take-up plates at the right. The picture mechanism handles film with either the normal photographic image or the squeezed one which has been photographed with the anamorphic lens for CinemaScope projection.

The machine is capable of reproducing both magnetic and photographic sound tracks and all film can be run at normal or high speed. When viewing a synchronized picture with sound track, a very simple control allows the sound track to be advanced or retarded in relation to the picture without removing any film from the sprockets. This can be of great use when no visual sync marks (page 92) have been put on the film and the separate sound track to indicate how they should be aligned in order to be in step. These synchronization methods are discussed on page 78.

The editing table can be operated either from foot controls or with a simple handle at the front of the table. Either method allows the film rolls to be run forward or backward as desired. The braking mechanism is very effective particularly when the handle is used. The film is arrested almost instantaneously.

Basic working parts of the horizontal editing machine which runs optical and magnetic married prints. Also separate picture and two sound tracks. (1) Viewing screen. (2) Feed plates for spooled film. (3) Speaker. (4) Take-up plates. (5) Hand controls. (6) Foot controls.

Viewing complete rolls of cut or uncut film is straightforward and the threading very simple with this machine. The operator can sit back and let the film run with no fear of spilling on to the floor. To view the same section of film several times is just a matter of reversing the control switch and then running through the section once more, without unthreading.

When the table is used by an editor for assembling cut sequences, however, and this technique is a favourite with many editors on the continent of Europe, certain preparations are necessary. The uncut film must be assembled into script continuity order, which is not necessarily the order in which it was photographed. And, in the case of bigger sequences, close angle shots which are to be intercut with long shots may well have to be assembled in separate rolls of film. The editor then runs backwards and forwards through these rolls, using his wax pencil to make marks, or possibly numbers, on the film as he decides the order and sequence of the shots to be assembled. This, of course, takes time and calls for a certain amount of memorized thinking when matching the action of one shot to its continuation in another and rolls of picture and sound may have to be changed back and forth while the cutting takes place.

Certainly, Scandinavian film editors favour this system but they often do not start the cutting phase of a film until the entire project has been photographed and the whole mass of film has been completely assembled into order of continuity. They then start at the beginning of the story and gradually work their way through to the end, cutting as they go. This presupposes that all the required film has been correctly shot and matched and that no disastrous errors have been made. At this late stage it would be impossible to repeat a shot. To watch a skilled Dane, or Swede, editing film at one of these tables is quite a revelation for the editor who has never used one. He will cut and splice as he goes along, gradually building up a cut sequence directly on the table, changing the rolls of uncut film back and forth, as required, and is obviously completely at home with the system. Those not used to the method will still think it a cumbersome and time-consuming operation, full of frustrations when a large amount of film material has to be handled.

Moviola

This upright viewing machine is completely different from the horizontal table, and as unfamiliar to the Scandinavian editor as the table is to his American counterpart. It is, however, in wider use than any other type throughout the world in major feature and documentary production. It seems that although there are many manufacturers of this kind of equipment it will always be known as the "Moviola", following the name of the famous North Hollywood company who originated, and still manufacture it, regardless of the name on the maker's plate. "Let's look at it on the Moviola", is an expression heard throughout the film-making world.

This machine is also designed for viewing the picture with a separate synchronous sound track and, although the size of the picture image is usually considerably smaller than that produced on the viewing table, the Moviola requires far less space and is very easily moved from place to place.

It is capable of reproducing the images of normal and Cinema-Scope photography, the image being projected, through mirrors and a simple lens, on to a ground glass screen. Picture and sound track can be run synchronously or independently with a very simple coupling bar connecting the picture and sound films when required. When running the sound only, or picture and sound synchronized, the drive is by a constant speed motor to ensure the correct speed and reproduction of sound. When the picture alone

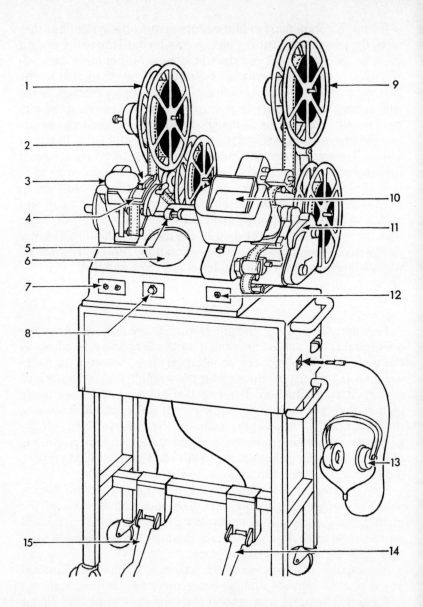

Basic operating parts of the Moviola. (1) Sound take-up. (2) Magnetic reproducing head. (3) Photographic sound reproducer. (4) Sound gate. (5) Coupling bar for synchronous picture and sound viewing. (6) Speaker. (7) Constant speed motor switches. (8) Amplifier/volume switch. (9) Picture take-up. (10) Viewing screen. (11) Hand-brake. (12) Variable speed motor switch. (13) Optional head-phone outlet. (14) Variable speed foot switch. (15) Constant speed foot switch.

is to be run, this too can be driven by the same constant speed motor if the coupling bar of picture and sound systems is not disconnected. However, a separate variable speed motor is situated in the picture drive mechanism, and if desired this can be used to drive the picture through the machine at varying speeds as required. Selecting forward or reverse running is a simple matter of throwing a switch. The machine is normally operated from foot pedals, although hand switches are also mounted on the control panel. The Moviola is equipped with both magnetic and photographic sound reproducing heads.

Unfortunately, in this machine there is no synchronizing control of the kind incorporated in the cutting table. Any alteration in synchronized relationship between picture and sound is done by physically moving one or the other strip of film.

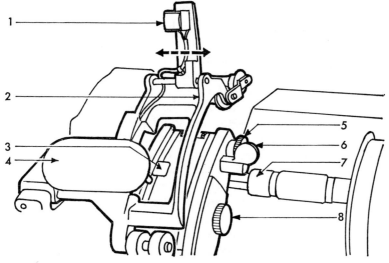

Detail of the Moviola sound gate. (1) Over-film magnetic head, movable over full width of 35 mm sound recordings. (2) Sound gate, open. (3) Under-film magnetic head. (4) Photographic sound exciter lamp. (5) Knurled wheel to "free" the driving sprocket. Sound film can then be pulled back and forth to locate individual sounds. (6) Gate release. (7) Picture/sound coupling bar. (8) Wheel to retract under-film magnetic head.

Whereas the viewing table has its feed plates and take-up plates, always in position, the film travelling from one to the other across the table, the Moviola operates in rather a different way. Very simple "gate" mechanisms are mounted on both sound and picture positions. The film is placed with the perforations over the appropriate driving sprockets, the gate clamped shut and the machine is ready to run.

45

For the editor to be able to view and select his sections of film for cutting, there is also a different film preparation procedure. Film rolls are fed from a source independent of the machine and, having passed through its gates, both picture and sound fall to the floor unless some form of container is put into position at the rear of the machine. Unlike the editor who works at the viewing table, the Moviola user needs all the film available for cutting broken down into individual takes, each being a reasonably small separate roll which can be fed into the machine. As will be seen later, it is one of the tasks of the assistant editor to collect matching picture and sound takes and wind them together in one roll.

An editor working with a Moviola usually feeds the film directly into the machine from his hand, allowing the small roll to unwind as it is drawn through the machine. He lets the film fall into a film bin suspended at the back. As with the viewing table, the editor can stop the film at will, using the small handbrake or wheel mounted near the picture head and run the film backward or forward as he wishes.

All the shots or angles, as the editor often refers to them, separated into individual rolls are placed on a rack at his side. He has great flexibility in handling the various shots when selecting pieces and deciding the cutting points. As the method of clamping sound and picture into the film gates is so simple, he can stop at any time, without having necessarily to run all the way through one scene, put in new piece of film, perhaps a different angle, and examine this. Now, he can go back to the first section again, which he has just removed. In this way he works through the film comparing one shot with another, and if necessary referring back to the previous one. He becomes so skilled in using the machine that the mechanics of operation are automatic and his attention is given fully to the task of film editing. Progress is smooth and fast. He has plenty of scope for trying various arrangements of shot or making direct comparisons between one shot and the next. It would seem that where editing is to be done from day to day as the film is being photographed, rather than wait until all has been finished, this is perhaps the better system and, certainly, the majority of film editors work with this machine.

Film viewed in the Moviola can also be put on to metal or plastic film reels, and by attaching feed and take-up arms with flexible belts attached to the main drive, complete reels can be examined. The reels can be run forward or backward with the film travelling from feed reel to take-up reel without falling into a

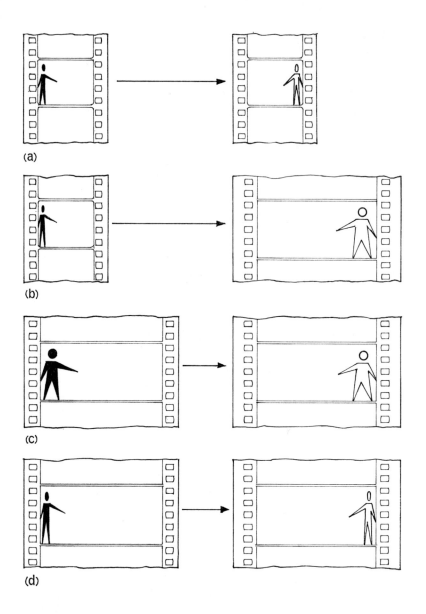

Some of the negative/positive formats. (a) Panavision 35. *Squeezed* 35 mm negative—*squeezed* 35 mm release print. (b) Panavision 70. Squeezed 35 mm neg.—*flat* 70 mm release print. (c) Super Panavision. *Flat* 65 mm neg.—*flat* 70 mm release print. (d) Ultra Panavision. *Squeezed* 65 mm neg.—*squeezed* 70 mm release print.

47

film bin. Not all Moviolas are fitted with these reel arms, as there are many film editors who prefer to work without them. But they are available.

Anamorphic lenses for Moviolas

Normal lens photography produces a straightforward negative which, after development, can be printed to give a normal image for viewing and cutting.

Some systems of photography are designed to produce a projected image whose ratio of width to height is much greater than normal. Such systems are CinemaScope and Panavision, trade names that have become synonyms for wide-screen work. In order to achieve this effect with film materials of normal proportions an anamorphic lens is used on the camera for original photography.

An anamorphic lens is designed to squeeze the image laterally as it reaches the film. Were the prints subsequently made from this projected or viewed with normal projection or viewing lenses, the overall area of the picture would be as usual but the objects photographed would appear vertically elongated—tall and thin. In order to spread the image back into a natural form (thus giving a projected picture of great width in relation to its height) special projection lenses have to be used. But in the case of a viewing machine, some form of simple converter is often adequate to spread the image to normal proportions. Of course, it is not essential that the editor have an elaborate and expensive converter to view the film. Indeed some editors do without them altogether and very quickly

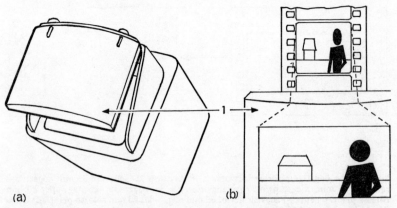

(a)   (b)

Viewing the anamorphized image. (a) Moviola viewing screen with simple plastic lens converter (l). (b) Squeezed image converted into normal image through the converting lens.

adjust to seeing the image in its squeezed form. However, if required, a very simple plastic lens, curved to the correct shape and mounted above the glass screen of the Moviola allows the image to be viewed normally.

On viewing tables, a supplementary lens is normally available, ready to be swung into position when this sort of film is being worked at.

Film benches

When viewing and selecting various pieces of picture and sound for the assembled sequence, the editor needs some means of mounting them into rolls and joining them together as he goes. Alternatively he can clip the pieces together in the correct order and wind them on to reels ready for splicing by an assistant. At the early stage he is dealing with one picture film and one sound film and needs one metal or plastic reel for each. Later, he will be dealing with additional sound tracks, all belonging with the same section of picture. But, because there must be a limit to how much film can be handled at any given time, the bench is designed to handle up to four strips of film simultaneously and has the means of winding them on to reels. The winding mechanism can accommodate four reels mounted side by side on a common spindle. A spring-

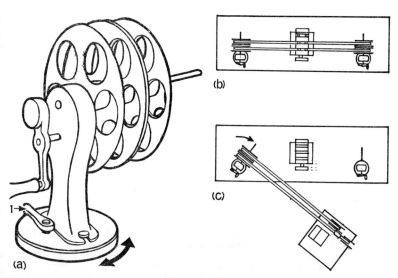

(b)

(c)

(a)

Film winding equipment. (a) American swivel winder. (I) Swivel lock and release. (b) Normal position for winding film through synchronizer. (c) Swivelled position for feeding film into viewing machine.

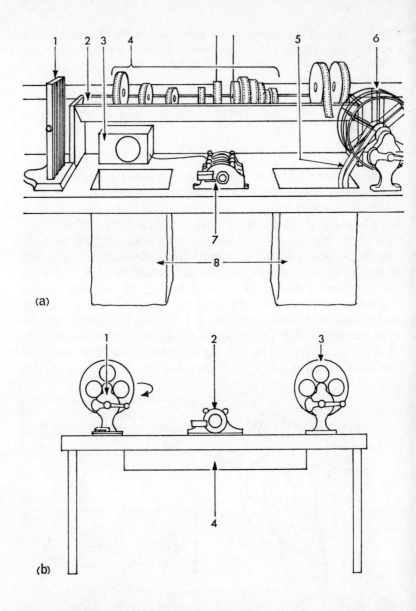

Cutting bench layout. (a) European style. (I) Film horse. (2) Film rack. (3) Amplifier/
speaker for synchronizer sound heads. (4) Broken down film to be cut, picture and
sound wound together. (5) Picture and sound leaders. (6) Take-up spools. (7) Film
synchronizer. (8) Film bags. (b) American style. (I) Winder, capable of being swivelled.
(2) Film synchronizer. (3) Winder. (4) Under-lighting.

loaded clamp slides on to the spindle against the outside reel to prevent any of the reels slipping and not winding up the film when the handle of the spindle is turned. This rewind mechanism is on the editor's right when he is facing the bench. At the left end of the bench there may be another similar four-way rewind.

Benches in the USA

The inclusion of a second four-way rewind at the left end of the bench depends on whether all film handled in the cutting room, and also in projection is mounted on reels, or just wound in rolls on to small plastic "centres" or "cores". The accepted practice in American studios is that uncut film should be wound on to metal or plastic reels at the moment it is received from the film laboratory. From then on, all the operations of assembly, projection, recutting and rewinding can be done from reel to reel, never winding film off reels on to centres. In this situation, the editor works from reels of film on the left winder to reels on the right winder and can wind back and forth at will. The film always remains under control and can never spill on to the floor or wander in coils across the bench.

Benches in Europe

For some unknown reason, except possibly because of the additional weight of the reels themselves, this system is not in general practice outside America. Cutting room work and studio projection is elsewhere geared for film handled in unmounted rolls wound on the plastic cores. Here, the editor works from rolls of film suspended on a spindle, each roll separated by an upright bar and the bars set into a heavy base plate so that the whole device will not topple over. This type of support is called the film horse. From this, he is able to feed the film into his viewing machine or wind on to the right-hand four-way rewind. The great disadvantage, of course, is that should he wish to re-examine a section of the film which has been wound on to the take-up reels at the right, he will have some difficulty in winding back and the film being pulled off the reels will spill over the bench. His bench, therefore, is constructed so that it has a solid centre section, to the right and left of which are large apertures through which the film can fall, if necessary, into linen or cotton bags suspended below.

American cutting benches normally have smooth flat surfaces,

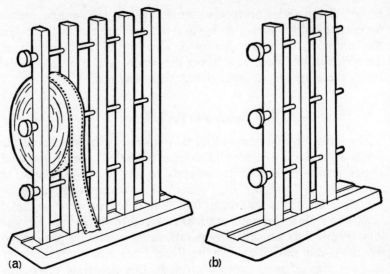

Film horses widely used in European cutting rooms. Many separate rolls of film are held in the way shown here with one roll. (a) 4-way model. (b) 2-way model.

underneath diffused lighting in the central area across which the film is wound, but no apertures and suspended film bags, since they are equipped with winders at each end. The European bench has the diffused under-lighting at the centre, a film horse (portable) at the left, a four-way winder at the right and cut-out apertures with suspended linen bags. If there is space for some drawers under

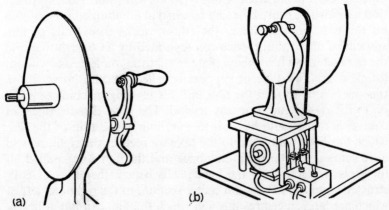

Plate rewinding. Rewinding mechanism used when film is not mounted on spools. (a) 35 mm rewind plate for approx. 1,000 feet of film on plastic centre. (b) Motorized version.

the bench surface, so much the better—small items soon become buried in the mass of material which accumulates on the bench. Here the American type bench has the advantage since nothing is suspended below and a drawer can be more easily fitted.

Film synchronizer

The basic film components produced by the picture camera and sound crews are recorded separately but synchronously. The editor must deal with these separate elements when assembling his sequences, yet maintain synchronization between them. Projection equipment of the special nature required will synchronously project separate picture and sound, as long as the components have been correctly built up and aligned into synchronous rolls. Viewing machines will handle these same rolls. Once the editor has started selecting *pieces* of these rolls, however, these pieces of picture and sound are wound on to reels, ready for splicing, always maintaining the overall synchronization between both component parts. If he were always cutting identical lengths of picture and sound for each piece, or "cut", there would be very little problem. The pieces would simply be wound on to the reels and spliced. In many cases, however, the appropriate sound for any relevant picture cut is a different length and assembly becomes more complicated. For example, it is often necessary that the dialogue being spoken by an artist presently "on-screen" be continued over the pictorial image of "off-scene" listeners, so that their reaction can be part of the overall effect. "Tight" cutting of dialogue scenes usually involves the last part of a sentence being "laid" over the next pictorial cut. Sound effects can often bridge the transition from one complete sequence to the next. It is an exception for picture and sound cuts to be of exactly the same length, since the sound of one picture cut is frequently continued over the cut which follows.

The editor must have some means of maintaining the *exact* synchronization between the sound and picture components. Otherwise the care taken to synchronize them when filming will have been wasted. Once correct synchronization has been established, it must be maintained throughout all future editing operations.

The item of equipment for keeping the picture film and several synchronized sound tracks in step is the film synchronizer. It is available in several forms for different gauges of film. Some models are designed to maintain the synchronization between two strips of film. Others can handle four. A synchronizer is a movable piece of equipment and when in use it is placed on the underlit section at the centre of the bench. It is weighty enough not to move about when being used. The film travels through it from the feed to the take up spools on the winders and is illuminated from below. Each strip of film is engaged on a sprocketed drum. The perforated film is then firmly clamped to the drum by rollers which are mounted on a hinged retaining bar. All the drums on the synchronizer revolve on a common spindle and, provided that the strips of film are engaged at a common start mark on the beginning of the roll, they will keep exactly parallel as they are wound forward. No matter how often the editor needs to overlap the sound from one picture cut to the next, he knows that the *overall* length of picture and sound will always remain the same. Provided that he compensates for any overlap in the incoming cut the synchronizer guarantees overall sync.

The drum on the end of the synchronizer nearest to the editor is normally used for the picture strip, the other drum or drums being occupied by synchronized sound strips.

Synchronizers with sound heads

The drums used for sound tracks are often equipped with magnetic sound reproducing heads which are in contact with the sound film as it moves through the synchronizer. Coupled to a simple amplifier, these heads reproduce the sound reasonably well (depending on the speed at which the film is being wound through) and with sufficient intelligibility to be of great use to the editor at all times. Each reproducing head has its own volume control mounted at the front of the synchronizer. Apart from assisting the editor in finding the beginnings and ends of words when making his cuts, they are useful for giving an idea of how several separate sound tracks will sound when eventually mixed together on the final track.

The synchronizer incorporates a footage counting device which indicates visually how much film has passed through and on many models also gives the number of individual picture frames in addition. Equipment used in Europe allows one revolution of the drums for each one foot length of 35 mm film in use.

Synchronizers in USA

Once again, the American editor uses equipment of a slightly different design. The drums of his synchronizer are much lighter

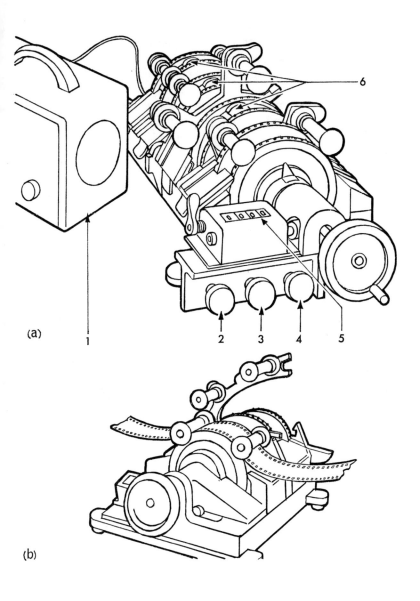

(a)

1

2   3   4   5

6

(b)

Synchronizing equipment: 35 mm film synchronizers. (a) 4-way synchronizer connected to amplifier/loud speaker (I). (2), (3) and (4), Volume controls. (5) Footage counter. (6) Under-film magnetic sound heads. Front drum of synchronizer for picture. (b) 2-way synchronizer.

and smaller and are rarely found with the useful magnetic heads incorporated. In American feature film studios, the sound editor very often uses a synchronizer with a 35 mm front drum for picture and 17·5 mm (split 35) drums to take sound tracks. It is attached to the cutting bench by a slotted bayonet-type fixing device, yet can be easily removed when not needed. Once having seen the synchronizer equipped with sound reproducing heads, however, the American editor is generally quite envious of his European colleagues.

Magnetic sound film reader

If the synchronizer is not fitted with sound reproducing heads, there must be some other means of locating individual sound modulations on the invisible magnetic sound track. Synchronizing start marks must be found and marked by the editorial assistant as one of his routine daily tasks. If the fitted synchronizer is not available he can use a small portable piece of equipment, with a reproducing head connected to an amplifier, which allows the film to be drawn through slowly, back and forth, until the sound to be located has been accurately found. This operation can, of course, be performed on the viewing table or on the Moviola but it would be uneconomic to tie up such an elaborate and expensive piece of equipment just for this one task.

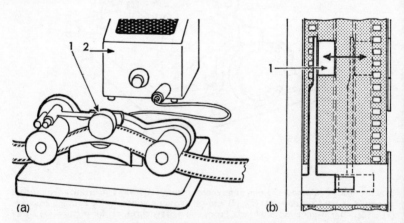

"Reading" the sound track. (a) Magnetic sound film reader. (1) Reproducing head. (2) Amplifier/speaker. (b) Head movable to scan three recording positions on 35 mm full coat track.

Splicing machine

At one time, all splicing on both negative and positive film was done by a liquid solvent process. Having scraped away a narrow strip of emulsion from one of the pieces to be joined, the area was coated with a special film cement fluid which partially dissolved the film base. The other piece of film was then brought into contact with it, and the two were held under slightly heated pressure for a short time. This method is still in use for the joining of negative film, but it does call for an overlapped join and each time it is made a portion of the film on each side of the join is lost.

The system was once used widely by the editor in the assembly of positive work prints. But when he wanted to change the sequence of cuts, perhaps extending one scene which had been previously cut and spliced, the small section of film which had been lost in making that splice would have long since been thrown into the waste bin. This loss would have to be allowed for in order to make the scene its exact original length by inserting a piece of blank film. It would then maintain exact synchronization with the sound track concerned, and also the picture negative from which the print was made. The loss was usually one frame, and a similar length in the sound film. Editor's work prints, certainly difficult sequences which had to be cut and re-cut before the final shape was acceptable, often became full of such "slugs" of blank film. Apart from being visually disturbing, when the sound track became filled with them the sound would be very jarring and disconnected. Reprints could, of course, be ordered and the mutilated film replaced, but this would amount to quite an additional expense in the editorial budget, particularly with colour film.

Tape splicer

A new system, very simple in design and operation, was evolved for splicing positive prints and is now in almost universal use in film cutting rooms. The splice is not overlapped, and pieces of film to be joined together are cut very accurately along the frame line of the picture, butted together and covered with narrow, self-adhesive, transparent tape. The small machine which performs this operation has register pins on which the perforations of the film are located. This ensures that the cut made by the guillotine type cutter at the side of the machine is always made exactly at right angles to the length of the film and that the butted splices will have no gap

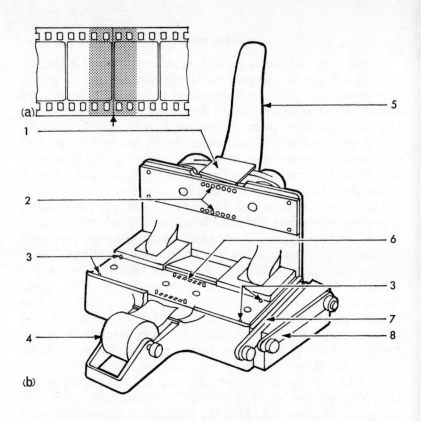

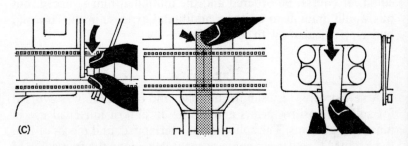

One of the methods of tape-splicing positive film. (a) Area of transparent tape across splice. It can be narrower and several sizes of tape are available. (b) Tape splicing machine. (1) Cutting blades (also one at rear). (2) Punches to perforate the transparent tape. (3) Register pins. (4) Transparent tape. (5) Operating handle. (6) Punch holes. (7) Straight cutting knife. (8) Diagonal cutting knife. (c) Operation. The straight cutting knife cuts the film along the frame line. Two picture cuts are brought together in register and transparent tape is positioned over the two pieces. The top of the splicer is brought down and the operating handle pressed sharply. This cuts the tape level with the sides of the film and punches the perforations.

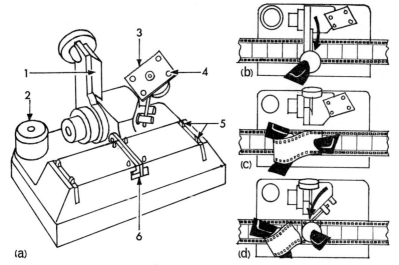

American tape splicing machine (a). (1) Straight cutting knife. (2) Tape retainer. (3) Serrated tape cutting blade. (4) Clearance for register pins. (5) Register pins. (6) Spring loaded cutting guide. Method of operation (b). Film held on register pins and cut along the frame line. (c) Pre-perforated tape positioned over two pieces of film to be spliced. (d) Tape cutter swung down, pressing the tape on to the film and the tape torn off against the serrated edge.

between them. Further, as no overlap is necessary, film is not lost when the splice is made and sequences can be cut and re-cut by simply unpeeling the transparent tape, and rejoining the film without small insertions of blank film. Picture splices are usually made by taping both sides, across the splice, as the film suffers

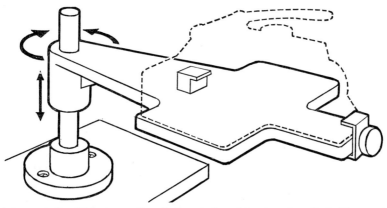

Joiner rest for C.I.R. tape splicer (splicer indicated by dotted outline). The stand swings through 360° and is adjustable for height. Mounted in a convenient position on the cutting bench it is ideal for the editor who splices as he works.

considerable stress when travelling through the viewing machine and the film projector which have intermittent movements. Because sound film travels smoothly through its machine at this stage, it is usual to tape the splice only on one surface, that which the reproducing head does not contact.

To make a tape join the pieces of film are placed in the joining machine, cut and butted together and located on the register pins. Tape is placed across the join. Pressure on the operating handle cuts the tape parallel with both edges of the film, and at the same time punch holes in the tape at the perforations.

The type of tape splicing machine currently used in American studios employs the same principle but, uses self-adhesive tape which has previously been perforated for the size of film being used. This tape has to be specially made for the purpose and is, therefore, more expensive.

Neg and pos splices

An important point must be made here about using the butt (non-overlap) splice in the assembly of positive editorial work prints which, as we shall see later are used as the guide for picture negative cutting. As the negative film splice is made by the overlap system, and a small additional amount of film is needed at either side of the splice, allowance must be made for this eventuality

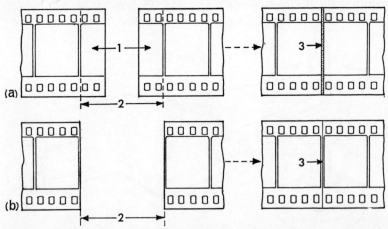

Positive and negative splicing methods showing the overlapped (negative) splice and the butted (positive) splice. (a) Overlapped splice with two pieces of 35 mm film to be joined. (1) The half frame allowance on each cut. (2) The eventual splice line.(3) The overlapped splice. (b) The butt splice. (2) The eventual splice line. (3) The butted splice.

when the positive work print is first assembled. In theory, only a very narrow overlap is required on the negative splice. But in practice, the negative splicing machine used at the laboratory requires a half of one picture frame to allow the film to be aligned correctly. As there is little use in preserving half a frame, a whole picture frame is lost in these joins. In any case, it will only be necessary when "cut-backs" are made. That is when cutting away from a scene at some point during the action, to another piece of film of a different camera angle, then back to the first scene and continuing the action of this scene on the frame at which the cutaway was made. At this point, the first frame of the incoming scene should be removed to allow for the negative splice. It would seem from this perhaps, that the advantage of not losing any film when making a splice with the tape-splicer will now have been lost. In this case we are going to lose a frame of positive picture anyway. But as these are *whole* frames they are well worth preserving carefully, filing them in envelopes sequence by sequence, available to be re-inserted into the cut film if the shot has to be extended.

Film bins

There must be several portable film bins, lined with linen or cotton which can be easily laundered, for use by both editor and assistants. They should be of reasonable capacity with a batten

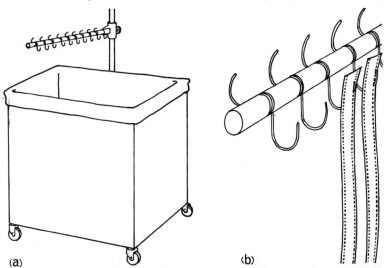

(a)   (b)

Holding the film trims. (a) Typical film trims bin with suspended hooks. (b) Detail of film trims on hooks. The ends of film fall into the bin which is lined with linen to prevent abrasion.

61

mounted in each. The batten has a row of pins so that sections of film can be suspended from it by their perforations, the bulk hanging down into the bin.

Film can be held aside in this way by the editor as he selects pieces for incorporation into an assembly. Bins can also be used to take the unwanted sections of takes, these "trims" occupying one pin for each take, so that the assistant can file these away for future use if needed.

It is useful to have one or two extra lined film bins without the supported battens so that small rolls of film can be quickly unrolled for identification and examination without having to use the rewind bench.

Waste facilities

These are the basic requirements of equipment and furnishings in the film cutting room. How the items will be laid out to best advantage will be a matter of individual taste according to the space available. How many benches, how many bins and how many people are needed depends, within obvious limits, on the size of the production. Above all, it must be clean and orderly and kept so. Documents must never be allowed to stray around the room and film must never be just thrown into a corner.

There is always a certain amount of waste film, particularly when it first arrives from the laboratory, with lengths of blank film put into rolls for processing convenience. Film may be damaged, no matter how careful one may be, and it will have to be replaced before the damaged film is thrown away. Perhaps the last requirement, therefore, is a film waste bin so that lengths of unwanted blank, and damaged film which has now been replaced, in fact, all the unwanted "junk" which will otherwise accumulate and confuse can be thrown away. There must never be any doubt about which film is to be thrown into the waste bin and, therefore, film to be filed should be filed at once and never left in disorderly bundles on a bench. In spite of all precautions, there are times when film is lost, or certainly mislaid, and there can be no greater frustration to the editor than taking part in the massive "search" which ensues, when he knows he should be getting on with the cutting, perhaps with an important deadline to meet.

The worst crime in the positive cutting room is to lose film, even though it can be replaced by a reprint. Routines may be dull; documentation and filing laborious; but as long as each assistant is aware of his responsibility the loss of film will be a rarity.

4

ASSISTANTS' DAILY ROUTINE

A SYSTEM of film identification is necessary from the moment the camera team start photographing the production. The action and the sound, both dialogue and sound effects must be fully documented for the benefit of the film editor.

Receiving the daily shipments of picture and sound film, synchronizing them and making them into rolls for the first viewing in the studio are the daily tasks of editorial assistants. These tasks become a matter of routine, but nevertheless an important one to simplify the film editing which will follow, regardless of the quantities of film received.

Film identification

To quickly identify any section of film from among the thousands and possibly hundreds of thousands of feet which may be shot is of prime importance for the editor and processing laboratory alike. Let us first examine the system of numbering each shot as it is photographed. This will clarify the purpose of camera, sound and continuity reports which are explained later.

The following example is a straightforward action and sound scene which is synchronously photographed in the studio where conditions are normal and no tricks are involved.

The editor, the film laboratory, and the sound transfer department must have some common reference when orders are placed for reprints of picture, retransfers of sound, and the final sorting and preparation of the negative to be cut to match the editor's work print. There has to be a visual identification on the picture negative at the start of each shot and a corresponding audible identification at the beginning of the accompanying sound track.

Slate board

For visual identification the simple slate board is used on which is printed the name of the production, the names of the cameraman and film director, the date of photography and the number of the shot, known as the slate number. It also indicates if the shot is interior or exterior, and whether a day or night effect is intended. As it is most unusual for the first "take" of any scene to produce the desired result to the satisfaction of the film director, the board also indicates the number of the take. The slate is photographed at the beginning of each scene and, while this is taking place, an announcement is made into the microphone calling out the slate and take number so that this information is also recorded on to the sound track. All relevant information is now contained on the picture negative and the sound track master recording and will reproduce on the prints as they are made.

All sync picture and sound shots require some form of visual and audible marks so that they can be synchronized for projection and viewing machines. These are put on to the film at this time. The methods used will be explained later when the synchronizing of film as it is received in the cutting room is discussed.

There are two main methods of slate numbering; that normally used in Europe and the slightly different system used on American productions. In either case it is usually the responsibility of the continuity girl to ensure that the correct number is marked on the slate, that it is changed to a new number at the beginning of each new set-up, or shot, and that the take numbers are advanced each time a new take is started.

European system

The European slate numbering system is very simple. On the first day of shooting, regardless of the number of the script scene being photographed, the first shot of the day is numbered "slate one", "take one". The take number is advanced each time a further take of the same scene is to be photographed and, as long as the set-up, or angle, remains the same the number, "slate one", will be unchanged. After a satisfactory take, or series of takes, the director may decide to cover the same action from a different, perhaps closer angle. The slate board will now be marked "slate two", "take one". Thus, the system of numbering the slate continues throughout the entire production and, although there is no direct

64

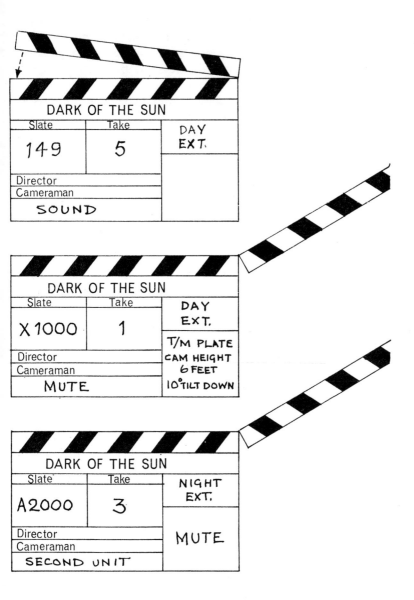

DARK OF THE SUN

Slate	Take	DAY
149	5	EXT.
Director		
Cameraman		
SOUND		

DARK OF THE SUN

Slate	Take	DAY
X 1000	1	EXT.
		T/M PLATE
Director		CAM HEIGHT
Cameraman		6 FEET
MUTE		10° TILT DOWN

DARK OF THE SUN

Slate	Take	NIGHT
A2000	3	EXT.
Director		
Cameraman		MUTE
SECOND UNIT		

Examples of the clapper board. For silent shots the clapper is usually left in the open position as an obvious indication that the shot is silent.

reference to the script scene number on the slate, the system works well without complications as long as a slate number is never accidentally repeated. Such a mistake could happen if a second photographic unit is at work for the same production, perhaps making establishing shots on some distant location. If it does, it can cause endless confusion in identifying film. The continuity girl and the film editor should take every precaution to avoid this.

American system

In America the script scene number is used on the slate board and if the first shot on the first day is to be script scene 145, the slate will be marked "scene 145, take one". New angles of the same scene are marked 145A, 145B, and so on with many combinations of the alphabet being used.

The advantages of having the actual script scene numbers projected on to the screen during the first viewings of the daily rush prints, as compared with a vague and non-connected slate number, are fairly obvious. Less obvious, but equally advantageous, is the fact that, since film is always filed in containers in the cutting room according to the slate number, all film made for one scene must be filed in the same container, or at least in consecutive containers. This makes the handling of any film required for recutting a sequence much easier and less spread about. For example, pick-up shots (additional shots taken at a later date) made with this script numbering system, and made probably much later in the production than the main photography, still carry the same basic script scene number and will be filed accordingly. With the European system, however, the slate number of the pick-up shot might be hundreds of numbers away from those originally used for the sequence and now all the shots involved will be separated in many different filing containers.

The main objections to the script scene method of slate numbering seem to be based on the sometimes very complex series of letters of the alphabet which have to be devised to follow the scene number when complicated scenes involving many different angles of the same action have to be photographed.

Whichever method is used, each separate shot is referred to in the cutting room and in the film laboratory by its slate number and take number.

There is another and very valuable means of identification, indeed the one by which all negative work, trick shots, dissolves

66

and fades are dealt with. This is the negative key number and will be explained later (see page 98).

Documentation and reports

Once the system of slating has been established and the first shooting has started, reports are made in great detail as the day's work progresses to give the fullest possible information to the technicians processing and editing the film.

On all types of production there are times when shooting is done in difficult areas, perhaps in confined space in an aeroplane or boat, when documentary records of the shooting may be minimal, even non-existent. This is unfortunate, to say the least. It makes developing and printing of film more difficult and the film editing task which follows becomes much more formidable. The most crude reports made at the time of shooting would be of some help even if they only give details of the numbers of the shots made, which takes are to be printed, and the script scene numbers relating to the shots.

Full reports should be completed at the end of each day by the key members of each department of the production team concerned. The editorial assistant then collects the editor's copy at the beginning of his day's work. Everyone in the cutting room then has complete details of the quantity and nature of the film which was shot on the previous day.

Naturally, when a unit is working on a distant location with perhaps a slow mail delivery, documents may not reach the cutting room until after the film has been received. So it will have to be sorted initially without the aid of reports. Later, when the papers are received, a thorough check and identification of film can be made.

Now we can examine individual reports in detail.

Picture negative report

The junior member of the camera crew responsible for the loading and unloading of the film magazines for the camera, also keeps the slate board ready with the information to be photographed at the head of each take. Additionally, he keeps a log of the individual footages photographed in each take and, at the end of the day, packs the film for shipment to the processing laboratory together with all the information they need.

During the day he keeps a record for each magazine of film placed on the camera. Usually this is on a card which is taped to the side of the magazine. This card gives the following information:

1. The number of the magazine. Each magazine has its own number to enable quick checks to be made if it is discovered that the picture negative is being marked and scratched in any way.
2. The type of film stock loaded and the total footage of unexposed film put into the magazine.
3. The numbers of each slate and take as photography continues, and the individual footage of each take.
4. Whether or not the take is to be printed, in accordance with the film director's instructions, and if the print is to be made in black and white film or in colour. Even if colour negative is being used, it will sometimes be necessary to make monochrome positive prints for cutting purposes to keep costs down.
5. The amount of unexposed footage (if any) left in the magazine when it is removed from the camera.

From this information he prepares the picture negative report, copies of which are available to all the people concerned. It gives the name of the film producing company, the title of the production, the name of the processing laboratory, and where the positive prints should be delivered.

It also gives, in the order in which they were photographed, the slate numbers and each individual take number, together with their respective footages. Alongside each take number the assistant marks a symbol to indicate the director's requirements after the negative has been developed. The three symbols normally used are as follows:

1. "NG" and "H"

   The first (no good) is an instruction to the negative department at the laboratory that the film is to be developed only, no prints being required.

   The second symbol "H" indicates that the director wishes to "hold" this negative after it has been developed. No print is wanted for the time being but he may call for it to be printed at a later date. (When the editor is in trouble with the assembly of the printed material, the first thing he may look for is the availability of a "hold" take on the troublesome scene).

2. "P"

   This symbol is obvious and is the instruction to the negative

CUTTING ROOMS COPY

PICTURE NEGATIVE REPORT

CONTINUED FROM SHEET No.	51875	SHEET NUMBER	1	CONTINUED ON SHEET No.	51877

THE SHEET NUMBERS MUST BE QUOTED ON ALL DELIVERY NOTES, INVOICES AND OTHER COMMUNICATIONS RELATING THERETO

PRODUCING COMPANY __M G M__   STUDIOS OR LOCATION __RICHMOND__

PRODUCTION __DARK OF THE SUN__   PRODUCTION No. __64__

DIRECTOR _____ CAMERAMAN _____ DATE __6·3·67__

STATE IF COLOUR OR B & W __E/COLOUR__

ORDER TO __TECHNICOLOR__ LABORATORIES

STOCK AND CODE No. __5251__   LABORATORY INSTRUCTIONS RE INVOICING, DELIVERY ETC. __Rush to M.G.M. cutting rooms,__   CAMERA AND NUMBER __BNC/S35/ARRI.__

EASTMAN COLOUR   EMULSION AND ROLL No. __693__   CAMERA OPERATOR

MAG. No.	LENGTH LOADED	SLATE No.	TAKE No.	COUNTER READING	TAKE LENGTH	'P' FOR PRINT B & W	COL'R	LENS F/L & STOP	ESSENTIAL INFORMATION	CAN No.
3B	830	325A	1	60	60	P		40--	BNC EXT TWILIGHT Roll 1	
			2	150	90		P			
		326A	1	310	160	P		260+	} 835	
			2	460	150		P	·	} SHOT AT DAY TIME.	
		327	1	550	90		P	··	B.N.C. FOR TWILIGHT EFFECT	
		328	1	620	70		P	·		
		329	1	660	40		··		} 835	
			2	710	50	P	··			
			3	780	70	P	··			
		WASTE			50					
1	390	325B	1	40	40	P		40--	EXT TWILIGHT Roll 2.	
			2	80	40		P	··		
	ARRI	326B	1	240	160	P		··		
		WASTE 2			10			··	140 S.E	
2	405	326B	2	90	90	P		40--	EXT TWILIGHT Roll 3.	
		330	1	160	70			··		
	ARRI		2	210	50	P		··		
		WASTE			10			·	185 S.E	

FOR OFFICE USE ONLY | TOTAL CANS | 2 |

TOTAL EXPOSED	1230	TOTAL EXPOSED	1230	TOTAL PRINTED		TOTAL FOOTAGE PREVIOUSLY DRAWN	
SHORT ENDS	325	HELD OR NOT SENT		B & W 420		FOOTAGE DRAWN TODAY	
WASTE	70	TOTAL DEVELOPED	1230	COLOUR 700		PREVIOUSLY EXPOSED	
FOOTAGE LOADED	1625					EXPOSED TODAY	·

SIGNED : _____

★COLOUR DESCRIPTION OF SCENE. FILTER AND/OR DIFFUSION USED. DAY, NIGHT OR OTHER EFFECTS. DAYLIGHT, ARCS, INKIES OR MIXED LIGHTING. INTERIOR/EXTERIOR A.M., P.M.

R.L.P. 102

A typical picture negative report, or camera sheet. Vital to the laboratory when breaking out developed negative for separate colour and black and white printing. Three cameras were in use on this sequence—BNC, Arriflex and S35. Figures followed by the letters SE indicate the "short end" footage left when the magazine was unloaded from the camera.

department at the lab. for a positive print to be made. The report usually has separate columns for black and white or colour printing, the symbol being placed in the appropriate column.

Other information written on the form includes the type of stock in use, and probably the emulsion number provided by the film manufacturer at the time of coating the film. Any special instructions for film development and/or printing which have been given by the director of photography. Apart from the individual take footages, the total amount of film loaded, the total to be developed, and the amounts to be printed in black and white or colour are written into the appropriate spaces at the foot of the form.

The top, and most legible copy of the report, accompanies the exposed, undeveloped negative to the lab. since without this information they really would be working in the dark.

Other duplicate copies are received by the accounts department so that checks can be made against costs and invoices for processing. The production department can, from their copy, check on progress and the diminishing rate of film stock. The film editor (unfortunately, he usually receives the last and least legible copy), can see from his copy how much print he is to expect, whether in black and white or colour. His assistant can check that all takes marked with the symbol, "P", have in fact been printed.

Sound master report

Perhaps different in layout, but similar in intention is the report made out by the member of the sound crew who has the responsibility for loading and operating the sound recorder.

Here, too, is the list of slate numbers and take numbers, with individual footages, and the same type of "symbol" instruction for the sound transfer cutting print required by the editor. It indicates whether there have been problems with synchronizing sound and picture, so that the editing staff are aware of this, and, for example if a wrong slate number has been called into the microphone, even though the correct one has been photographed on picture.

Unlike the picture negative, rolls of master magnetic film for sound recording have no laboratory processing requirement and are available for the manufacture of transfer cutting "prints" immediately. The sound recorder operator therefore gives each

SOUND FILM DAILY REPORT — ORIGINAL MAGNETIC   No. 3125/2

Title: "DARK OF THE SUN"

Director _____   Stageman _____
Mixer _____   Recorder _____

Prod. No. M.G.M. 64	Machine M.G.M 64	Machine No 3	E.M. No	Total Rolls 3	Bias 1	X 600	Date	Erase Date	Operator
	Total Cans 3				Total Footage 1,800	Authority			

Left recording report

Scene	Take	Footage	Disp.	Roll No.	Remarks
T'ONE.	1	20	P	N54	SON PULSE.
314	1	115	P	NON SYNC	T'ONE @ -6DB
315	1	90	P	" "	7½ I.P.S
316	1	60	P	SYNC	ANN: ON START OF R.
317	1	100	P		314 REHEARSAL
318	1	50	P	NON SYNC	PLEASE IGNORE.
	2	30	P	" "	ANN 319 IN ERROR
	3	30	P	" "	
	4	30	P	" "	
REHEARSAL FOR 319		35	P		
319	1	90	P		NO CLAP
320	1	45	P	" "	"
322	2	40	P	" "	"
	3	40	P	" "	
323	1	90	P	" "	
T'ONE	1	15	P	N.SS	NON SYNC
324	1	60	P	NON SYNC	"
325	2	90	P	" "	"
REHEARSAL FOR 326		50	P		
326	1	90	P		NON SYNC
	2	150	P		"
327	1	135	P	← ANN TK3	
328	1	75	P		
REHEARSAL FOR 329		45	P		
		30	P		

Right recording report

Scene	Take	E.M. No	Footage	Disp.	Roll No.	Remarks
329	1		45		(N.SS)	
	2		50	P		
	3		50	P		
T'ONE	1		15		N.54	
FX31	1		75	P	TRAIN BELL	
331	1		30	P		
	2		30	P		
	3		30	P	NON SYNC	
332	1		30	P		
333	1		45	P		
334	1		60	P	NON SYNC	
335	2		100	P		
	3		85	P		
336	1		90	P		
	2		60			
337	1		45	P	No PULSE	
	2		90	P	NON SYNC	
			90	P	"	
BATCH 22						

Master sound recording report. This material was shot on location, hence the number of "non-sync" recordings. Rehearsals of scenes are sometimes recorded wild and left for the editor to print if required. Such rehearsals are usually clear of generator noise and other unwanted effects and might serve as a guide track for the work print if the selected take is very noisy. This is good thinking on the part of the sound mixer.

roll a master sound roll number as it is loaded on to the machine and his report indicates very clearly, which slate and take numbers are contained in each roll, for future identification.

A and B master recordings

In the cause of economy, recordings may be made, first on one edge of the magnetic coating, then (reversing the roll on the machine when the first edge is full) on the other. This is possible because a single-track magnetic recording head only occupies a small area of the total width of the film, when 35 mm is the recording medium. Such master rolls are given a roll number, and the double-sided recordings "A" and "B" side designations. This information is also included in the report.

Wild recordings

Apart from shooting synchronously with the picture camera, the film director and the senior sound engineer may have thought it valuable to record independent sounds for future use by the editing department. For example, the sound of a large crowd murmuring, applauding or laughing, may well be difficult to reproduce later on. Exterior sound effects of a specialized nature are extremely useful when sound tracks are being prepared for the final sound mixing. It is most valuable to have a reasonable footage of these effects, clear of dialogue. Separate recordings allow easy adjustment of balance of overall sound at a later stage. Such independent recordings, as opposed to those which are synchronous, are known as "wild" recordings. The report always indicates where such wild recordings have been made, together with special slate numbers which these are usually given. It probably gives a brief description of the sound recorded, perhaps with an indication of which script scene will benefit from its inclusion.

A sound recording made when the recorder is not running in synchronization with the picture camera (for example if the camera were to be running at high speed to achieve some special photographic effect) is also called a wild recording.

Cutting transfers

Sound "prints" are made by a simple transfer from the master film on to a new piece of magnetic cutting film. Such transfers are the responsibility of the sound department concerned and usually take place in the section of the sound department equipped only for this type of work. This certainly applies in film studios and the transfer department handle the work of all the productions which may be shooting at any one time.

The top copy of the sound master report, therefore, accompanies the completed rolls to the transfer department at the end of the day's work. All that is required then is a transfer of each take number which has been marked, "P", for printing. The operator loads the master roll on to a sound reproducing machine, or re-recorder, and a new unused roll of magnetic film on to an electrically interlocked recording machine. Monitoring the sound and listening for the announcements, easily found within the master roll by reference to the footage lengths written on the report, he transfers the takes to be printed on to the new film for shipment to the editor. The master roll, therefore, is never cut and is stored carefully in a film vault at the transfer department, ready for further transfers which may be necessary from time to time.

If the master sound was made by a tape machine, for example on a $\frac{1}{4}$-in. tape, the transfer department would use different reproducing equipment but would still provide the editor with transfers of the printed takes on 35 mm perforated magnetic film.

When the editor receives his copy of the sound master report, he checks that everything marked for printing has been received, then can use it as a means of identifying the contents of each roll for any further transfers which may be needed.

Daily continuity report

The script, or continuity girl, working with the shooting unit, and very close to the film director, watches the movements of artists to help them repeat these with accuracy on the various angles which will be made. She times the sequences, ensuring that every shot is given its correct slate number and that the numbers are recorded on to the film. She ensures that the director's requirements for prints to be ordered are understood correctly by both picture and sound crews. She really does an enormous amount of work which greatly benefits the editorial department and is in fact, a very important member of that department.

Throughout the production, a close system of co-operation between editor, editorial staff and continuity girl is of great mutual value.

Armed with her script, stop watch, notebook and her very observant eyes, she is at the director's side during rehearsals, checking the action and movements, listening to the dialogue and checking against the script, all the time filling her notebook with information which will be incorporated into her continuity report.

When actual shooting begins, rehearsals satisfactorily completed, she times the shot, watches movements of artists and camera, notes any variations in dialogue which differ from the script, at the same time making sure that props and furnishings and the mass of things which may be used to "dress" the set are in correct position. When the camera angle is changed or, after changing the lens, the action is repeated, she uses her notes to ensure that dialogue is consistent, movements and gestures the same as before. Consequently the editor is not frustrated by being unable to intercut the angles because some artist picks something up with the wrong hand, or sits down during a different line of dialogue.

All editors should be (and usually are) grateful for the way in which her constant vigilance makes the free editing of film so much easier.

Each separate camera angle photographed is given its appropriate slate number, then the various take numbers. For each angle a continuity report is prepared and typed by the continuity girl on a printed form. This time, the editor is more fortunate and usually receives the top and one further copy, another being sent to the production manager and one kept with the shooting unit.

Details on the report

The continuity report contains a wealth of information and it is almost entirely designed for the benefit of the film editor. It indicates the slate number and the script scene number for which it is intended; it also shows how many takes are made, the length of each take and if the take is to be printed. The camera in use is quoted by its reference number and the lens focal length, the aperture of the lens and the various "key" focus distances measured by the focus operator are included. It also mentions whether the shot is an interior or exterior, day or night effect, regardless of studio or location shooting.

The bulk of the information, however, is contained in the main body of the report. Here is given the details of movement of artists, camera movement in relation to dialogue, if spoken, and the

Form 138

Metro-Goldwyn-Mayer British Studios Ltd.

DAILY CONTINUITY REPORT

Production No. __MGM 64__   Title __DARK OF THE SUN__

Camera No.   Cameraman   Set Up

__BNC 179_____ 40mm 5'3" t.4 _____

Slate No.	Script No.
473	17pt

_____ _____ _____ 1½ L Diopter_____ Date __THURS:6.4.67_____

_____ _____ _____   Set __Int. Mercenary HQ_____

_____ _____ _____   Night or Day __Day__

Print ———	nvg posn.	COL PRINT	COL PRINT							
Take No. ———	1	2	3	4	5	6	7	8	9	10
Footage ———	25	50	25							

Action and Dialogue :-

CLOSE SHOT ADAMS & RUFFO F.G.

Camera shooting from high angle down towards Adams
seated, Ruffo standing L f.g.

JANSEN: (OFF) What about a beer or something?

cue: No thanks I'm having one with the Sergeant.

ADAMS: BIG APE ISN'T HE?

Ruffo looks up, reacts then looks down at Adams.

Typical layout of the Continuity Report. Dialogue and "prints" usually typed in red on the editor's copy. Note the information of camera lens and focus distance, useful when retakes are needed. Script No. indicates part of Scene 17. This is a simple close shot. Complicated slates often occupy two, even three continuity sheets.

complete relationship between dialogue and action as it has taken place. Further, since there are probably several takes photographed on the same angle, the variations between dialogue, action, and camera movement will be noted for each take. Notes are included on those takes which are not to be printed, whether they are to be regarded as NG or held. These notes, in particular, are of great assistance to the editor when the shooting unit have long since gone their various ways, employed on other films, and he is in the final stage of editing his picture. The notes form a complete "diary" of the events as they were photographed by the shooting unit, particularly in relation to the comments of the film director at that time.

For the editor it is better if the dialogue is typed in red, and the actions and movements in black. This is why he, luckily, receives the top sheet.

The reports are an immediate indication to the editor on the coverage of any sequence. When received, and sorted into separate sequences, he need only pick them up and "weigh" them in one hand, to know how much film coverage has been devoted to any one sequence, each report representing one camera angle. They are also a useful indication of the amount of film waiting to be assembled, particularly if sequences are sufficiently incomplete at the time of original photography to make immediate cutting inadvisable.

Reports covering film which has been assembled are gathered into a folder in script scene order. Reports relating to film which has not yet been cut are separated and, since each individual report represents one camera angle in the film, the editor can readily see how much film is waiting for assembly by referring to the "To be cut" folder of continuity reports.

Missing documents

These are the basic and very essential documents received by the editor from the shooting unit. Just how essential and useful they are is always confirmed when they are not available at the time of film delivery from the lab., as in the case of foreign location shooting.

It is an unfortunate fact that film shot on difficult locations is invariably more complicated to check, sort out, and put into some sort of order. These are the types of location when more than one camera might be in simultaneous use on a difficult scene, and the cameras will not all necessarily be shot with synchronized sound. Physical difficulties with aerial shots, sea shots, and those made in very confined spaces may make impossible the normal inclusion of the slate board, and announcements on the sound track may well be inaudible. This is the time when the information contained in the reports is most needed, yet very often unavailable.

Document checks

One of the first daily routine tasks of the assistant, therefore, is to collect these important documents. Back at the cutting room, a quick examination of their contents can be made and, initially, a list made of the slate numbers and take numbers of both picture and sound to be expected. An immediate check can be made for example, if the continuity report indicates that a certain take is to be printed, yet the relevant camera or sound report shows that this is regarded as "NG". Checks made now will avoid confusion when the film actually arrives.

Daily sound rushes

The transfers made by the sound department from master sound to cutting print are normally available in the cutting room before delivery of the picture from the laboratory. Rather than wait for the arrival of picture prints, and in order to save time when they do arrive, sound transfer cutting prints can be sorted, identified and, where sync picture and sound shots are involved, sync start marks can be established. When the picture does reach the cutting room, less time is then taken in assembling the rolls of film which the entire unit will be anxious to view at the earliest break in their activities.

Sorting and marking sound

The rolls of magnetic daily rush prints received in the cutting room at this time, representing the shooting of the previous day, will have no visual indication of the starts and ends of takes or even the order in which the rolls have been assembled in transfer.

The assistant must identify each section of film, using the magnetic heads on a synchronizer, or a separate magnetic sound reader. Starting from the head of each roll of transferred sound, he positions a magnetic reproducing sound head in contact with the emulsion of the film and slowly winds through the rolls, listening to the recorded information. The sounds will be audible in a loudspeaker connected to the amplifying system attached to the sound heads. A fairly crude, but intelligible reproduction will be heard.

The assistant listens for the announcements of slate and take numbers at the beginning of each take, marking the numbers with wax pencil on the surface of the film as they occur. He is assisted in this task by reference to the sound report, which gives him an accurate indication of the lengths of each take. If he uses the synchronizer with magnetic heads and a footage counter, the task is very simple.

He also searches for the sound synchronizing mark in the case of sound-and-picture sequences. Since the methods of recording these were previously mentioned only briefly, they will now be explained in greater detail.

Synchronizing start marks

Synchronized sound and picture shots (picture recorded on to one film and sound recorded on to another) must be shot with both films running at precisely the same speed. Electrically interlocked mechanisms must be started together and a synchronized point must be made between the two at the beginning of the shot. When the prints of each are received they can then be viewed synchronously. A visual mark is photographed at the beginning of the picture, and, at the same time, an audible sound must be recorded on the sound track.

The old method of using a hinged "clapper" on the slate board is still in general use and is simple, yet effective. As the slate is photographed, with both picture and sound films running at the correct standard speed, the hinged bar of the clapper is brought sharply down on the slate, thus providing a visual identification on the picture negative and, at the same time, recording a short "clap" on the sound track.

When the picture frames on the print are examined the clapper is seen slightly blurred and falling in progressive stages towards the main slate board until the two make contact. At this point the blurr ceases and this is the *sync frame* of the picture. Providing that it has been photographed correctly, positioned carefully in front of the camera, the clapper will be easily seen, both in movement and when static, since this portion of the clapper and slate is usually marked with broad black and white stripes.

The clapper noise recorded on to the sound film is very short and sharp. It is found quite easily when the sound film is wound past the reproducing magnetic sound head. Near this sync mark, the voice of the assistant making the announcement of slate number and take number completes the identification of the shot.

Once these common picture and sound sync marks are marked on the films, and are aligned in picture and sound reproducing systems in projectors, viewing machines or film synchronizers, the

78

Marks used to indicate the synchronizing point on sound and picture showing (a) the visual clap and (b) the clap recorded on the sound track.

picture and sound films remain synchronized to each other while being run through the equipment until the end of the shot.

Electronic sync mark

This method of clapping the sync mark, however, can be extremely annoying to an artist when, for a close shot the clapper is banged down right in front of his or her nose. Alternative electronic methods of producing a picture and sound mark which would not be disturbing to the artists have been evolved.

The most common electronic system (also known as "silent turnover") used in studios consists of an automatic "fogging" of the picture negative for a specified number of frames. The fogging takes effect at one side of the negative, while at the same time an audible sound signal is recorded on to the sound film, the signal being exactly the same length as the picture fogging. Picture and sound marks would not come into effect until camera and recorder were "run-up" to standard speed.

Aligning the two marks on the prints gives synchronization, but this system is not always foolproof. For some unknown reason the picture camera very often fails to record the foglight and sometimes the system operates before either camera or recorder are up to true speed. When functioning properly, however, it dispenses with the need for a clapper boy, who has to scramble out of picture the moment he has recorded the clap. And, naturally the electronic system causes no annoyance to the artist.

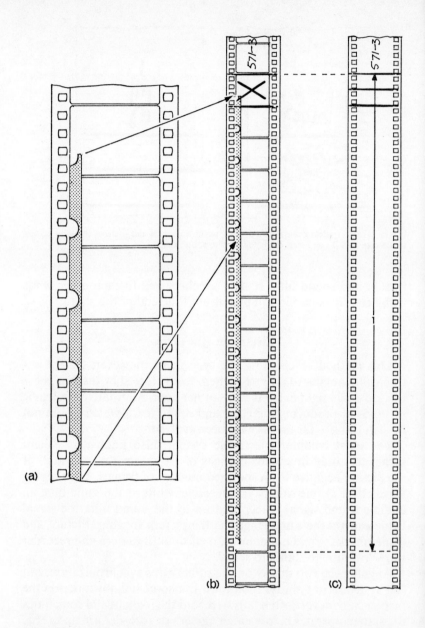

(a)

(b)

(c)

Alternative automatic method of establishing picture/sound synchronism. (a) Each picture frame over a pre-set length records a light which "fogs" an area on the negative. (b) The length of the fogged area on the positive print. (c) (l) the matching length of the sound "buzz" on the sound recording. Aligning the two achieves synchronism.

Whichever system is used, synchronizing the picture with the appropriate sound track consists of matching a visual mark with an audible mark at the beginning of each take.

The assistant editor still has to identify the various slates and takes of the daily sound transfers and the synchronizing marks in readiness for the receipt of the picture daily rush print.

Processing routine

Development of picture negative, making and processing the required prints, is usually an operation carried out during the night at the laboratory. Exposed negative received before the hour of midnight, possibly an hour or so later by arrangement, is developed by the night crew, and is then sorted so that those scenes required for printing are assembled together in rolls, the remaining NG and held negative being assembled separately. The rolls to be printed are assessed for grading, both in print density and colour (where colour is used) are cleaned and handed to the positive printer, who then makes the prints according to the grading assessment. The undeveloped print is processed examined and cleaned, and is then available for the first viewing by the lab contact man assigned to the production.

This first viewing takes place very early in the morning in the laboratory projection room and, in special circumstances when a shot relating to the present day's work has to be seen as quickly as possible, even without sound, it is usually possible to arrange for the film editor to be present. With so many other productions to handle and view, the times of viewing being dependent on the quantities of film involved, it is understandable that the laboratory technicians normally prefer to view the film alone.

Processor's viewing report

The Lab Contact will check the quality of the print, bearing in mind the style of the photography, noting any deficiencies in processing and grading, watching for any scratches or blemishes that may call for a check to be made through all the processing and camera equipment. He then makes out his viewing report, listing all the slates and takes in the order of viewing and how each roll of positive has been assembled. The number of the printer machine light from which each take was exposed for printing is noted, with any necessary comment regarding photographic quality or defects.

The daily rush print is then sent to the film cutting room together with a copy of the viewing report. But any serious defect seen at this stage would be immediately telephoned to the shooting unit, or to the editor if the unit is away on a location. If short positive grading test strips were made as a guide to the printing operation, these would be included with the rush print, together with a further copy of the report to be handed to the director of photography as a check on the previous day's photography.

TECHNICOLOR ROLL No.	CAMERA REPORT OR YOUR ORDER No.	SCENE & TAKE	PRINTS REQUIRED COL.	PRINTS REQUIRED B & W	RUSH PRINT TIMINGS.	FINAL RATING	COMMENTS
90694	51874	314A-1	C		17	16	Oc
		315A-1	C		17	16	Oc
		316-1	C		17	15	RP LIGHTER
		317A-1	C		16	15	Oc
		319A-1	C		18	17	Oc
		320A-1	C		17	15	RP u
90695	"	314B-1	C		18	18	D.A. T.S. EDGE
90696	"	315B-1	C		17	17	Oc
		317B-1	C		16	16	Oc
		318-1	C		18	16	Oc
		2	C		18	16	Oc
		3	C		18	16	a
		4	C		18	16	Oc
		319B-1	C		19	19	a
		320B-1	C		17	13	R.P. LIGHTER
90697	51875	323B-1	C		16	14	RP u

Technicolor Ltd 39006

RUSH PRINT VIEWING REPORT
FOR COLOUR/XXXXXX
5251–693

Consignment No. P24
Date of Photography 4-3-67

Prod. DARK OF THE SUN
Sold to M.G.M.
G.P.O. No. 1811

8/366

TO SHEET TWO

Viewed by:

GENERAL COMMENTS:

SHIP TO: M.G.M. CUTTING ROOMS, ELSTREE

Abbreviations as used in reporting defects:

NTS—TS	Non Track side (right) Track side (left)
—D	Minus density (white) on screen.
+D	Plus density (black) on screen.
DA	Dirty camera aperture.
X	Indicates negative will be examined and any serious defects confirmed later.
RP	Indicates positive print will be replaced. (Print is punched in slate). We would prefer negatives that print between 12 and 15 on our printer scale.

Daily rushes laboratory viewing report. RP written in the right-hand column indicates order to reprint, in this case lighter.

82

ADDITIONAL REPORT ON NEGATIVE DEFECTS
SEE ALSO OUR VIEWING REPORTS Nos. ....27601.............

To ....The Production Manager.................   Date...25th May, 1967................

Copies to ..The Editor.............................   Subject ...."DARK OF THE SUN"...............

....   Photographed ....24-5-67..........................

M. G. M. Productions.

Scene	Take	Nature and Position of Defect (Edge Nos.)	REMARKS
Roll-96112 Scene 710B	3	As a result of negative perforation damage found prior to processing, five frames of picture had to be extracted at a point 1-ft. from the tail-end of your non printed scene 710B take 3, at footage number - A4X24038+1/5.	Sample of damaged film enclosed herewith.

ST. 3661

Negative defects report sent to the production manager and the editor detailing the location and nature of the defect, and in this case enclosing a sample of the damaged film.

Picture negative filing

The rolls of negative of that day's work are then handed over to the negative breakdown department at the laboratory. The staff there document all the information they need for their own filing system. They store the negative in a clean and safe place where it is instantly available. Individual scenes and takes are clearly identified for any reprinting which may be called for and the eventual negative cutting. The negative is usually kept in numbered rolls at this stage. The numbers correspond to those which were given to the rolls of positive prints at the time they were made and, therefore, incorporated in the viewing report sent to the editor.

The processing itinerary and subsequent print viewing may vary if the laboratory is part of a large studio organization and situated on the studio site. But, in general, the processing of daily rushes is done as a night operation. Close contact is maintained between the laboratory and the film cutting room during the course of the entire production, the supervisor at the lab. co-ordinating all the editor's film requirements.

Daily rush picture print

These "dailies", or "rushes", as they are commonly known can be expected at approximately the same time each day during the shooting period of the film. A disruption to this routine delivery can, of course, be caused if the laboratory production supervisor has been dissatisfied with the print quality and has called for reprints. A major disaster of machine breakdown during processing with resultant negative damage could be another reason. Regular and prompt delivery is to be expected normally however.

The daily routine of the film cutting room must be arranged to deal with the film as it arrives so that synchronizing picture and sound is achieved with no delay. This is probably the most vital operation which the editorial assistant performs during the shooting period. Synchronizing has to be fast and accurate since picture has to be viewed with sound at the very earliest opportunity. Producer, director, and cameraman want to see the result of the day's work, which perhaps has a direct bearing on something which they are presently shooting and, certainly, any serious shortcomings in direction, performance or photographic quality will have to be rectified at once. Sets are, perhaps, about to be "struck", artists finishing their commitment, and any delay in discovering such unfortunate shortcomings may be extremely costly. It is usual to have a regular daily projection room reservation at the same hour. So the synchronizing of film and assembly into viewing rolls goes forward to meet this deadline.

Planning rolls of dailies

Having consulted the reports on picture negative, sound master and continuity, the assistant editor knows exactly which slate numbers and take numbers are to be printed. He knows the individual footages, and can plan in advance how he intends to assemble the roll or rolls for projection. He will know that rolls of 35 mm film begin to reach the point of unmanageability if they are much over 1,000 ft. in length, particularly with the routines which still have to be performed before editing starts, and so he plans the contents of each roll with this in mind. He consults the viewing report immediately and lets the editor see any unusual comments which may have been made, particularly when negative blemishes or defects have been noted. Now, he can begin the synchronizing operation.

Synchronizing rushes

In normal circumstances, as we have seen, the sound tracks have already been sorted, each take marked at the head with its identifying slate and take number. The sound clap or alternative synchronizing mark has been established and visibly indicated with a wax pencil cross.

Now, the assistant finds each appropriate slate and take of the picture, establishes the visible picture clapper, or alternative visual synchronizing mark, and starts to assemble these sections into synchronized picture and sound rolls. He works at a film cutting bench equipped with whichever method of "feeding" the film is in use, e.g., the film horse for rolls not mounted on reels, or the winding spindle if reels are to be used. The film synchronizer is in position over the diffused lighting panel, and empty reels mounted on the right-hand winding spindle.

Preparing the leaders

The projection machines require enough blank footage to thread the film from feed to take-up mechanism and so the assistant should have prepared leader film for picture and sound rolls, numbered with the daily rushes roll number and with synchronized start marks in the form of a cross occupying one frame on each leader. The requisite number of pairs of film leaders, one for picture and one for sound are prepared by using the synchronizer.

The drums of the synchronizer are marked around their circumference with picture frame lines (e.g., in the case of 35 mm film a line after every forth sprocket) to aid the consistent framing of blank leader film which has no visible frames. This ensures that whatever length the leader maybe the first picture frame eventually spliced to it is correctly presented in the gate aperture of the projector so that the entire frame is projected on to the viewing screen. As each splice in a picture roll is made across the visible frame line of each cut it presents no problem. But blank leader film must be correctly spliced even though the frame line cannot be seen. The lines on the synchronizer drum will make this possible.

The synchronizing start mark crosses are made to occupy the depth of one frame, coinciding with the lines on the synchronizer drum. A sufficient length of leader (say 10 ft. after the start marks) is drawn through the synchronizer, and the picture and sound leaders are cut exactly level where any one of the lines on the drum occurs. When the assembled rolls eventually reach the projection room, the picture cross is placed centrally in the picture gate aperture, the sound cross centrally over the magnetic reproducing head.

With the leaders mounted on the take-up reels, and before the first scene is synchronized and attached, a focus and aperture film of the correct type should be spliced on to the picture leader. This is of benefit to the projectionist. A similar length of blank film is spliced to the sound leader to maintain synchronization. This focus leader must be of the same type as the picture to be projected. If it is a CinemaScope picture then the information on the focus leader must also be in CinemaScope. Focus leader consists of horizontal and vertical lines and sharply defined lettering. This makes it easier to focus accurately with the projector lens. Arrows at top, bottom and sides of the frame pointing to the correct position for the screen

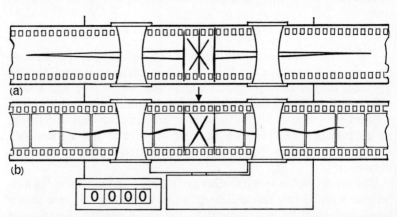

Film synchronizing procedure. Picture and sound start marks are shown here placed at level sync in the film synchronizer. (a) Sound. (b) Picture.

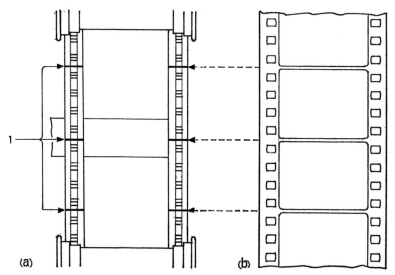

Correctly "framing" film in the synchronizer. This is particularly important with blank leader film which has no frame lines printed in. (a) Close detail of a synchronizer drum for 35 mm film with (I) the frame lines marked after every fourth sprocket. (b) All picture should be mounted in the synchronizer with its frame lines placed over these marks. All blank leader to be joined to picture must also be "framed" correctly.

masking. Quite often, the picture camera is of the type which photographs slightly more on the negative than is finally required and, unless the projectionist is given some guidance, he will not know how to mask the projected image. He needs sufficient time to adjust the focus and correctly frame the aperture before the first shot appears. Something like 15 ft. of focus leader is usually adequate.

The picture leader at the head of each roll also indicates the title of the production and the format of the film e.g., wide screen, CinemaScope, standard, so that the correct projector lens and gate aperture plate are used.

Synchronizing

Synchronizing of each take now takes place and the assistant assembles them in the order of viewing. As long as the sync indications on picture and sound have been correctly located and marked by him, the operation is simple.

Placing the film in the synchronizer with picture and sound start marks level, situated correctly over the frame lines on the synchronizer drum, the assistant rolls both films *backwards* through the

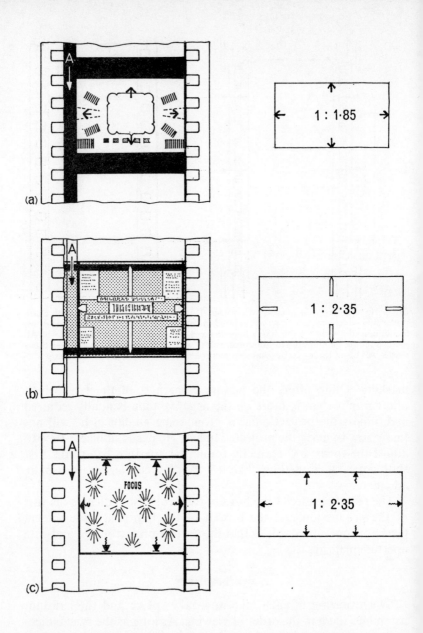

Types of focus leader film, designed as an aid to the projectionist for focus and frame alignment. The arrows in each case are a guide so that the screen image can be adjusted to a correct marking on the screen to avoid the image being cut off at top, bottom or sides. (A) is the sound track area. (a) Normal lens focus leader. (b) and (c) Types of Panavision leader. The projected area in each case is shown on the right.

synchronizer so that the footage containing the slate board information photographed ahead of the "clap", is retained. Marking with a wax pencil at this point the slate and take number, for future reference, he cuts both films exactly level and *on a frame line*. Picture and sound are spliced to the leaders and then, winding through the synchronizer on to the take up reels he eventually reaches the end of the take. This is fairly easily seen on the picture print since the camera was running down in speed at this point and the density of the print changes. In any case there is usually at least one frame of clear film at this point. Where dark scenes and poorly illuminated slate boards make this a more difficult point to see, the sound track will generally have the voice of the director shouting "cut!"—and this will narrow the search. If the picture was made silent and does not have this vocal aid, the approximate area of the end of the take can be established by checking the length of film which was noted on the appropriate report and using the footage counter on the synchronizer as a guide. Having found the end of the take, both picture and sound films can be cut exactly level on a frame line, before the film is allowed to pass out of the synchronizer.

Locating the start marks, cutting picture and sound level on a frame line at the start of the slate board, winding them through the

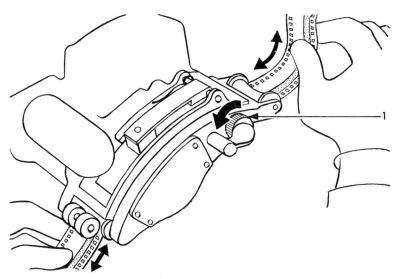

Magnetic sound track searching. This is another method, often used by the editor when cutting dialogue scenes. Turning the knurled wheel (I) releases the drive sprocket, allowing the sound to be freely moved back and forth beneath the sound head.

synchronizer together and then cutting each level on a frame line at the end of the take, is then continued. The slates and takes are assembled in the correct viewing order as these synchronized rushes are built into rolls, ready for projection. A short length of blank film is spliced at the end of each completed roll as a protective measure and, in the case of picture, to avoid a dazzling white light appearing on the screen at the end of the roll. Any clear film contained in the print (a result of lab. printing requirements) should be removed as the synchronized rolls are assembled. White light on the screen between takes can be most disturbing when viewing darkly illuminated night scenes.

Documents for projection room

During assembly, the assistant prepares the daily rushes book, noting the slate and take numbers in the order of assembly. This is for the editor to use when in the projection room. The continuity report and lab viewing report should accompany this book at the first viewing so that unprinted takes can be discussed if necessary. The viewing report serves as a reminder of any blemishes to be watched for. The printer light information is used as a basis for reprint discussion where these are contemplated.

Viewing order

Viewing order mainly depends on the director's requirements. Some are quite happy to see the assembled rushes in the order in which they were photographed, others are insistent on a rearrangement so that they are viewed in continuity order. In this case master scenes are immediately followed by the medium and closer angles, even though some of the close shots were made right at the end of the day's work. This request presents no great difficulty and will simply call for the correct breaking down and sorting of the picture and sound before synchronizing begins. It may mean that an occasional silent shot must be inserted into the rushes roll when further sound shots are to follow. This is simply a matter of inserting the correct amount of blank film in the sound roll at this point to maintain overall synchronization.

Where takes are assembled in order of photography, silent shots are generally held out of the roll until all sound shots have finished, then assembled at the end.

90

Non-standard-speed shots

If all the takes have been made at normal camera speed, all visual and recorded sound sync marks correctly included, correct announcements made and information for printing properly documented, then synchronizing the picture and sound is very straightforward. Unfortunately, the day will rarely pass without one complication or another and sometimes a problem which has never been met before. A little thought will usually provide the solution.

An obvious complication, is where the picture camera speed is non-standard and, therefore, not running at speed with the sound. Clappers may have been outside the camera viewing range when clapped, or even left out altogether. Several picture cameras may be simultaneously photographing a spectacular scene but only one of them was interlocked with the sound recorder. And so on.

If the picture camera is at non-standard speed then it is most unlikely that the scene being recorded will have dialogue, although this can happen. It is more likely that the camera has been under-cranked to exaggerate the action of a fight, or speed up the travel of some vehicle. So only an overall sound effect is needed initially for this scene.

A slate board, not included at the front of a shot, is normally inserted at the end, upside down so that the fact is obvious, and cannot be confused as the start of another take. Slate boards are sometimes included at the end of a scene where the camera started close to a subject and pulled back to reveal the scene if at the beginning there was insufficient space to insert the board between lens and subject.

Multiple camera set-ups are usually employed on some spectacular battle scene or a stunt which is difficult to repeat. Once again, only a sound effects track may be initially required, though it may be advisable to order a sound track for each camera angle, even if the sync is only approximate on some.

Missing slate boards

The complete absence of a board is possible and particulars of this should be noted in the various reports. The shot is allocated its missing number as though it had been recorded on film in the usual way. Or it can be designated NS meaning "no slate". In any event when synchronizing daily rushes, the few pieces of film which *are* unslated can be reasonably easily identified by viewing the first few feet of action on the Moviola in conjunction with the information given on the continuity report.

Visual synchronizing

If synchronizing marks have been left out altogether there is no alternative than to put picture and track on to the Moviola and start visual matching of picture and sound. Overall effects tracks present little problem where such noises as door slams and similar movements are almost as good as the omitted clapper. Dialogue scenes are very simple having found the first spoken sentence. Visual matching in such cases is made easier by working with words which have a slightly explosive beginning. Good examples are those beginning with the letter "P" and "B", which call for a much more obvious and easily matched mouth movement. The picture should be moved back and forth in the Moviola one frame at a time in relation to the sound track. Each time a change in relationship is made, the result can be viewed for its synchronized effect and the correct sync can soon be established. Pencil marks can be made on the film in the picture gate and in the sound head. With these temporary marks aligned in the film synchronizer, the two filmstrips can be wound back to the head of the scene and cut level on a frame line.

Where picture and sound units have not been interlocked at the time of shooting, it may be necessary to go all the way through the take on the Moviola, synchronizing visually and making temporary sync marks at intervals throughout the take. The picture and sound would then be clamped into the synchronizer using the first set of temporary marks and, after cutting level at the front, winding through and making an adjustment to the sound track as each new mark enters the synchronizer. All the adjustments must be made in the sound track only, removing excess, or lengthening the sound in clear areas between words or effects so that the overall sync is as perfect as possible in such circumstances. Such sound tracks would be regarded only as temporary working tracks for initial cutting purposes to be used eventually as guides for making correctly synchronized replacements.

Film damage

Whatever complications are encountered, the assistant's prime objective is to do the synchronizing work as fast as possible using

92

the information given in the reports, where this will be helpful. He must handle the film with great care, never allowing it to come into contact with dirt or to be scratched by some of the hard metal parts of equipment. He must be particularly careful to avoid such damage if visual synchronizing on the Moviola becomes necessary.

The difference between positive and negative film damage is normally quite obvious. Positive scratches and blemishes are usually plus-density when viewed on the screen, whereas a minus-density effect is apparent if scratches and blemishes have been printed from the negative. There are occasions when negative damage, involving light scratches, can be corrected by a laboratory treatment applied to the cell side of the negative film and it is often possible to polish the surface to remove the offending scratch. A check reprint, to ensure that the damage has been removed can then be ordered. Careful film handling before the first synchronized viewing eliminates doubt of the origin of any scratches and marks seen, and leaves the viewing free from distraction.

The rolls of daily rushes are finally taken to the projection room and, at the appointed hour, the editor is joined by the authorized members of the producing company for the first important viewing.

5

DAILY ROUTINES

DAILY viewing of synchronized rush prints of the previous day's work is never delayed. If costly re-shooting becomes necessary, for whatever reason, this situation must be established with all speed, however unfortunate the circumstances may be.

Deciding who must attend these daily screenings is the responsibility of the producer. Often the first viewing is not attended by the director or members of the shooting unit, unless some vital check is necessary. He and the crew are no doubt, fully occupied with the shooting of the day, and any time lost in this area represents considerable expense. The director and key crew members may leave their viewing to the end of the day or possibly during the lunch break. Meanwhile, the producer and editor screen the film and make their assessment.

If the entire production team is away from the studio, perhaps on foreign location, then it is the editor's responsibility to view the film alone, making his assessment and preparing a brief report to be telephoned or cabled to the producer and director, wherever they may be. In preparing such a report, the editor considers the quality of the day's work, the amount of coverage for editing provided by the director and the quality of photography and artist performance. He must also watch out for any physical damage to the picture negative. The opinion of the experienced editor is always respected at such times and, although his telephoned or cabled reports might bring bad tidings, his praise of work well done helps to maintain the morale of a unit faced with many physical hardships on such a location. He is expected to be honest and objective in his comments and, for the time being, will be the "eyes" of the director until such time as he returns to the studio.

Daily studio screenings

The producer must be satisfied that the story is developing into a photoplay which accords with the artistic requirements of the script. The director must be assured that his use of the camera, and performances of artists are as good as he thought they were at the time of shooting. The cameraman assesses the quality of the rush print in relation to his lighting and the mechanics of camera movement, focus, composition of the shot, and so on. Art director, wardrobe, make-up, hairdressing and continuity—in fact all the key personnel should attend these screenings, particularly during the early days of the production so that corrections and adjustments called for by the director and producer can be discussed and understood immediately.

Very often during the early days of a production, the laboratory supervisor will make himself available to make an on-the-spot assessment of the print with the director of photography. The early scenes may not have been graded and printed as the cameraman visualized. It is usually at this stage, too, that any reprints are made to the standard required so that a "key" can be established for the whole project. Any scratches and defects are checked at once. A laboratory check on the negative establishes if the damage is permanently contained in the negative calling for retakes. Careful research may reveal a faulty camera, film magazine, or other misaligned equipment which must be discarded or corrected to avoid further negative damage.

Selection and coverage

The editor and the director discuss the coverage of the story, and where several takes of the same angle have been printed, selections are made and preferences indicated. Armed with his daily rushes book, the editor notes these preferences throughout the screening. This determines the choice of shots for his first assemblies.

But any take chosen is not necessarily required in its entirety. The editor and director discuss the merit of sections of each take, bearing in mind the other angles available and the constant cutting back and forth between angles which may take place.

There must always be sufficient film coverage to give the editor flexibility in the cutting of the film. The film "jigsaw" should ideally, be capable of assembly in many different ways around a basic plan. To be forced to assemble film in a one-way pattern is very unsatisfactory, usually fatal in the later stage of fine cutting when deep cuts have to be made to reduce a sequence which may be overlength.

Director and editor must bear such things in mind at these screenings and, if the coverage is "thin", arrange for additional shooting. A small amount of additional coverage at this stage is relatively easy to supply—with sets still available, artists still on the payroll. To wait until the closing days of the production when fine cutting is under way might be too late—even impossible.

Sound quality

While noting the selected visuals, the editor listens carefully to the quality of the sound tracks. He, the director and the chief sound engineer must determine which, if any, sound takes are of unsuitable quality to be used in the final product.

In normal studio conditions the dialogue recordings are of high enough quality for the final sound track. There are times, however, when this high quality cannot be maintained and unwanted sounds are unavoidably mixed in with dialogue. Wind machines, aircraft passing overhead and difficulty in positioning the microphone close enough to the actor can all ruin the quality of dialogue recording, particularly when shooting on exterior locations. Although these sound tracks are quite suitable for assembling the editor's working copy they must eventually be replaced by "clean" recordings, synchronized with picture, and made under the controlled conditions of the recording studio. The editor makes notes of all such scenes so that the necessary film can be ordered and preparations made in advance. Where such notes are made, the assistant editor orders as routine, a picture reprint and a sound transfer of each shot involved in readiness for eventual post-synchronization. The cheapest black and white prints of picture are ordered, although if the cameraman had asked for reprints on a sequence to correct grading errors, the rejected prints could well be used for this work.

When everyone concerned has attended the screening of daily rushes, editorial activity returns to the cutting room. There are further routines before the film is available for editing.

Film logging and coding

The identifying marks made at the time of shooting enable records and reports to be compiled. The picture negative, however, carries an additional form of identification that plays a vital part in most of the editing and laboratory procedures which follow. This is the original negative key number or edge number. During manufacture, each roll of film is printed with special numbers at 1-ft. intervals along its entire length, outside the perforations on one outer edge. The numbers consist of a letter prefix, followed by a series of numerals, and the numerals advance by a unit at each 1-ft. interval. It might be 35YG,89400; or A12X,149328, for example.

In the two examples quoted the 35G section and the A12X section of the key number remains constant, and the following number advances by one unit per foot. The prefix differs for each type of photographic emulsion giving an indication of the emulsion speed and grain characteristics and whether the emulsion is for original negative photography or for a duplicating process.

These numbers are printed by a machine which uses a rotating numbering block and ink of a type impervious to erasure by photographic processing. Thus, when the exposed picture negative is developed at the film laboratory the numbers not only remain visible on the clear edge of the film but, during the printing process, they are photographically transferred to the positive print giving a direct reference from original to print throughout the roll. In theory, prefixes and numerals are never repeated on any two rolls of film in current use so matching of negative to positive film is simple down to a single frame. The editor, working with the posi-

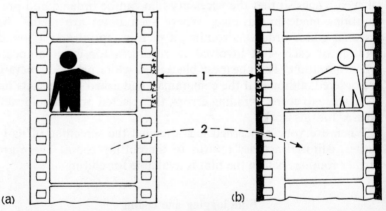

For film identification and reference, the key number (1) transferred from (a) negative to (b) positive print (both here seen emulsion uppermost). The frames when printed (2), incorporate a masking to provide for the sound track between perforations and image.

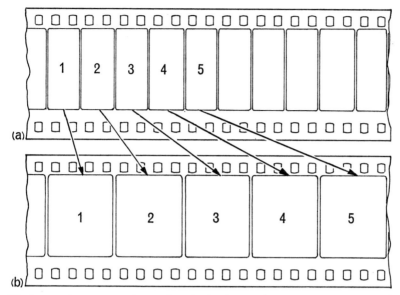

The key number: an exception to the rule that key numbers appear one per running foot of 35 mm positive film. (a) Techniscope half-frame picture negative with normal one-per-foot key numbers. (b) The positive print, enlarged and squeezed so that each negative half-frame now occupies a positive full frame. The key numbers transferred to the positive print, therefore, will now occur at intervals of two feet.

tive in the cutting room can identify any piece of negative stored at the laboratory.

Photographic sound negative film also carries a similar key number. Magnetic sound film normally has no key numbers printed at the time of manufacture.

It would seem that there are now enough forms of identification on the film—slate numbers, take numbers, picture key numbers, but one more equally important numbering operation must take place *after* the daily rushes have been synchronized into rolls.

Editorial code numbering

The two basic reasons for carrying out this further operation are:

1. *Identification*: Whereas the picture has visual slate boards and an identifying key number printed at the edge, the magnetic sound cutting print has none, and once editing starts any short pieces of film severed from that initial announcement and clapper board will have no identification.

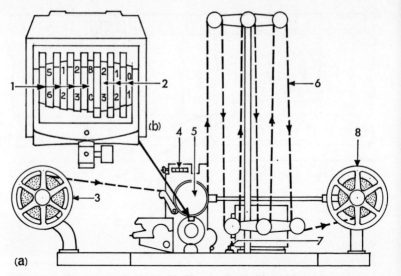

Editorial code-numbering machine (a). The numbering block (b). In this example, the first four rings (1) remain static after being set by hand. (2) These three rings are set at 000 and, during the numbering operation, automatically increase by one unit per foot of film passing through the machine. (3) Feed spool. (4) Footage counter. (5) Sprocketed main driving wheel. (6) Film passing through the drying period. (7) On/off switch. (8) Take-up spool.

2. *Maintaining synchronism*: Picture and sound films are constantly removed and replaced as they are viewed on the Moviola and film synchronizer. It would be very time consuming to have to go back to the beginning of each scene every time to find sync marks, particularly with lengthy takes. Further, when cutting starts, and slate boards are removed, no synchronizing marks remain on the selected pieces. The editor, therefore, needs some visual synchronizing reference between picture and sound *throughout* the length of each take.

Where picture has been shot without sound, and where sound has been shot wild as in the case of additional dialogue tracks, all such film must be code numbered if only for the future identification of short lengths.

Code numbering is usually done on a machine of the type used by the film manufacturer when printing the negative key numbers on the stock as it is made.

The rolls of film are fed from a feed reel over the main drive sprocketed drum, where the self-inking numbering block makes contact with the film edge at 1-ft. intervals, over rollers on a

100

number of drying arms and then on to the take-up reel. The numbers on the rotating block indicate the slate or scene number, this remaining static during the numbering operation but being easily altered by hand for each separate take, followed by further numbers which automatically advance by one unit as each foot of film passes over the drum.

Method

Sound and picture rolls of assembled and synchronized daily rushes are put on to the machines. The start mark cross which has already been marked with wax pencil at the head of each take is placed on the appropriate mark on the drum of the machine. As the drum starts to rotate the first number is printed. The two groups of numbers (static and rotating group) are set at exactly the same combination on the picture start and sound start of each synchronized take. By aligning corresponding numbers at any point during the take the correct sync between sound and picture can be found. The operator of the numbering machine is provided with a list of the contents of each roll of picture and sound track and the numbers to be set at each start mark. If he is also given the approximate length of each take this, too, will be helpful. Watching for the beginning of each new take, he will stop the machine, reset the series of numbers for the new take, line up the film with the start mark on the drum and restart the machine.

For a synchronizing reference it does not really matter which

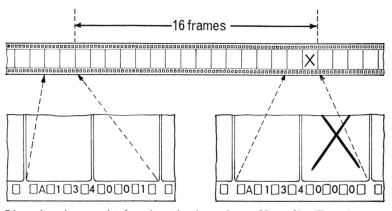

Film coding. An example of an editorial code number on 35 mm film. The code represents the number for Slate 134A and is zeroed at the start mark. The machine will now print an advancing number after every 16 frames (1 foot). The type of numbering block used here prints the numerals between the film perforations.

combination of numbers is used as long as picture and sound carry identical numerals. For identifying short lengths of film separated from the slate board and announcement, however, the static numerals should give clear reference to the original slate or scene numbers.

Numbering methods

A simple numbering block has six letters; the first three moveable by hand but remaining static during printing; the second group of three capable of rotating from 000 to 999 automatically. Suppose that slate 143 has been photographed and three takes have been printed, the first take 150 ft. long, the second 155 ft. and the third 148 ft. The numbers for take one are set at 143 000 and, at the end of the take read somewhere around 143 150, depending on the length of original camera run-up on the slate board. The numbers for take two are now reset at 143 200 and, at the end of the take read 143 355. Take three is numbered from 143 400 and ends at 143 548.

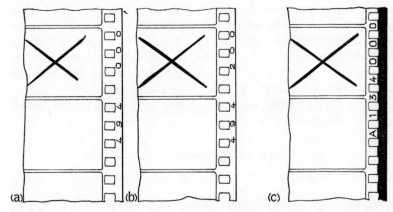

Machine operated editorial code numbering, with different types of number block. (a) Numerals on the outer edge for the first printed take of slate 494. (b) Numerals for the second printed take of 494. (c) Numbers between perforations, useful where the outer edge of the print is opaque.

More sophisticated numbering blocks may indicate scene numbers in greater detail by incorporating a choice of alphabet letters in addition to the series of figures. Both types are in wide use around the world.

Where machines are not available, hand stamping methods may be employed. The film is stamped at regular and matched intervals with a repeating stamp of the kind used to mark prices on goods

102

in supermarkets. When handling large quantities of synchronized film, however, the assistant using this method will be affected in rather the same way as was Charlie Chaplin in *Modern Times*.

On the continent of Europe some assistants still number the film by hand, using a fine paint brush and quick drying white ink.

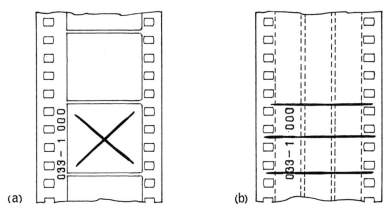

(a)　　　　　　　　　　　　　　(b)

Editorial code numbering. Manually operated stamp. Here, the hand-operated method prints the numerals in the blank sound track area on the positive picture and on the cell side of the magnetic sound film. This can be troublesome if the stamp becomes magnetized. Note the very clear indication of slate, take and footage numbers. In this case, slate 33 take 1. (a) Picture start frame. (b) Synchronous sound start frame.

In some countries, particularly where the editing table is used for cutting, such code numbering systems are thought unnecessary since editing progresses steadily without the constant removal of rolls of film from the synchronizing mechanism. This does seem a poor policy, bearing in mind the cutting and re-cutting, eliminating and reshaping which usually follows first assembly.

Master record book

At this stage the daily rushes are *almost* available for the editor— but not quite!

Apart from the reports already gathered, a master record book must be compiled. This applies in all film cutting rooms except those involved in minor productions.

The assistant editor takes all the additional information available and tabulates it in this book. Against each slate and take number in progressive order he records the date of photography, the number of the negative roll stored at the laboratory, the first and last negative key number of the take, the first and last code

Slate	Take	Key Number	Code Nº	Negative Roll	Sound Master Roll	Date
1	1	A 12x 14914 – 980	001000 –066	4981	A1	29 MAR.
	2	14981 –15052	100 –171	4981	A1	
	3	15053 –15130	200 –277	4981	A1	
2	1	A 12X 15134 – 194	002000 –060	4981	A1	
	4	15258 –320	100 –162	4982	A1	
3	2.	A 29X 39180 –480	003000 –300	4982	B1	
	5	39870 –40178	400 –708	4983	B1	

Cutting room records: extract from a master record book showing entries for three slates. This information is recorded throughout the production.

number of the take, and the number of the master sound roll in which the take can be located for future re-transfers.

Breaking down rushes

Now the film can be cut and assembled and if the editor is using a Moviola for viewing and cutting, he probably wants the film to be broken into individual takes, picture and sound rolled in together for convenience in handling. These will be set out on film racks, either in slate order or in script scene order of continuity, whichever

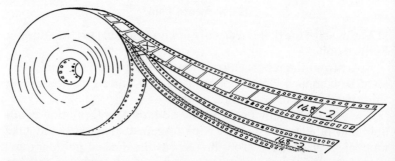

Breaking down rushes and preparing for film assembly. Usual method of preparing individual takes for cutting on the Moviola. Picture and sound wrapped together.

is preferred by the editor. No matter which method is employed, each take should have clear wax pencil indications of slate and take number in full view.

First assembly

Despite the haphazard chronology of shooting, each day's work often includes at least a small self-contained sequence which can now be assembled by the editor. Certainly, after a few days of shooting some sequences will be complete. Assembly must begin at once, no matter how short or isolated the sequences may be, unless the producer or director have agreed that they need the film to remain in an uncut state for some specific reason. There are times when film may have to be held for visiting executives and, they often choose the early days before much film has been assembled. It probably gives them the feeling that they are seeing a lot for their money when they view many rolls of uncut film.

The aim must be to have all film completely assembled in the shortest possible time after the final day of photography and this is achieved only by avoiding delays in starting these first rough assemblies and continuing such work as shooting progresses.

For the sake of economy, studio sets must be "struck" as soon as all work on them has been completed, often as soon as the film laboratory has given a clearance on the satisfactory and safe development of the negative. Such released stage space is then available for new construction and shooting can proceed smoothly from set to set throughout the production.

On occasions, a set is held until a doubtful or difficult scene has been assembled by the editor so that everyone can see, at least, the basic result. Doubtful performances, accidental negative damage during processing, "thin" coverage by the film director, all call for fast assembly. On these occasions set routines in the cutting room may have to be passed over. Coding and logging of records can be dealt with later, and the editorial staff must always be prepared for such possibilities.

Detailed scrutiny of material

It is also important that the editor begin to familiarize himself with the film at his disposal by examining it in great detail. He may have gained an overall impression from the screening of daily rushes, but by physically handling the film during the early assemblies and watching it on his viewing machine, a much more critical examination is possible. Takes initially rejected by the director may reveal subtle differences in certain areas related to the selected take. Although selections and preferences were established with the director at these viewings, they should never be rigidly followed at the expense of the overall result and directors are invariably happy to have a new thought at such times if it results in an improvement.

More important, the editor can gain complete familiarity with all the takes and angles available within sequences, and unconsciously build up a complete memory picture of all film, particularly that which is not incorporated in the assembly. This will be invaluable in the weeks that follow and during the eventual fine cutting.

Script marking

The continuity report made for each camera set-up serves initially as an immediate indication of the quantity and nature of the film which is about to be delivered. In addition, as we have seen, the mass of detailed information on each sheet is invaluable to the editor for his first assemblies. At this stage the information on the camera angle i.e. long shot, close shot, medium shot, etc., given at the head of the report is especially useful. Details of action and dialogue tell the editor where each shot starts and ends, in relation to his script.

The editor marks up his script pages when he receives the reports each morning. He writes the slate number at a point on the script page where the shot starts, indicating the size of the angle, and draws a vertical line down the page, or pages, finishing at the point where the shot ends. Not every script scene is covered in its entirety by each camera angle, but broken down by the director into the most effective segments, varying in angle so that visual continuity of the cutting can be done in several ways. Marking the script pages in this way for each shot gives the editor an immediate overall indication of the amount of film available to him as he looks at the script pages before him. He sees how many angles cover the same action and dialogue, and how far into the sequence he can expect to be able to use each shot if he wishes.

Editorial assistants are sometimes given this script marking task as one of their regular morning routines but it will be more beneficial to the editor if he does it himself. By doing so, he can build up a mental image of the coverage and probably begin to "feel" the cutting pattern even before he sees the film on the screen.

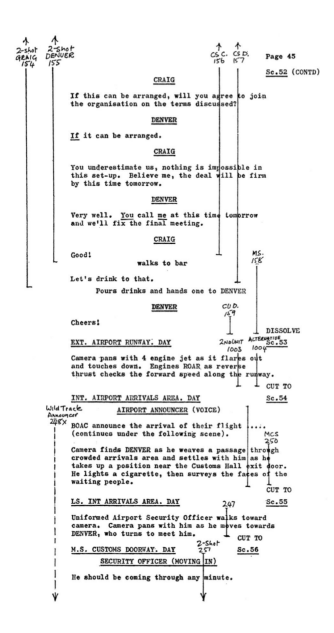

2-shot GRAIG 154   2-Shot DENVER 155   CS C. 156   CS D. 157   Page 45

Sc.52 (CONTD)

CRAIG

If this can be arranged, will you agree to join
the organisation on the terms discussed?

DENVER

If it can be arranged.

CRAIG

You underestimate us, nothing is impossible in
this set-up. Believe me, the deal will be firm
by this time tomorrow.

DENVER

Very well. You call me at this time tomorrow
and we'll fix the final meeting.

CRAIG

Good!

MS. 158

walks to bar

Let's drink to that.

Pours drinks and hands one to DENVER

DENVER   CU D. 159

Cheers!

DISSOLVE

EXT. AIRPORT RUNWAY. DAY   2ND UNIT 1003   ALTERNATIVE 1004   Sc.53

Camera pans with 4 engine jet as it flares out
and touches down. Engines ROAR as reverse
thrust checks the forward speed along the runway.

CUT TO

INT. AIRPORT ARRIVALS AREA. DAY   Sc.54

Wild Track Announcer 248X

AIRPORT ANNOUNCER (VOICE)

BOAC announce the arrival of their flight ....
(continues under the following scene).

MCS 250

Camera finds DENVER as he weaves a passage through
crowded arrivals area and settles with him as he
takes up a position near the Customs Hall exit door.
He lights a cigarette, then surveys the faces of the
waiting people.

CUT TO

LS. INT ARRIVALS AREA. DAY   247   Sc.55

Uniformed Airport Security Officer walks toward
camera. Camera pans with him as he moves towards
DENVER, who turns to meet him.

CUT TO

M.S. CUSTOMS DOORWAY. DAY   2-Shot 257   Sc.56

SECURITY OFFICER (MOVING IN)

He should be coming through any minute.

Method of script marking, indicating the film coverage available to the editor. In
complicated scenes, there would be many more slates and, therefore, many more lines.

107

The first cut

Using this information and the details in the continuity report the editor must now consider the pattern of first assembly, bearing in mind that the script will never tell him how to cut the sequence, even if it indicates specific angles.

He can review the film for each progressive section of the scene, perhaps reviewing it several times before making the first cut. He can run through on his viewer any section of sound take quickly and synchronously by using the code numbers.

Perhaps the most difficult decision is the choice of the first angle where there are several alternatives, and how best to open the sequence, because this will often govern the pattern of cutting for a considerable way into the scene. The thing which makes us all brave at such times is the knowledge that if an experimental assembly is unsuccessful, the print can be respliced in its original form and another, different, assembly made. Flexibility in cutting is not designed to aid the editor of uncertain ability, however. But the film director should provide enough coverage for several patterns of cutting to be achieved before the best result is established and set.

It will have been noticed, particularly by female editors, that the editor and assistants have been referred to constantly as "he". The feminine counterparts throughout the world will perhaps be more forgiving if it is made clear here that their skill, technical knowledge and ability is no less appreciated than that of the male!

The editor now gradually selects the film pieces and establishes the order of the cuts, passing each cut section of picture and track through the synchronizer to avoid any errors in synchronization and picture framing. He clips the sections together with paper clips ready for splicing when the sequence is finished, gradually winding them on to reels mounted on the rewinding spindle. Picture and sound leader film with an identification of the sequence number and correctly framed synchronizing start marks is previously attached to the empty reels ready to receive the first cut.

Splicing

Some editors prefer to splice the cut film as they go along, rather than clip it together and leave it to the assistant. This is quite simple with the small portable tape splicer and enables them to view sections of cut material as they progress. If paper clips are

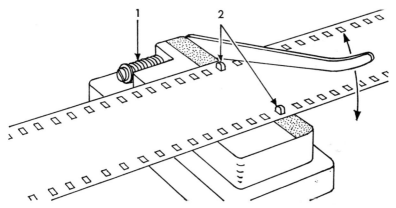

Making the physical cut. If the editor prefers the assistant to perform the splicing, he will need such a device to ensure that he makes all picture and sound cuts exactly at 90° to the film edge so that all pieces to be spliced will correctly "butt" together. (1) Spring tensioner to aid a "clean" cutting action. (2) register pins to ensure a 90° cut.

used, however, and cuts wound unspliced, a brass, or non-magnetized type of clip is better. This avoids any possible interference with magnetic sound film with which they come in contact during assembly.

If the tape splicer is used, therefore, no positive film is lost on a join, the editor must remember that the overlapped join on the final negative assembly will claim an extra frame (p. 60). This is of particular importance when employing the "cut-back" technique.

Additional viewing facilities

A second silent picture viewing machine, attached to the main one (and sometimes considered a luxury) is a considerable advantage when the Moviola-type equipment is used. Simultaneous matching of action where movement is involved is thus simplified.

The editor will now steadily build up the sequence, marking the sound and picture film in the viewing machine with pencil symbols where cuts are to be made. We have seen that the sound cut is often longer than that of the picture, allowing the dialogue or sound effect to continue over the next picture cut. This is not only to smooth the effect of subsequent viewings but also to include visual reactions and perhaps to tie in a spoken commentary with the picture being viewed. The synchronizer must be used constantly so that compensations are made in the overall length of each sound cut to maintain synchronization throughout the scene.

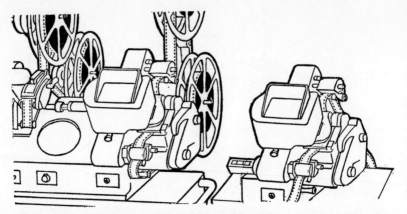

Film assembly. Second picture head alongside main Moviola, as an aid to matching visual cuts, particularly for movement.

Organizing and filing trims

As cuts are made and wound on to the reels, unwanted sections including the front picture slate boards and the sound announcements are suspended on pins in the film cuts bin. They are available for a re-examination if necessary while the sequence is still being

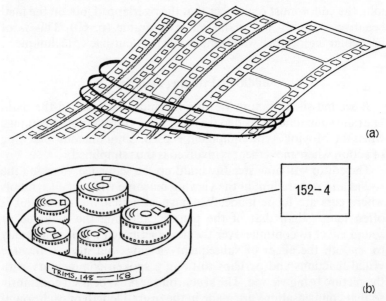

(a)

152-4

TRIMS, 148 — 158

(b)

Filing trims and unused film. (a) Trims bound together with a rubber band before being wound into a roll. (b) Individual rolls of trims, tagged for quick reference.

assembled. As soon as cutting has been finished the assistant winds them up take by take.

The editor will, no doubt, always aim to keep separate all the trims of one take together on one pin. The assistant is advised, however, to check that this has in fact been done when the film in the bin is handed to him for winding into individual rolls for filing. Sections of slates intermingled with other slates, or separate takes mixed together, will cause much frustration and time-wasting searches if the sequence needs to be recut later. The assistant should arrange the trims before wrapping them up, so that each take is suspended on the pin of the cuts bin with the head trim at the front, the tail trim at the rear and any other trims from the take sandwiched in sequence. Where there are many trims from one take it is relatively easy to find the required trim for re-examination at some future time.

The assistant then takes each bundle of trims, picture and sound together, binds the head of the bundle with a rubber band and winds it into a roll for filing. Filing of trims and unused takes is simplified if the rolls of individual takes, cut or uncut, are stored in a series of tins of adequate size in slate-number order. Each tin should be marked with the first and last slate number of the film inside and each roll should be tagged with a small tape so that it can be immediately identified when required. Much time is saved later with a little intelligent checking and effort made during the sorting and filing of all film.

Assembly screenings

Assembly of the film now proceeds from day to day even though the sequences are probably isolated with no direct continuity between each.

As more screen time is accumulated and more scenes are assembled, it becomes important that a reasonably frequent examination is made in the projection room. A weekly screening with producer and director, allows a careful watch on the progression of the filmed story. It also serves to establish mutual confidence between a producer, director and editor who may be working together for the first time. On such a relationship depends to a large extent, the successful outcome of the film. With the editor conscientiously assembling the film, any problems can be brought to light immediately, and not put to one side. Such weekly screenings also speed up the eventual arrival at the fine cut, rather than hold it up until

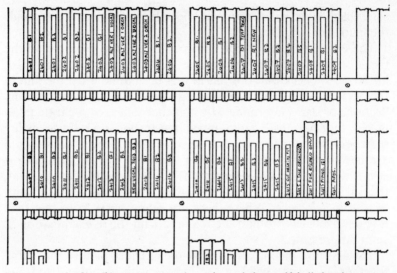

Filing system for film. Film tins are stored upright on shelves and labelled with summary of contents for quick reference. Trims are arranged in sequence of progressive slate numbers, each tin label indicating the first and last slate number contained inside. Picture and sound trims of individual slates are filed in one area; wild tracks; production effects; playback tracks; matte or rear projection backgrounds, in separated areas. This diagram shows many music recordings and playback tracks for a major musical production.

all shooting has been completed. They are of the utmost importance to the director, enabling him to evaluate the quality of his work and the performance of artists as the weeks go by. Retakes may be needed, an additional angle might be justified and it will help greatly if such necessities are revealed as early as possible.

Sound for screenings

During these early assemblies of film, in fact throughout the entire preparation of the editor's working copy, the use of temporary sound tracks should not be ignored. Scenes shot on location, particularly isolated "bridging" and establishing picture shots are often made by a small camera unit without simultaneous recording of sound. Sound crews working with the main unit always try to provide the editor with a selection of overall sound effects which cover the activities of such second-unit photography. But this is not always possible.

The director will not want to hold up main photography while the sound crew are away shooting sound effects. But sometimes the recording of effects can be carried out at the end of a day's shooting, or even on a "rest" day. Sound crews are usually very co-operative in this respect, particularly if the editor supplies the sound recordist with a list of the effects he will need.

It can be very disturbing to all concerned when the sound track of sequences incorporating mute shots suddenly goes dead on the cut. It is better to incorporate even a temporary sound effect to cover these shots so that the normal flow of sound is uninterrupted. Eventually, a good quality, well-synchronized track can be produced and fitted by the sound editor. But almost anything is better than a blank sound section at this stage.

Temporary music tracks from a library can be used to create an impression of the final sound track, and time taken in putting in such sound is well spent.

Dialogue recording may have been extremely difficult where the unwanted noise of aeroplanes and traffic, for example, has intruded on the scene. At times, the dialogue recorded may be inaudible on the sound track and, since the sound engineer is well aware of this situation as he monitors the take, he tries wherever possible to make a clean recording independent of picture.

If such a recording is made immediately after the take is approved, and in a quieter area away from wind, generator or traffic noise, the artists can generally closely match the rhythm of speech they used when the take was photographed. Synchronizing picture to such wild dialogue recordings is a question of visual adjustment when the film is received in the cutting room. Gradual alterations are made throughout the take, and the sound is cut or stretched as necessary. The resulting sound track is much more use in the cut work print than one which was irritatingly noisy, perhaps inaudible. Eventually, the entire scene will probably have to be post-synchronized to picture in a properly equipped recording theatre.

Temporary visuals

Picture shots, too, can be used in a temporary way. Stock shots from the film library may not provide exactly what is needed but, until such shots can be made, the temporary stock shot may provide the valuable links between sequences which would otherwise be missing.

Proposed dissolves and picture fades, merging one scene into the next or indicating the end of a phase of the story, are indicated by the editor on the picture work print as he continues the

113

assemblies. These markings are visible on the screen, and are a useful reference for everyone concerned in the subsequent screenings.

Identifying unslated material

On some productions the editing staff may receive a mass of unslated film, perhaps shot on a difficult location where the regular inclusion of the slate board was virtually impossible.

Operators shooting from small aeroplanes and helicopters, for example, may shoot thousands of feet of film without using a slate board. The continuity girl will probably be miles away working with the main unit and there will be no notes for cutting room guidance.

In this case there is no alternative but to gather descriptions of the angles and action by viewing the film, making notes, and preparing brief continuity reports containing the basic facts. As the very existence of each continuity report is a constant reminder to the editor of the existence of each piece of film, if he marks these reports as he cuts each shot for inclusion in the work print he will know which film is yet uncut. Continuity reports for unslated film are, therefore, very useful. Such film would then be code numbered on the numbering machine using any arbitrary numbers which are unlikely to be repeated on future shooting. Logging and filing can then be done in the usual way.

Reference rolls

There are times, on large productions, when thousands of feet of film are shot, perhaps only for one sequence, with very little documentary information. Here, perhaps even brief notes for the preparation of continuity reports would entail a major operation unworthy of the time involved. Each roll of such film contains shot after shot, separated only by a camera stop and a few blank frames on the print, without any slate board information.

To avoid a time-consuming search through all the rolls looking for just one piece of suitable action for cutting purposes, smaller reference rolls can be made by taking a few frames representative of each shot and splicing them together in order of appearance in the main roll. One thousand feet of such film containing ten separate shots could be condensed for reference and selection to less than 3 ft. of film by taking a 4-frame section from each shot and joining these together in the correct order. Such a reference roll, kept in the tin with the appropriate film, saves many hours of laborious viewing. The small sections are examined at leisure, section by section, on the Moviola (viewing a static frame) and the most suitable shot located. The assistant then breaks out the third, seventh, or whatever shot is required from the main reel ready for the editor to make the cut.

Temporary inserts: picture

As we have seen, early assembly of sequence will probably involve isolated material and, although scenes may be complete in themselves, they will not necessarily be continuous in flow from one to the other. Also, a required picture insert may be held over and not photographed until towards the end of production, present work being concentrated on all shots involving artists.

Sound, too, may be incomplete and it is not always possible to fill up the blank areas with library sound effects, particularly with interior scenes which have been shot silent. In other words, there are going to be many occasions during early assembly of sequences when blank areas are left in both picture and sound. As a temporary measure lengths of white leader film can be inserted to separate unconnected sequences. But the editor usually has a roll of special framed film, each frame of which is printed "sequence missing", or "scene missing", whichever is more appropriate to the occasion, making the situation obvious to all who view the sequences in their present form.

Temporary inserts: sound

As far as the sound track is concerned, it is very useful to have a small supply of magnetic "fill" track available at all times during assembly—an open microphone sound track which will give either an interior or an exterior atmosphere when reproduced. Any short length of interior or exterior sound track without any obviously repetitive noise can be made into a continuous film loop so that a roll of sound transfer can be made from each for use by the editor.

The situation can be dealt with quickly by always having this film at hand on a spare film horse at the left end of the cutting bench, ready for immediate use. The assistant should check that four rolls are always at the ready and they are:

1. "Scene", or "sequence missing" film.
2. Interior "fill" track.
3. Exterior "fill" track.
4. White coated leader film.

115

Checking sync

One further precaution should be taken at this, and all future stages of assembly, particularly when recutting takes place. All sequences involving separate picture and sound track, whether they be first assemblies or recuts, or perhaps the inclusion of a new picture insert, should always be checked for correct synchronism as soon as the editor has finished the work and the film has been spliced. It is surprisingly easy to lose synchronism between picture and sound, even when passing all film through the film synchronizer. A misread code number could be the cause.

It saves much embarrassment in the viewing room if a rigid routine is established. *All* sequences should be checked for synchronism after the first assembly and after *any* change is made in the cutting copy.

Missing keys on reprints

There will always be the rare occasion when the positive print is made that, through an error on the part of the printing machine operator the negative key numbers do not appear on the print. For some unknown reason this happens more frequently when reprints are made. It is usually discovered when the routine recording of information in the master record book is done and the laboratory must provide a new print at their expense for the all-important future reference between negative and positive. The eventual ordering of trick work and negative cutting will be impossible without them.

Picture reprints are requested by the cameraman to correct faults in grading. They may also become necessary in the editor's work print due to some unfortunate physical damage which is beyond repair. Such reprints, when received, are viewed and checked as though they were new daily rushes. Grading and density of print are checked so that a high standard is maintained. Synchronizing marks are pencilled on as before with the original print, and they will receive exactly the same code numbering.

Cutting in reprints

When instructed to do so, the assistant exchanges the old for the new print, be it in an uncut roll or in an assembled sequence. If it is in a sequence he will have to ensure that each cut is replaced if there is more than one cut incorporated from this slate, regardless of whether all have in fact been damaged. This is to ensure consistency of density and colour which tend to fluctuate from print to print. Even small differences cannot be tolerated.

If two prints are in existence because of grading corrections, there is still only one negative at the laboratory. To avoid confusion, only one print should be in circulation and available to the editor for cutting. Ideally, NG prints should be thrown away immediately to avoid any danger of cutting a second print. But they can be used where post-synchronizing may be necessary as grading defects are not bothersome in this operation. Also sound editors never seem to have enough waste film to enable them to space out the sound effects as they are building their reels for final sound dubbing. Long sections of NG film are often used by them for this operation.

If the rejected prints are to be kept for these purposes, they must be clearly marked in such a way that they can never again be incorporated in the editor's work print. It is unlikely that an editor would accidentally cut a second print and repeat a piece of positive film involving a dialogue scene, for obvious reasons. It can easily happen when cutting silent establishing shots, however, particularly when he is desparately searching for film to bridge two sequences and there is a shortage of such coverage.

Marks on mag sound film

Picture prints are normally handled in viewing machines and synchronizers with the emulsion surface uppermost. They are also wound this way on to reels. Magnetic sound track may be used either with the emulsion or, alternatively, with the film base uppermost, depending on the position of the reproducing sound heads on the machines. This does vary.

It is poor policy to allow pencilled information to be written on the emulsion surface of magnetic tracks when using wax pencils as the wax will eventually soften, spread, and be collected on the head of the reproducer. Sound quality becomes distorted and time is lost in cleaning the head and locating the area of wax causing the damage. All writing and sync start marks should be on the shiny base surface.

Splicing magnetic film

Blank film is spliced on to the head and tail of the magnetic rolls for projection purposes and included within the roll whenever sound track is not yet available and the shot is silent. Many sound reels are needed for each completed picture reel during the preparation for final sound mixing and involve the use of hundreds of feet of blank film to maintain overall synchronization with the picture. Blank film can be purchased from manufacturers and it is specially designed for this purpose but, generally, either white coated leader film is used or, where hundreds and hundreds of feet are required by the sound editor, he will use any correct gauge film that he can find, even rejected picture prints. When film of this nature is used it, too, will have an emulsion surface and a shiny base surface.

Leader film spliced to a picture roll in the cutting room will always have both leader and picture emulsion surfaces uppermost. The reverse is the case when splicing such film to a magnetic sound track. Like the wax pencil, the emulsion surface of any film is relatively soft, particularly as it becomes warm, and since the magnetic reproducing sound head is always in contact with the film surface as it passes through the machine, leader film or old picture prints used as blank spacing will gradually leave some of their emulsion coating on the sound head and distortion will result. Leaders at the head of a roll, and blank lengths inserted to maintain sync within a reel, are always spliced so that their hard shiny surface contacts the reproducing head and the head will slide clean and dirt-free as the film passes through.

It would, perhaps, seem stupid not to use blank magnetic film for such purposes since the sound head is unaffected in this way by the magnetic emulsion, and for short lengths this can be done. On the other hand, magnetic film is relatively expensive, it can be degaussed and used again and again so it is unlikely that any quantity of waste magnetic film is available for this purpose. Furthermore, the sound editor in particular likes to be able to see clearly which part of his reels are blank and which sections have the spaced out sound tracks and if all magnetic film were to be used he would have difficulty in quickly telling the difference between blank and sound.

Head and tail leaders of all rolls of magnetic sound are therefore spliced so that their hard cellulose surface makes contact with the sound head. When using "butt" splices this means that blank leader and magnetic film are joined cellulose to emulsion. Blank sections cut into reels to maintain sync are spliced in the same way.

6

SPECIAL SHOOTING PERIOD
PROCEDURES

WITH daily routines established, work in the film cutting room would normally proceed towards the fine cut and final sound mixing without any further complication. This, of course, is not always so. So many major productions nowadays rely heavily on special effects of one kind or another that photography and sound recordings are rarely simple and straightforward. Editors and assistants have to receive and handle various forms of effect film during the course of any production programme other than those of the most simple and modest nature. Apart from ordering optical processes the editor often has to prepare film in advance of shooting a special scene. In this work the time factor is of great importance. He must plan the processes concerned in advance to ensure no delay when shooting does take place. Such pre-production processes and post-production liaison with film laboratory or special photographic effects department are the complete responsibility of the staff in the film cutting room.

All the processes may be met on one production, even though perhaps one system may appear to completely replace another, and so they will be examined individually in so far as they involve editor and assistant.

Rear projection photography

There are many times when *physical* effects are used by the director and his shooting crew to create reality. Smoke, fire, fog, snow, rain can be introduced into the scene artificially to create whichever additional effect is needed. This calls for skill and knowledge on the part of specialists in this department and does not directly affect the editor.

Two special processes of composite photography do involve

119

editing departments very fully, however, and, the first of these is the rear projection system.

Difficulty of photographing the actions of artists against a real background in awkward, expensive, and dangerous circumstances can be overcome by projecting a filmed scene on to a special translucent screen behind the artists. The artists are then photographed from the front, so that they are combined with their special background.

Rear projector

A particular type of projection machine is used. This has the finely manufactured intermittent movement of a motion picture camera instead of the normal projector mechanism, which ensures a rock-steady image on the screen. A foreground set is constructed and the screen and projection machine will be aligned in relation to this so that the angle of the projected image and the height and angle of the motion picture camera photographing the combined foreground and background will be correctly related. As the movements of projector and motion picture camera are intermittent, they have to be electrically interlocked at the beginning of each take to ensure that the shutters of each are opening and closing at the same time as one another throughout the take. If sound recordings are to be simultaneous, these too are made synchronously in the normal way.

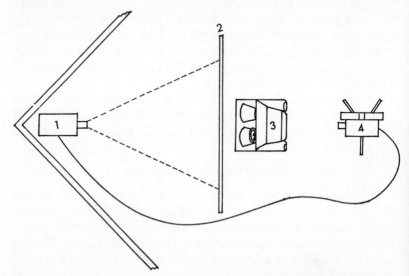

Layout on shooting stage for rear projection. (1) Rear projector. (2) Translucent screen. (3) Mock up foreground, car. (4) Film camera, interlocked with rear projector.

Using the foreground set, perhaps a mock-up of a car interior, speed-boat, aeroplane, or whatever is necessary, the photographic angle of the projected background image must be changed each time the angle of the camera photographing the combined scene is altered. The projector and camera must always face one another. Various angles of the same photographic background are made in advance to fit the director's anticipated requirements on the stage. These are necessary regardless of whether the backgrounds are moving or static. To shoot such a scene the background photography must be done in advance and sufficient time has to be allowed to process the negative and make the special prints needed for the special projector.

Shooting the background plates

Very often, the film director is unable to be present when the projection background "keys", or "plates" are photographed and a small camera unit will go off to a location, shooting the required angles with the correct lenses. Where background movement is needed, such as when the foreground is supposed to be a moving vehicle, the speed of travel is important and the camera unit shooting the "plates" must be armed with precise instructions. Moving backgrounds are shot with cameras mounted in cars, boats, in aeroplanes, or wherever necessary and always from the correct angles so that background movement will match the subject. Steadiness of the projected image is of vital importance in the case of background film photographed for a static scene. The camera is locked off on its mount, anchored and weighed down firmly to avoid camera vibration.

Whereas the motion picture camera on the shooting stage often masks the negative in the area to be occupied by the sound track on the final combined print for exhibition, the camera used for photographing background film almost invariably exposes the full area of the negative frame. The larger the available area the better the chance of positioning and selecting a section of the background when the combined photography takes place.

Viewing back projection rushes

Special slate numbers are chosen for background material, perhaps with a prefix letter of the alphabet, so that the daily rush print shows clearly that it is for the rear projection process.

When rush prints are received in the cutting room they are kept in rolls separated from the normal daily rushes. They can now be viewed by editor, director and cameraman, and takes and angles chosen in anticipation of the combined shooting. They are kept in separate rolls because, even if the production in progress is of the CinemaScope type, photography of background film for rear projection is always made with the normal camera lens. Only the lens of the camera photographing the combined foreground and background applies an anamorphic "squeeze" (p. 48). For this reason the rush prints must be viewed in the projection room with a normal projection lens, even though the production dailies are seen in CinemaScope.

The rush print must be viewed as soon as possible after receipt for selection of takes and angles. It may be incorrectly graded for day or night and colour balance may be wrong. Rush prints are made purely for selection purposes, to check movement and speed of action, to choose the angles required by the director and as a basis for grading density and colour on the final prints. They are useless for the rear projector, which uses a film stock with special perforations. The final prints are made on this specially perforated material.

Steadiness test

A selection of takes having been made, steadiness prints on static backgrounds are ordered by the editor.

The laboratory is given information on the slate number, key numbers, negative roll numbers, etc., so that the negative can be brought out and given its steadiness test. For this a special print is made, over which a static grid in the form of a series of vertical and horizontal lines is superimposed. When this print is viewed any movement apparent between grid (known to be completely steady) and image proves unsteadiness in the negative. In that case background film may have to be reshot. It is not necessary to have such check prints made on every single take, particularly where the action is of great length. Usually one shot from each camera magazine is enough. Where the camera set-up is being constantly changed on static backgrounds, however, these steady prints are advisable on all angles and it may be that making a "grid print" of just the first section of the take will be sufficient. Prints need not be made in colour if a colour process is being used. The cheaper black and white print is just as suitable to prove steadiness. Deciding the quantity and range of steadiness checks is just a matter of commonsense in any particular circumstance.

122

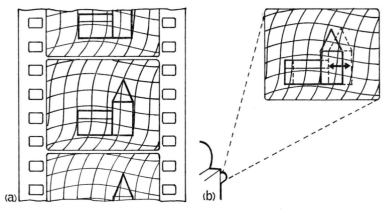

Proving image steadiness for rear projection and matte shots. (a) Print made from the negative to be steadiness-checked where a static grid incorporated in the printing mechanism registers on the print. (b) When the print is projected on to a screen, any movement of the pictorial image relative to the grid lines indicates that the image on the negative is unsteady.

Plates: grading and colour balance

Having chosen takes and angles, proved steadiness where this check is necessary, the editor asks the laboratory to provide a short density and colour grading strip on each shot. A few frames of negative, representative of the scene, and of "even density" (i.e. before the exposure varies as the camera runs down at the end of the shot) are printed at varying printer lights (p. 81) and with varying combinations of colour printing filters. These short lengths of print, each producing a slightly different quality, are examined by the cameraman, the technician in charge of the rear projection, and the laboratory. Their combined assessment of the grading of each print required is noted and the selected grading strip used as a guide when making the full length rear projection prints. Further balancing is possible at the time of combined shooting by fitting neutral density or colour filters on the projector lens. But if these are used, a more powerful light is needed in the projector. So the closer the grading to the cameraman's requirements in the first place the better.

Negative perforated prints

Special prints are now made at the laboratory, on positive film designed for this purpose with negative type perforations. These are a requirement of the special movement in the rear projector and are an aid to image steadiness.

Enough prints of each angle and set-up are ordered so that a "clean" projection print is always in reserve no matter how many rehearsals are made before shooting. These also cover the possibility of accidental damage to a print. Normally, one rehearsal and two "shooting" prints are ordered.

Focus leader

As an aid to focusing the rear projector, the laboratory splices a focus leader film to the beginning of each take of the *negative*. No physical splice exists on the positive print made from this, and the focus can be carried smoothly from the leader to the image without being disturbed by the extra thickness of a splice passing through the projector.

Editing backgrounds

The editor may well have to edit the backgrounds, "jumping" out sections that are unwanted, making cuts where these do not visibly intrude. If this is necessary, his edited print is needed at the laboratory so that negative can be matched to his edited positive and cut similarly. Such edited sections must be carefully checked and approved before negative cutting is allowed.

Prints received for rear projection, specially prepared on to negative-type perforation stock are often delivered direct to the cutting room together with the daily rushes. These prints should never be handled in a positive film cutting room and not even removed from the tin. They must be kept spotlessly clean, and, although positive prints, should only be handled by people who have been trained in the handling of negative film and with the correct equipment.

Pros and cons of combined photography

Combined photography has obvious limitations. Considerable space is required between the projector and screen and a fairly large shooting stage is needed.

Photographic duplicating of a projected image must also result in a loss in quality, however small. Its great advantage, however, is the fact that the results of the combination photography are available for viewing with the daily rushes as soon as these are processed, within 24 hours, and if any disasters are apparent, all components are still available and a re-take immediately possible.

Travelling matte system

The travelling matte process is a means of producing a combined scene where the actors actually appear to be in their surroundings. It saves taking a production team to a location which may be expensive or dangerous. It also allows composite scenes to be made up which would otherwise be quite impossible, i.e., in science fiction films.

The matte is a form of mask used to exclude details from some part of the picture so that later a separately prepared image may be printed in to the blank areas. The result is a composite of foreground and background film components without any effect of superimposition.

In the travelling matte process these blank areas automatically follow the movements of the actors.

Such optical photographic processes are the responsibilities of specialist technicians, but the editor is involved in choosing the two basic films concerned for foreground and background and aligning them side by side to visualize their final relationship. He supplies information to the specialist "matte" operators necessary to ensure a correct "marriage" of the component films.

Unlike the rear projection system, the travelling matte process is lengthy and costly. To wait several weeks for a final composite print, only to discover that the marriage was incorrectly ordered in the first place would be obviously disastrous. The marriage must be aligned with care.

 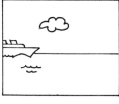 

(a)   (b)   (c)

Blue backing process shots showing the three components with which the editor is involved. (a) The foreground action, photographed against a special backing. (b) The photographic background film. (c) The optically produced positive composite which the editor will eventually receive and cut into his work print.

125

The foreground action is photographed independently of the background, although it is done with the final relationship very clearly in the mind of the director and cameraman. Background photography may be deliberately delayed so that the exact requirements of action and movement are known. As with back projection a set or mock-up is first erected in the foreground. The foreground action is photographed against a special coloured backing. One of the most common systems uses a flat surface suspended background of an evenly applied and evenly lit blue colour. These are called blue backing shots.

Receiving travelling matte foregrounds

Often the first component the editor receives is the action photographed against the blue backing. This arrives with the usual delivery of daily rushes, and must be synchronized with sound in the normal way. In projection, if the film is in colour, the action appears as though suspended in a very even deep blue sky, the foreground figures and set being normally lit. Apart from this, the print is quite normal and the daily rushes are entered in the editorial records and edited in the usual way. Some sequences may be entirely made up from blue backing shots or, alternatively, there may be only one or two such shots to be cut into a scene. The assembly of such sequences is refined and recut, until the background film is shot and daily rush prints of this delivered to the cutting room. But before these appear the editor must order steadiness tests on the foreground materials in hand.

Steadiness of both foreground and background film are vital to the success of the travelling matte process, particularly when a static set-up is involved. Any unco-ordinated movement produces an unwanted gap, or "fringe" line between the two images when combined optically. Foreground steadiness can be proved at once so black and white grid steady tests are ordered immediately from the laboratory holding the negative, just as with rear projection backgrounds.

Receiving travelling matte backgrounds

The background prints received as normal daily rushes are slated wherever possible so that they are easily identifiable as film for this purpose. Although it is possible with certain trick shots it is unlikely for these to have a synchronized sound track. The film is

126

recorded, logged and coded and perhaps broken down and sorted into groups, as with normal rushes.

Normally, with the travelling matte process both backgrounds and foregrounds are photographed with the same type of lens system. If it is a CinemaScope production employing lenses giving an anamorphic "squeeze", the background too, is shot with an anamorphic lens.

Editors should bear in mind the difference between rear projection and travelling matte backgrounds when they select background film for use in these processes from stock film libraries. Either type *can* be handled, but it is better to have *normal* lens backgrounds for the rear projection system and *anamorphic* squeezed backgrounds for travelling matte work in a Cinema-Scope production.

Matching travelling matte components

When the background film becomes available, selections of takes are made once more with the director expressing his preferences. But, during the matching and aligning of the two main components in the cutting room, the editor is possibly in a better position to assess the future result of the optical combination. He may be able to gain an impression of the final result by placing both foreground and background films in the viewing machine simultaneously, one on top of the other, and run the films through the machine to watch the relationship as the scene progresses. This might be essential when, for example, the steering of a foreground vehicle must match the appropriate background movement, or a specific reference is made in the dialogue track to something passing by. It may not be very clearly seen in such circumstances, particularly when night shots are involved, but it does give a basic guide.

Throughout his assembled foreground sequence of blue backing shots, the editor looks for a suitably matching background, correct camera height, correct angle of shooting, and appropriate speed of action. The important thing is that it is done cut by cut so that, not only is each cut correctly matched with its proposed background, but the overall flow of the sequence is maintained. The obvious example is a sequence in a moving car. The speed of movement represented in the background must be consistent and the progression from one set of background details to another acceptable.

As each cut of foreground is suitably matched to the appropriate section of background, the editor makes notes for the travelling matte technicians, to enable them to make the final composite shots. They need to know the slate numbers of foreground and background to be married and where the negative can be located in the laboratory filing system. They must be given details of the right section of the shot involved in each cut, because to order the full take in each case would be enormously expensive. The notes must also tell them whether day or night effect is aimed at, and last, but most important, the synchronizing relationship between foreground and background film. Using the negative key numbers on each piece of film, this can be given without any misunderstandings.

The prints which the editor uses to match and assemble in his work print sequences are, of course, only for temporary use and as a guide. The final composite shots come from the travelling matte department and, if approved and satisfactory in every respect, replace these temporary ones.

Overlay check print

In view of the somewhat lengthy optical process, orders for composite shots must be sent to the technicians concerned as soon as possible. This is unlikely until the sequence is "fine" cut and everyone happy with its shape. Composite mattes are too expensive to re-order through recutting a sequence. But the editor can order a relatively inexpensive black and white temporary overlay of every combined foreground and background which he is fairly certain will be used in the final cut. The laboratory simply superimpose one on top of the other in printing. The foreground image is completely transparent and useless for cutting, but the expense is well worth while for several reasons. The temporary overlay can be made very quickly and will give some idea of the final result, however crude. The relationship between foreground and background on dark scenes may not be successfully achieved in the hand or on the Moviola and may only be possible by making an overlay. Also, any apparent unsteadiness can be observed. A minute combination of movement which is now visible between two scenes may not have been apparent in individual steadiness tests.

Background/foreground control

Before shooting, when rear projection is being used, the background image is positioned on the screen at the correct height and angle. In photographing the foreground action, only a small portion of the projected screen image might be included in the overall shot. The projected image can to some extent be raised and lowered and a different projection lens can, within limits, produce an image of different size. The film can be turned over in the projector mechanism so that the *direction* of the action is reversed; the film can also be run in reverse so that the *action itself* is reversed. This degree of control is possible at the time of shooting according to specific requirements.

Similar controls in making the composite travelling matte shot are available but only if specified by the editor. He can order the background to be "flopped over", thus reversing the direction of the action. Running the film from tail to head when making the matte components reverses the action itself. Skipping every other frame of the background during the optical process when preparing the composite exactly doubles the speed of any movement. And, since the whole process is a carefully controlled optical one, the possibility of using a day effect background to reproduce a suitable night effect in the final result should never be overlooked, particularly when stock library film has to be used.

But with any of these systems, there is some loss of general photographic quality. A photographic copy of the rear projection image is never quite as good as the original, as the grain of one emulsion is then being added to another. Optical duplication of both foreground and background film in the travelling matte process also causes a loss of general quality, sometimes reaching unacceptable levels.

Painted mattes

There are occasions when artists have to be seen in surroundings which just do not exist. Live action can be backed up with a painting which is photographed separately and inserted later in an optical process.

The camera photographing the original scene is tied down with weights on a solid surface and no panning or tilting is possible during the shot. Various features on the set break off at a certain point, and these are eventually blended into the painted insert. The action is never allowed to wander into the area that will contain the painted scene.

The painting itself is prepared on glass. One projected frame of the live action is still-projected on to the glass and a line chosen at which the two must eventually blend. Making such paintings, choosing the blend lines and colours with great care and

129

subsequently photographing the completed painting is the work of skilled specialists.

The rush print of the original scene probably shows the action taking place in an area surrounded by arc lamps and the walls of the studio stage. An exterior shot may reveal a horseman riding across the drawbridge of a non-existent castle. The castle will eventually be added by painting.

The film is documented in the cutting room in the same way as daily rushes and, as soon as possible, a take is chosen and a steadiness check print ordered. The design and style of the painting originates from the production designer or art director. He may need a few frames of the editor's positive print in order to execute the design in relation to the action and set-up.

This process, too, can be a slow one and, the manufacture of mattes for the painted and the live action sections, a sometimes laborious task. The editor specifies the point at which his cut starts and ends allowing a small piece at each end for handling purposes as with all optical work. He then issues the appropriate order so that the action negative can be identified at the laboratory, and a special duplicating print made for the optical printer. Later, he receives a print from the new composite negative.

Split matte shots

This process involves separately photographing two scenes, parts of each eventually being amalgamated as one whole shot. The dividing line is chosen with great care so that it can not be seen.

A typical application of this technique would be an extreme long shot of a group of people, correctly positioned, for one set-up and a miniature or model set for another, bearing in mind the position of the group in the first shot. When these are combined into a composite split shot an impression is given of a group of tiny people photographed alongside an enormous structure. The requirements of the final shot depends on the nature of the script and are limited only by the skill of the technicians who carefully line up each portion as it is photographed.

Again, the editor's responsibility is, on receipt of such film, to have steadiness checks made. He then views the two pieces of action which are to be combined and moves them in relation to each other until the synchronized action is satisfactory, perhaps viewing them superimposed in his viewing machine. He can clamp both pieces in the film synchronizer as they are now aligned. Winding back in the synchronizer to the point at which the shot is usable and allowing a little extra for future handling, he chooses a frame on one film where a key number is visible and marks this frame. The level frame on the other film may be some distance from a key number to the point level with the mark made on the other film but he arrives at the synchronizing information required by the

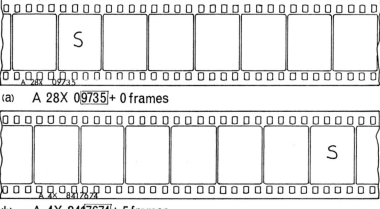

(a)   A 28X 0 9735 + 0 frames

(b)   A 4X 84 7674 + 5 frames

Synchronizing information required by optical printer operators to enable them to "marry" two picture components. Here, the two picture frames marked "S" are to be synchronized when making an optical composite. (a) The first synchronizing frame is situated on part of a key number. (b) The synchronizing frame on the second component is indicated by counting frames from the nearest preceding key number. The key number portion is boxed to ensure accuracy to the individual frame.

technician who will make the composite shot. In optical printing, synchronization is achieved by lining up the key number on the first film, with the key number plus or minus X number of frames, on the other, as indicated by the editor.

Sound for shooting stage playback

When photographing a musical number or perhaps a song with instrumental accompaniment, circumstances may make it impossible to obtain a sound recording of high enough quality for the final product. Microphone positioning may be difficult, perhaps impossible, when large complicated tracking shots are contemplated, and overall sound balance will be poor.

The sound for such sequences is often pre-recorded in a sound studio, completely independent of the problems of the studio set, lights and camera position, and a correctly balanced sound track

131

produced. Several takes may be made, and some editing may be needed before the sound tracks are suitable for use. These original sound pre-recordings are regarded as master recordings, transfers being made in the usual way for editing in readiness for the playback operation on the shooting stage.

Playback machines on the shooting stage may be designed to use magnetic tape, or disc. Whichever type is needed it is prepared from the master edited recording.

One small music number in a sequence causes little problem to the editing staff. But a full scale music production is a different affair and may well call for a specialist music editor who, with his skilled knowledge of music and film, attends the many pre-recording sessions and takes care of the pre-production requirements.

Warning clicks

When shooting the sequence, in order that singers and instrumentalists can have some advance warning of the beginning of such playback sounds, correctly placed and rhythmic audible "clicks" must be inserted into the leader of the master magnetic recording and thus transferred to the playback track being used on the studio stage. The "beat" of the clicks, and their quantity, guides the artists to the point at which the sound track starts to play. Vocal and instrumental miming to the track thus has a greater chance of starting in synchronization.

The editor creates the clicks in a magnetic master track by cutting one frame of 1,000 cycle "tone" into the leader at appropriate intervals. Such tone is available in lengths from the sound department. Very often it is found at the beginning of rolls of daily sound transfers.

Cutting playback sequences

After shooting, picture and sound of such playback sequences are received from the lab and synchronized in the usual way. The reproduction of the disc or tape playback sound will naturally be of inferior quality, the sound rushes being for guide and cutting purposes only. When the sequence is eventually cut and "set" the master track of the original recording is used for final sound dubbing.

Playback track coding

Keeping the synchronization between picture and guide track when cutting a sequence involving music is done with the usual code-numbering system with matching numbers on picture and sound but now the editor has another problem—to maintain overall sync between the guide sound and master sound. It assists him greatly if the master track is code-numbered as soon as it is available to the cutting room staff and all picture and sound rushes for the sequence numbered synchronously to it. On any playback sequence where a large quantity of film is expected, such numbering allows the editor freedom of cutting and re-cutting, yet his guide track always remains synchronized to the master recording by numbers. It does mean, of course, that the daily rushes are not necessarily numbered from their start marks as would normally have been done.

To provide accurate cross-reference between picture, master and guide tracks the guide track must first be matched to the master track—finding the matching word or phrase of music and synchronizing the two by using the magnetic heads in the film synchronizer. A matching code-number is then made at the beginning of the take (as near the start mark as possible as these are points unlikely to exactly co-incide) and the guide track numbered accordingly. Picture for that piece of sound is also numbered with the same series of numbers. Naturally, all angles of picture covering the same section of the playback sound will receive the same set of footage code numbers and any recutting will always remain synchronized to the master track.

Effects playback

Playback sequences are normally used in the big musical production but there are occasions when sound effects must be edited and prepared for playback use. For example, the noise of a huge cheering crowd can help an artist to react realistically as the guide sound is played on the stage. "Thought" voices are sometimes used in scenes and an actor's spoken thoughts may have to be heard on the stage so that his performance is timed correctly.

All such tracks are prepared in the cutting room as an aid to the director.

7

LATER SHOOTING PROCEDURES

THE last period of shooting calls for very close co-operation between editing staff and shooting crew. At this point final editing work will soon be free of the arrival of any further daily film. After many weeks of editorial work isolated sequences grow into longer complete sections of the script as they are joined together. Retakes may be needed, pick-up shots made necessary by recent assemblies and close up inserts required to cut into the work print. Unsatisfactory dialogue tracks must be post-synchronized to provide recordings of acceptable quality for final sound mixing. All these must be done before sets are struck, props returned, and artists leave the production.

Retakes and inserts

When retakes and pick-up shots are needed, the editor's cut sequences may be viewed on the shooting stage. The director, cameraman, continuity girl and artists can then see exactly what is needed to replace, or fit in with the existing material. For this purpose, rather than have complete and lengthy scenes exposed to the dust and dirt found on some shooting stages, the assistant editor may break out just the section of the original sequence which has to be matched to the new shooting.

The value of an insert may only be realized when the assembled film is viewed. This is another reason for constantly assessing cut film throughout the course of the production and leaving insert shooting until the end, often the very last day.

The editor compiles a list of proposed insert shots as the production moves along. He notes the scene, the form of the required insert, whether it involves any section of the set and whether props or furnishings are required. He indicates if any wardrobe is necessary, where for example, an arm wearing the appropriate clothing is to be seen in the insert. This list is sent from time to time to the production manager of the unit so that the furniture, props and clothing can be held back, as necessary.

During insert shooting the editor comes to the shooting stage with the cut film, for matching. Usually, there is only one point at which the insert can be successfully cut into the work print to produce its full value. Nobody knows this cutting point better than the editor, so he is often expected to direct the shooting of such material.

Post synchronizing

One of the most important tasks which the editing department performs during these final days of shooting is the post-synchronizing of dialogue scenes.

Each day when viewing daily rushes, the editor notes scenes with unacceptable dialogue sound quality and the cutting room assistant orders a picture reprint and an extra sound transfer on all such scenes in readiness for post-synchronized recordings. When the film is received it is synchronized in the usual way, assembled into rolls and code numbered if there is time, although coding is not greatly important.

One would not expect an artist to re-record a dialogue scene of any length and maintain the original synchronization as well as quality of performance. Long scenes *are* post-synchronized in the manufacture of foreign language dubbed films. But lip synchronization is usually very approximate and would not be acceptable in any major feature production.

Scenes to be post-synchronized are broken down into dialogue sentences of convenient length. This takes account of any natural pauses which occur in the delivery of the dialogue. At the same time, the artist must be able to retain the original rhythm of his speech.

In a specially equipped recording theatre, sections of the scene are projected on to a screen for the benefit of the artist. At the same time, he listens to the original sound to recall the exact dialogue and rhythm of speech. The original sound is then switched off and he speaks the dialogue in sync with picture as recording equipment makes a new, clean, sound recording. Were the short section projected as a normal piece of film it would have to be constantly projected and rewound until a satisfactory recording was made. This would take up too much time. If the required section is made up into a loop, the projector can repeat the same film section, as long as required. These are the "work" loops.

Preparing post-sync loops

The editor takes the scenes one at a time, views them on the Moviola and marks them for breaking down into loops of convenient length. Each section of picture and guide sound track is cut to the same length and a picture and sound leader film incorporated into the loop for projector threading. The editor usually marks the scene initially on the viewing machine dividing the speech into sections. Then, after transferring the film into the synchronizer he cuts synchronized sections of picture and track according to the marks he has made and, giving each section a number hangs them on the pins of the cuts bin. At the same time, he notes the actual dialogue contained in each numbered section. The assistant prepares picture and sound leaders, splicing these to each picture and sound section in the form of a continuous loop of film. All leaders are naturally of the same length and are marked with synchronous start marks for projection purposes. The synchronized picture and sound loops are marked with a wax pencil number. The name or names of the artist or artists concerned are noted and a typed report prepared for each loop indicating the loop number, names of artists concerned, and the exact dialogue to be spoken.

Loops and reports are filed so that whenever an artist is available for post-synchronizing work, they can be quickly sorted and taken to the recording theatre. Typed reports are assembled in similar order and given to the recording artist. The cutting room filing system must ensure that nothing is missed and all loops are, in fact, post-synchronized in the theatre. Once an artist has finished on the film it may be difficult, perhaps impossible, to call him back for this work.

Cueing the loops

When recording the worst thing that the artist can do is to try and follow lip movement while he is speaking into the microphone. Such an attempt creates an inevitable time lag and his speech will always be late. He must be given an aid to start speaking in sync with the image on the screen without watching lip movement and continue from the beginning of the section by repeating the original speech rhythm. Some visual or audible warning of the time to start speaking must be provided. Clicks are sometimes used. Numbers printed on the picture leader, one, two, three, leading rhythmically to the beginning of the sentence can also be employed. But the most common and successful visual aid is a cue line drawn diagonally on the picture leader, moving across the screen as the picture is about to appear, disappearing at the side of the screen as the image appears and speech should begin. There is now no need to watch the lips as they move. The visual line cues the start of dialogue. It is then a matter of matching the original rhythm of speech. If the loop is a long one with few breaks in dialogue delivery, further cue lines drawn to the beginnings of each key word in the original delivery can be of great assistance to the artist. Lines must be drawn with discretion, as there is nothing worse than "over-cueing" a loop. Post-synchronizing is generally regarded as nerve-racking and a difficult art to acquire. So anything which can help the artist must be done. Artists have their own preferences. Some prefer short loops, others like to repeat the dialogue in longer sections and are disconcerted if the scene has been separated into too many small sections. They may find that although synchronizing is easy, it is impossible to have time to regain the quality of original performance. The operation then becomes too mechanical for them.

It is always a good scheme, particularly with a major artist whose preferences are unknown to the editor and where there are many loops, to ask them which way he prefers to work in the post-synchronizing theatre. Artists are always grateful for such consideration and it certainly saves much time-wasting and re-cueing of picture when the session is in progress. It may even avoid complete reassembly of the loops themselves.

As far as the physical preparation of loops is concerned, the cutting, splicing, logging and filing ready for the recording session is time consuming work but must be done in a methodical manner if scenes are not to be forgotten and loops mislaid when filing. As with all other work in the cutting room, systems must be established and routines maintained. Any advance preparations possible must be put into effect in order to save time. Suitable post-sync leader film can usually be obtained from the film laboratory printed with synchronizing start marks and cued with a line to the beginning of the picture cut. Where many loops are needed such leaders enable the assistant to prepare them in advance in readiness for splicing.

Post-sync coverage

Loops prepared during the course of shooting when the fine cut is not yet available are made from the complete angles for each sequence concerned, regardless of whether or not these angles have, at that stage been included in the cut sequence. They are shot so that long after the artist has finished his part in the picture, flexibility is still possible for recutting and angles changed as desired. Occasionally such repeated post-synchronizing of all angles would take an artist several weeks. So the artist may arrange to make himself available just after the approval of the fine cut of the entire picture, post-synchronizing only those angles actually used in the cut. The situation has to be quite clear here. The fine cut *must* be firmly approved and the artist *must* be available and not on the other side of the globe working on a new assignment.

Post-sync recording supervision

The artist needs some sort of direction or supervision when "looping" his dialogue. He is usually the worst judge of his own performance and, very often it is not just a matter of matching the original performance but of attempting an improvement. Post-sync dialogue is often needed where the original voice turns out to be unsuitable. An accent may be unacceptable as a result of changes to the script, or perhaps it may even be unintelligible. The artist providing the replacement voice needs directing, and, as the scene is recorded in small sections continuity of voice pitch and strength must be maintained. It is surprising how much vocal "energy" is lost in post-synchronized dialogue unless careful supervision is made throughout the recording session. The obvious person for the task is the film director himself. But frequently, artists who are not involved in a day's filming are called upon to loop scenes to save time at the end of their commitment. In this case, the director will not be available. If the director agrees and has confidence in the capability of the editor, then he is entrusted with supervising this post-synchronization.

Three things must be closely watched:

1. That no loops are missed or forgotten.
2. That lip-sync is perfect.
3. That quality of performance is not allowed to drop in the struggle to achieve perfect sync.

Major artists may refuse (and they are often right) to do this work in the absence of the director. So evening or weekend sessions may be necessary.

Post-sync recording systems

Some decision must be made about the actual system of the new dialogue recording; alternatives affect the editorial staff.

Master roll

In one system the post-synchronized dialogue can be recorded on to a roll on a tape machine, or on to a 35 mm magnetic sound roll with a maximum length of around 1,000 ft. In either case these recordings are regarded as master rolls and provide the editor with a cutting transfer print. They are recorded in sync with the picture loop, and a new take is made by the artist during each revolution of the work loop. There are times, particularly with a lengthy speech, when part of one reading must be used in conjunction with part of another. Notes are made, perhaps playing the master roll back to select the useable takes.

When transfers are made from the master roll the editor needs some synchronizing reference. This is provided if a click, or sync plop as it is very often known, is inserted into one of the loop leaders and recorded on to the master roll at each revolution of the loop. Lining up the sync plop on the new transfer with that on the working loop enables the editor to sync sound to picture in the film synchronizer. He can then write one of the picture key numbers on the sound track at level sync for future permanent reference.

Virgin loop

The other recording system used at these sessions is by "virgin loop". When originally preparing the loops, the editor makes, not only a picture and synchronized guide sound loop but a third loop of new magnetic recording film of the same length as the other two. All three have a common start mark. At the session, the three loops are run synchronously and continue until a satisfactory new dialogue recording has been achieved on the virgin loop. The sound recordist is then instructed to play back the take.

As long as the system is on "record", all signals received on each revolution of the loop are automatically "wiped" on the following revolution. Otherwise each new recording would be added to previous recordings on the virgin loop. When playback of a recording is requested and the switch turned to "playback", wiping automatically ceases and that particular recording can be

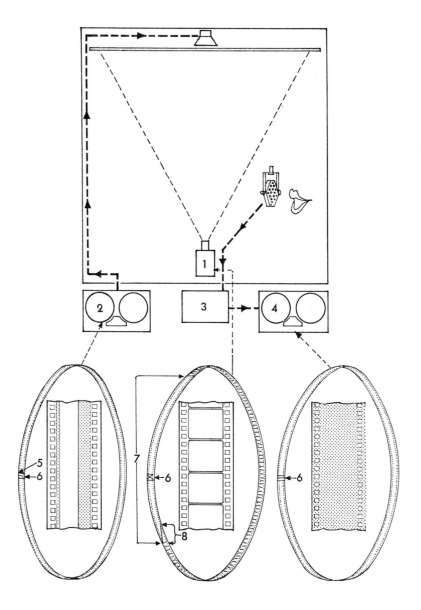

Post-synchronizing theatre, using the virgin magnetic looping system. (I) Picture projector running the picture work loop. (2) Re-recording machine running the dialogue work loop. (3) Sound monitor and recording room. (4) Recording machine running the virgin magnetic loop on which the new dialogue is recorded. (5) Sync plop. (6) Synchronous start marks on all loops. (7) Leader length, on which is printed (8) cue line leading the artist to the beginning of the speech.

heard over and over so that it can be checked for sync and quality.

It is clear, therefore, that communication between director and recordist must be established without any confusion, otherwise a good recording will possibly be wiped on the next revolution of the loop before the recordist switches to "playback".

Each new recording is checked for quality, performance, and correct lip-sync with the picture loop which is still running. If, on checking, the quality is not yet perfect, the switch is returned to the "record" position and further attempts made. This does mean, of course, that only one final reading is recorded unless more than one virgin loop is prepared for each pair of work loops. This is in fact nearly always done. If full coat magnetic 35 mm film is used, recording capability can be doubled by stopping all three machines, turning the virgin loop in the recording machine so that the opposite edge of the film is presented at the recording head, re-aligning the three start marks and running up once again for further attempts by the artist. Such double recordings on to virgin loops are known as "A" and "B" side master recordings.

Here again, transfer of all the recordings are made for cutting purposes. All the virgin loops are broken after the new dialogue has been recorded, and then spliced into normal rolls for a transfer to be made.

When the virgin loop transfers are received in the cutting room synchronizing reference is still required, as with the "master roll" method, and a sync plop will still have had to be inserted into a leader on one of the working loops.

The obvious advantage of the virgin loop system is the capability of immediate playback of each good "take" *automatically synchronized to picture.*

Post-sync master roll numbers

As with all recordings, a sound report is prepared so that a master roll can always be identified by number and individual readings located from the loop number which is also included on the report. In the case of the virgin loop system, master roll numbers are given as they are assembled from the virgin loops.

Dialogue editor

The editor is so fully occupied in the preparation of the cut film that it is very doubtful that he has prepared and documented all the working loops. As the weeks go by, he not only deals with the new

142

daily film but also reshapes earlier cut sequences. Scenes that eventually have to be post-synchronized may be spread throughout the production on a major film project and, since the loop-preparing operation is quite a lengthy one, choosing the point at which the sentences are to be separated, drawing additional cue lines and having the loop sheets typed would become a full time occupation. Senior assistants are normally quite capable of doing the work but they are then taken away from the main task of organizing the routine work of the cutting room.

It is usually far better to employ a dialogue editor who specializes in doing all post-synchronizing work on films. Give him his own working and filing area. Give him his own assistant to prepare the reprints, splice the loops and sort them for projection, and let him get on with it. This is the only satisfactory way when a lot of loops are going to be needed. They will be ready whenever the artist is available and there is far less likelihood that any scene is missed or any loop forgotten and nothing can be more disastrous to the film editor.

The dialogue editor knows exactly how many loops have been prepared for each artist and the production manager can schedule this additional activity required from the artist. He can also attend the looping sessions, so that as the director is concentrating on getting the best performance, he can concentrate on the more mechanical problem of lip-sync. Perhaps most valuable, is that he can put picture key number synchronizing marks on all the new looped sound tracks as they are received from the sound transfer department, ready to be cut into the editor's work print. When any recutting of sequences is done, the appropriate looped sound track will be available with its synchronizing mark ready to put in to the reshaped sequence.

8

POST PRODUCTION

WHEN all the main photography has been completed the immediate task of producer, director and film editor is to screen the completely assembled work print so that they can make an assessment of the basic shape. All the routines of the cutting room have been geared during the whole of the shooting period so that this screening takes place with minimum delay once the film is shot.

Screening the first assembly

In earlier screenings, during the course of production, sequences in the assembled film are seen more for their individual value than the effect they may have on the story as a whole. The pace of a scene, excellent as it may have seemed at an isolated viewing, may now appear to flounder in context.

There is no magic length for any film story but, obviously, 100 min. of "tight" film, no matter what the subject may be, is more tolerable and entertaining than 120 min. of stretched story-telling. The script is timed to an estimated final length before shooting starts. But the work print in its assembled form often exceeds this expectation. The lengthy and slow scenes are now re-examined for their best effect in the overall story. But the main purpose of this first screening of the entire film is to assess the general shape.

At this stage sequences should not be broken by a reel change-over. Repeat viewings of any one sequence will thus not involve changing projectors midway. Where temporary changeovers do occur, dots can be marked on the print at the end of each reel. The first one is a cue to start the motor of the projector carrying the new reel, and 11 ft. later a second dot cues the change from one projector to the other. This second dot occurs $1\frac{1}{2}$ ft. before the end protective leader film. Each cue is marked over three or four

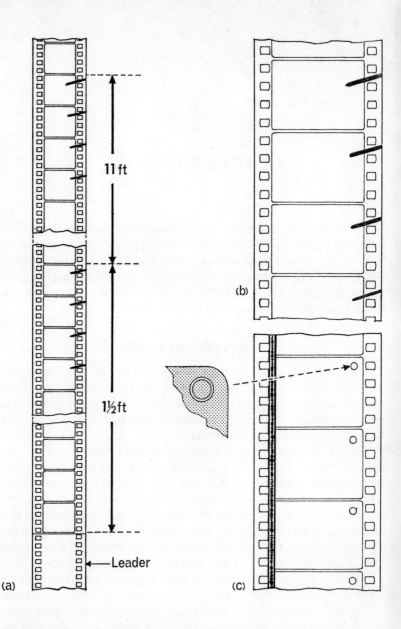

Temporary and permanent projection change-over cues. (a) Temporary cues marked on the work print, using wax pencil which can easily be removed if reels are changed. (b) Enlarged detail.
(c) Permanent changeover mark which is eventually printed into release prints, having been scribed on the negative.

consecutive picture frames so that a dot will appear at the top right corner of the screen. This is standard procedure for 35 mm film. These marks are, of course, only temporary ones for the screening of early assemblies. They do not determine the changeover points that will be used in the final release print.

Rough cut to fine cut

The transition from rough assembly to fine-cut work print is a gradual one. It may take days, or weeks, depending on the size and complexity of the film. It is very unusual not to have one "problem" sequence which needs cutting and re-cutting right to the end, even though all other reels have been set. Whatever the problems may be, the pattern is fairly standard for any feature production: viewing, discussion, recutting, viewing—repeated until the result is satisfactory to all. The director is very often present in the cutting room watching physical cuts being made, looking at them on the viewing machine and trying something else if he is not satisfied. Some directors prefer to be away from this activity, and would rather see any effect of recutting on the projection room screen. This is a matter of personal choice.

If a director prefers to work in the projection room, viewing the same sequence many times while making suggestions for reshaping, it is an advantage to have projectors capable of both forward and reverse running. If possible they should operate from a remote control switch in the viewing room. This system can be a disadvantage, of course, if the director is one who finds it difficult to make a decision.

Director's alterations

In the original assembly of the work print the editor will, no doubt, have been allowed complete freedom in the way that he has built each sequence. The pattern of cutting may be fairly obvious and, if not, then the editor establishes his own pattern, aiming to find the most effective combination of picture and sound from the material at his disposal. Even if there are only two shots covering a scene, finding the right cutting point is a matter of using his experience and skill. Finding the pattern is one problem; fitting the cuts together mechanically, another. If the director is not satisfied with the pattern, he searches for a new one. And if a picture cut disturbs him he says so, and an alternative cutting point may have to be found.

It is not always easy to be objective at these viewings. The more familiar people become with the film the more difficult it can be. Arguments can develop and, with a large and complicated production the atmosphere might sometimes be strained and tense. Startling suggestions may be made and revolutionary ideas proposed. Yet no apparently wild idea should necessarily be rejected as being stupid. Everything is worth trying and sometimes the changes brought about by repositioning complete sequences, splitting them, cutting away in the middle of a scene and then back again, are remarkable. Scenes may be eliminated altogether—they can always be put back—and this can sometimes create a problem.

Frequently the arguments for and against eliminating a complete scene can be very lengthy. Within itself it may be an excellently directed, photographed and edited scene. But, if retention adversely affects the overall result, then it obviously must go. The producer may want it "out" and the director is equally firm that it should be "in", and the editor will be right in the middle holding an unwanted casting vote. One has to be honest and objective, regardless of how good the scene itself may be.

Experimental recuts

Sometimes a scene is completely and drastically reshaped and recut in an experimental way, no one really knowing just what the result might be. Perhaps it may be a wasted effort. With a complicated sequence involving a large amount of film, it is disconcerting to have the director say at the end of several day's recutting, "Put it back the way it was . . .". Where such blatant experiment may not work, the editor can protect the original pattern of assembly by duplicating the pictorial sequence before the recutting is done. As quality is unimportant for this cutting pattern protection, a very simple and inexpensive duplicate film can be prepared. The original sequence is sent to the laboratory with an order for a rough dupe— usually referred to as a "cutting copy" or "work print" dupe. The laboratory will know that it is only for reference purposes and in this case will use the cheaper type of duplicating film. A rough negative is made on the printing machine from the positive cut sequence and a print made from that negative, thus providing a duplicate sequence. When such a dupe is ordered, the laboratory should be specifically instructed to ensure that the key numbers carried in the editor's cut sequence are also duplicated. If it has to go "back the way it was", the sequence can easily be re-assembled by reference to the key numbers on the dupe.

Eliminations

Sequence eliminations must be completely understood by the editorial assistant responsible for filing. Often the sequence is reinserted in the work print and, therefore, it should always be filed as a complete and assembled piece of film and never broken down into its component cuts. Occasionally only a part of the elimination is replaced. But, whatever is eliminated should always be kept intact. The script scene number can be written on the roll which will be filed in special tins kept solely for this purpose. This makes future identification easier.

Optical effects

Dissolves and fades seem to be less desirable nowadays. Sequences are often linked by a "time-cutting" technique, or the transition is performed by the use of sound effects. But where they are contemplated they are indicated on the editor's work print with lines giving a clear visual indication of the intended effect when the print is screened in the projection room. Such lines can be drawn on the film with a wax pencil or a felt-tipped marking pen. Wax pencil can, however, eventually create a minor annoyance. As the wax softens, it spreads beyond each side of the markings and the film becomes covered with streaks and blobs. A felt-tipped marker is much more satisfactory and it can easily be removed with a cleansing fluid if the planned optical effect is changed or eliminated.

Other optical effects may be planned at this stage. A cut, for example, may be more satisfactory if a piece of film is "flipped over" so that the direction of movement is reversed. Perhaps a section of action is too slow and would benefit from a "skip-frame" (p. 129) optical effect using alternate picture frames only. All this optical work is done in the trick and optical department at the film laboratory and the operator of the optical printing machine needs information from the film editor to accurately produce a new negative incorporating the desired effect.

Determining reel length

Gradually, however, recutting proceeds until the fine cut of the entire film is settled. Now that the shape of the film is right the editor must take a final look at the mechanics of his cutting. Every cut should be examined to ensure that it has been made in the best way. If an improvement will result by the removal of one or two frames at the point of the cut then this should be done. It is surprising how the overall effect can be further improved by taking this action throughout the film. Titles are considered and the length, style, and position of the series of opening main titles are discussed. If the film is a lengthy road-show type, an Intermission may be necessary. This requires an additional title. Finding the most suitable place to separate the two parts of the story can sometimes be quite a problem.

If the film is to be released by a major film distribution company, their standard trade mark may be required at the head of reel one.

For all such additional requirements the estimated footages involved must be allowed for when determining reel length as it is unlikely that titles will be agreed and available for some time.

With these additional footages in mind, the editor can now consider the permanent length and content of each reel, choosing the projector changeover points with great care so that screenings of exhibition prints take place with no apparent break between reels as they proceed from projector to projector. Few theatres are, as yet, equipped with an automatic projector changeover device. The operation is carried out manually by the skill and timing of the projectionist as he follows cue marks at the ends of reels. The type of scene where the reels change is very important. The projectionist may be a fraction late in following the cue mark and will screen a little more of the outgoing shot and a little less of the incoming one as he makes the change. So the editor must avoid any scene where action has been carefully matched, or dialogue is continuous. He will try to find an area of silence—perhaps an establishing shot or a silent reaction shot—where a minor error in changeover timing on the part of the projectionist will be unimportant.

Printing limitations

There is one other consideration when finalizing the contents of reels. There is a maximum allowable length for each reel when the printing operation takes place after cutting the picture negative. Each reel must be within the limit. Some examples of these limitations are given below. As they are a requirement of the film laboratory, the editor must establish the limits set by the laboratory operation.

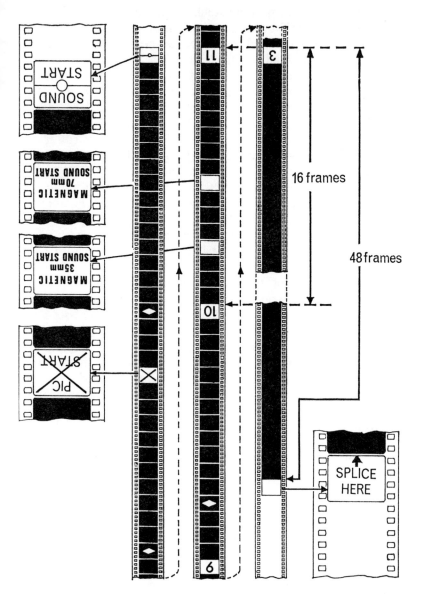

Standard Academy head leader. In positive form they provide projector "thread-up" information. The negative also carries information which assists the laboratory printing operators and ensures that correct sound synchronizing takes place. Inverted writing appears upright as the operator pulls the film *down* from the feed reel to thread up.

With 35 mm film, printing stock is manufactured in lengths of approximately 1,000 ft. and, other than in special circumstances, the editor's work print reel never exceeds about 960 ft. This footage allows for head and tail printing leaders.

A 70 mm release print presents different problems, particularly if the 70 mm print is an enlargement from a 35 mm negative. Reels of positive prints for exhibition are often combined by splicing together two or more single units after printing, so that the large joined reels involve fewer projection changeovers. The editor may be limited not only by individual reel lengths, but perhaps also by the combined footages of several consecutive reels.

With 35 mm release printing the procedure is usually standard, with the editor's reel length ideally a little over 900 ft. Each reel of his work print starts and ends on a scene unlikely to be affected by a changeover error. A standard Academy leader is also cut on to the head and the tail of each reel. The leaders, in negative form, provide printing information to the operators at the laboratory. In positive form, on the final release prints, they identify the reel number and give the projectionist a guide for correct lacing of the projector. Almost invariably, 35 mm release prints are issued as a combination of two consecutive reels. Reels one and two are printed from single negative reels, then the positive prints are spliced into one double reel for exhibition, the reel being called the A/B reel. Each pair of reels is dealt with in the same way, and if this is the only type of release contemplated, the editor is only concerned with the type of scene changeover at the end of alternate reels i.e. from the end of the "B" to the beginning of the next "A" reel.

Each production calls for variations of a standard procedure. Reel lengths and content are determined by the planned release printing.

Work print dupe

Once the reels are set in their final form with Academy head and tail leaders, a final check is made to ensure that synchronization between sound and picture has been correctly maintained during the re-mounting of reels. The major work of editorial post-production is now able to start and, as several of the staff will be working simultaneously on any one reel, a duplicate of the editor's work print must now be made. The laboratory is instructed to make a rough black and white work print duplicate (sometimes called a "slash dupe", or "printers dupe"), of each reel of picture ensuring that when the dupe prints are made the negative key

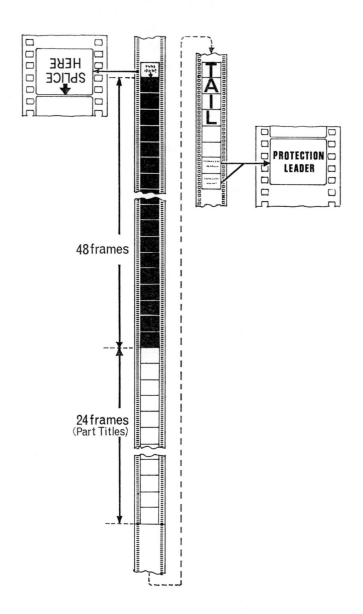

Standard tail leader. The part titles (indicating reel number and title of production) are inserted in standard positions on both head and tail leaders for ease of identification when making up complete copies, and for the guidance of projectionists.

numbers are printed through from the original work print. Two such dupe prints may be made on the larger type of production, one for the sound editor and one additional print for the music department. This, certainly, is standard procedure in America.

After the picture reels are duped a copy of the entire working sound track is made, reel by reel, so that while the sound editor is working with the original sound track, preparing for final sound mixing, a complete copy is still available for screenings.

Final phase-picture/sound

Two major phases can now be put into operation so that the laboratory can produce combined release prints for exhibition. Both operations proceed simultaneously now that duplicate reels are available, and they are to prepare for:

1. *Picture negative cutting*: Dissolves, fades, trick shots, titles and trade marks, have been indicated in the various reels by drawing dissolve or fade lines (or inserting blank film at the point where titles will subsequently occur) but, as yet, there is no negative to cover them. When the production negative is cut to match the editor's print each positive cut must obviously have been made from a negative, the negative stored at the laboratory awaiting negative cutting. The editor now orders new negatives so that a dissolve or fade can be incorporated, and so that titles can be photographed and combined with a suitable background. Negative cutting cannot take place until approved prints from such negatives are substituted into the work print.

2. *Final sound mixing*: All the sounds the editor has cut into reels, in synchronization with picture, are as yet contained in a single sound track. Some sounds are acceptable, some are not, and the sound editor now goes through the final reels taking out the unusable sounds. In conjunction with the remainder, the other sound tracks are now built. They are all synchronized to one picture reel, with dialogue, sound effects and music separated and sub-divided so that they can be finely balanced when mixed into the single master sound track.

Final picture preparation

Negatives incorporating a required optical or trick effect can now be made. The editor must supply certain information to the technicians so that the timings and lengths of the shots incorporating the optical effects are exactly as planned in the work print. Dissolves and fades must occur exactly where marked in the editor's print and, in dissolves synchronization must be maintained on both scenes. Positive prints are made from the new optical negatives and, as long as the opticals have been correctly timed, they can be substituted with temporary ones in the working copy without any adjustment to synchronization or length.

There is an automatic system for making a dissolve or a fade at the release printing stage. But, normally, optical work of this nature means incorporating an additional optical effect during duplication. The optical printer works from a positive film made from the original negative.

The optical process

Whereas the original camera photographed a live action scene the optical camera photographs a positive print of the scene. Shutter and iris mechanisms in the optical printer create the effects on the new negative. The positive film has a fine grain duplicating emulsion, specially designed for this work, to ensure the minimum loss of quality in the final dupe negative. Duplicate negatives *can* be made without going through the fine grain positive stage but, in general, are made in this way to create optical effects.

In a simple fade-out, the effect is achieved by copying the positive scene on to a new negative while, at the appropriate place in the scene, and for the correct length required, the shutter is smoothly and gradually closed to produce the transition from full exposure to blackness. With a fade-in, the reverse operation takes place, and the shutter gradually opens over the required length of scene until full exposure is reached on the correct frame of picture.

A simple 4-ft. dissolve from one scene to another involves firstly a 4-ft. fade out on the outgoing scene. The exposed negative is then wound back to the beginning of that fade and a 4-ft. fade in of the incoming scene superimposed over the first fade. The scenes gradually merge from one to the other. The editor allows for the superimposition of these scenes in his work print by making the splice joining the two halves of the proposed dissolve where the centre of the eventual visual effect occurs. This is at the centre of the 4-ft. dissolve. In his work print, the last 2 ft. of the outgoing scene, and the first 2 ft. of the incoming scene are removed at the splice.

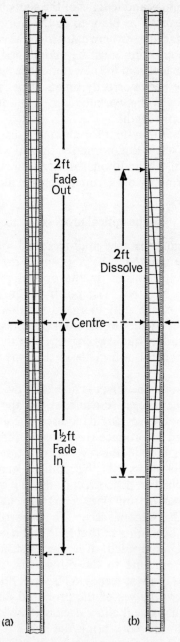

Markings for dissolves and fades—conventional lines marked on picture work prints.
(a) Indicates fade out and fade in. (b) A dissolve.

156

The dissolve is indicated by diagonal lines drawn from one edge of the film to the other on both sides of the splice, the lines meeting at the splice.

The frame on which the first line starts on the outgoing scene is known as the start dissolve frame. Where the line ends on the incoming scene it is the end dissolve frame. The overall length in this instance is exactly 4 ft. from start frame to end frame.

Fades only involve the one scene in which they occur. The conventional indication is by a pair of lines, starting at the edges of the film on the frame where a fade out begins and converging to meet at the frame on which the fade ends. Lines converge the opposite way for a fade in, but they should all be drawn to the correct length so that the start frame and the end frame is clearly indicated.

In cases where the fade or dissolve is so long that drawing a line of sufficient length is impractical, a token line is drawn, but the length of the proposed effect must be carefully measured and the start and end frames marked on the work print.

Information from the editor

The following information must be given to the laboratory so that they can prepare the necessary duplicating film, for use by the technician operating the optical printer. They mark the various start and end frames on this film from key number information supplied by the editor, taken from his work print:

1. The slate number and take number of each scene, and the negative roll number under which they are filed.
2. The length of the required dissolve or fade.
3. The exact frame on which the fade out starts, or on which the dissolve starts on the outgoing scene.
4. The exact frame on which the fade in ends or on which the dissolve ends on the incoming scene.
5. How many feet of additional duplicate scene is required before and after the optical effect for cutting purposes.
6. Any other helpful information, description of action and whether day or night effect.

It is interesting to note here the terms commonly used by technicians in reference to film components used in the duplicating process. They are:
The original negative.

Fine grain duplicating positive, which can be further subdivided as:

(*a*) "Fine grain" in black and white processes.
(*b*) "Inter-positive" in colour processes.

Duplicate negative which is known as:

(*a*) "Dupe Neg." in black and white processes.
(*b*) "Inter-neg." in colour processes.

Length and quality of optical

It would seem a simple matter to replace any cut in the picture which involves an optical effect by duplicating the entire length of the cut. Every photographic duplicating process must mean some loss in quality, however, and it would seem unfair to a cameraman to cut in a long duped scene just because it incorporates a fade or dissolve. Making optical dupes is also fairly expensive, particularly with a colour process.

As a general guide, any scene longer than about 10 ft. is not duped in its entirety. Only 2 or 3 ft. of duplicate film are ordered before and/or after the optical effect, whichever the case may be. Here is another reason for the technical operation to be done with accuracy, starting and finishing on the exact frame of picture. The dissolve or fade must be correctly made and the action must match exactly on both sides of the dissolve if the original scene is to be cut to the duped scene just before and just after the dissolve. And everything must be synchronous. Furthermore, the dupe negative incorporating the dissolve must be of sufficiently high quality to match the original negative closely. There must be no density or colour "jump" where such a cut takes place in continuous action. Often there is nothing to hide this in a static scene. It could be a deciding factor in whether or not to dupe a scene for its full length. At other times, a light switched on in the scene, or a piece of fast movement is enough to cover a minor density fluctuation on the cut.

Auto-opticals

With automation in dissolve and fade making there is no problem with consistent quality and length of the optical. But this system is not always available.

At the point in the cut negative reel where a dissolve is to occur, the original negative of the scene is cut in with the amount of additional footage needed for the dissolve. Using a "punched-

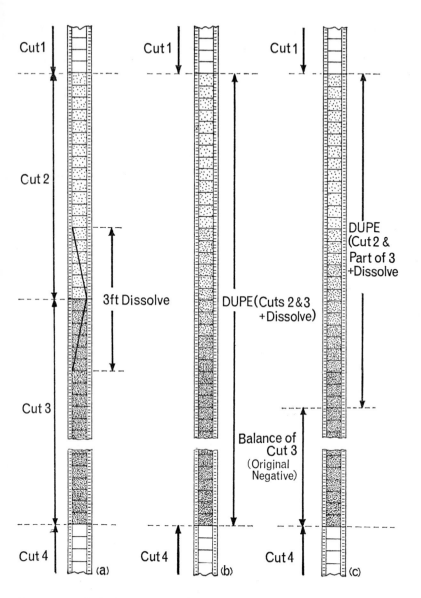

Alternative methods of cutting in completed optical dupe film. (a) 4 cuts in a work print, cuts 2 and 3 involved in a 3 foot dissolve which has been conventionally marked. (b) First method. The dissolve has been made and the entire lengths of cuts 2 and 3 have been duped at each side of the dissolve. (c) Second method. The dissolve has been made and cut 2 has been duped for its entire length. It was considered, however, that cut 3 was too long to be entirely duped. As soon as the dissolve is fully in, a cut is made in continuous action to the original print of cut 3. Both methods are an indication of how the negative will be cut.

159

tape" timing device and with the shutter mechanism incorporated in the film printer, dissolves and fades are automatically produced from the original negative when the release print is made. After printing (and fading) the first scene involved in the dissolve, the printer is "cued" to rewind the positive film for the length of the dissolve required and then runs forward again when the negative of the second half of the dissolve arrives in the printer aperture.

Alternatively, the cut negative is assembled in "A" and "B" rolls for printing. For this, the reel is split into two components so that scenes involved in optical work are separated on alternate rolls, overlapped in relation to each other for the dissolve and followed or preceded by blank film. This involves a double printing operation, with timed shutter mechanism. The system is no longer in general use although it is still available.

The advantage of either method is, of course, that optical effects are produced without any intermediate negative duplication. No loss in quality occurs, and no "jumps" through having to make matched cuts in continuous action. A disadvantage, on the other hand, is that the optical effect is not seen until a print is made from the cut negative and it isn't always possible to anticipate strange effects and untidy dissolves in advance.

Ordering manual fades and dissolves

If the dissolve and fade are to be done manually by optical printer, exact key number information, correct to the frame in each case, must be supplied by the editor when he specifies the order to the laboratory. It is an unfortunate fact that the negative key number which is printed through to the editor's positive print will rarely occupy the exact width of one picture frame. Usually occupying part of two frames, it can sometimes spread over three, according to the number of letters and numerals used. The editor selects one operative frame and encircles that part of the key number filling the frame when writing it on the order. The fine grain print from which the optical is made can then be marked with the start or end dissolve frame accurately, using this "zero" frame as the guide from which any number of plus or minus frames are to be counted. If all orders are specified correctly, fine grain prints marked accurately, and printing is carried out according to the start and end marks, the final duplicate negative will be exactly as planned in the work print.

160

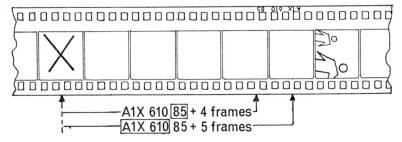

A1X 610 85 + 4 frames
A1X 610 85 + 5 frames

Alternative methods of choosing the "zero" frame. Either way, the information guides the operator to the correct operative picture frame—essential in all optical and trick work. The frame marked X is, thus, quite obviously indicated by either method.

Matching optical to original print

Prints made from these new negatives carry their own set of key numbers. Only the fine grain duplicating positive film carries the original key numbers, whereas the duplicate negative has its own special prefix which indicates the negative type. Duplicate negative key numbers should be logged in a section of the cutting room master record book reserved for such work. Unfortunately, unlike the simple picture reprint made from original negative, there is rarely any direct reference between the newly printed optical and the print in the editor's copy, other than the image itself. Synchronizing the two to check the accuracy of the mechanics prior to cutting the new print into the work print is usually a matter of finding a correctly matched frame of action on either side of the dissolve, or one matched frame in a fade, and then aligning both in the synchronizer to check the overall synchronism. If correct, in sync and grading, the section of new print is substituted in the work print ready for negative cutting.

Finding the matching frame is sometimes a problem in a scene with little movement but, even with the very best processing, there is usually a speck of dirt on the original negative which has been duplicated right through the processes, and will be visible on both prints.

As with all new film cut into the work print, and particularly with optical effects, it must never be assumed that matching prints in this manner has achieved correct synchronism. All optical work must be checked in the projection room to ensure that the dissolve, fade or effect is mechanically and photographically perfect.

161

Order format

A typical 4-ft. dissolve would require the following information on the order:

Dissolve

Slate 292–1. Day exterior. Train, right to left.
(Neg Roll 4821)

Start dupe	A29X 59084
Start dissolve out	A29X 59 089 + 3 frames
Dissolve full Out	A29X 59 093 + 2 frames

4-ft. Dissolve to:
Slate 192–4. Day interior. Railroad station.
(Neg Roll 4719)

Start dissolve in.	A8X 4034 1 + 6 frames
Dissolve full in	A8X 4034 5 + 5 frames
End dupe	A8X 40350

Special instruction: Neither dupe will cover the full length of the cut. Grade accurately to the original negative.

A typical fade-in:

Fade

Slate 302.1. Dawn effect. Open landscape. (Neg Roll 8892)
Make 4-ft. fade-in:

Start fade	35Y G4072 3 + 8 frames
Fade full in	35Y G4072 7 + 7 frames
End dupe	35Y G40734

A typical Fade-out:

Fade

Slate 432–4. Night exterior. Liner at sea:
(Neg Roll 8421)
Make 3 ft. fade-out.

Start dupe	A12X 402912
Start fade-out	A12X 40 2920 + 11 frames
Fade full Out	A12X 40 2923 + 10 frames

Special instruction: Please "flop over" so that direction becomes right to left.

Other opticals

Other simple optical effects may be required, to speed up a shot by printing every other frame, to reverse the direction or to reverse the action itself. Perhaps even an optical enlargement is needed.

TECHNICOLOR LTD. – OPTICAL SPECIFICATION

SUBJECT _Dark of the Sun_   DATE _2 October 1967_   ORDER NO. _6_

EDITOR _Ernest Walter_

PRODUCER

TECHNICOLOR ROLL NO.	OPT. NO.	FOR REEL	SCENE AND TAKE	SCENE START OR START FADE IN	LENGTH OF FADE	START DISSOLVE OUT	LENGTH OF DISSOLVE	END DISSOLVE IN	SCENE END OR FADE FULL OUT	LENGTH OF FADE	TIME OF DAY REQD	TECHNICOLOR ORIGINAL ROLL	TYPE OF NEGATIVE	LENGTH OF SCENE	FILM LOCATION
	22	4	211-3	A19X14318					A19X14-3[29] Plus 7 Frames	4 Ft.	Night	92763	E/Colour	75Ft.	
	23	4	392-8	A4X317729 Plus 2 Frames	3 Ft.				A4X317742		Dawn	94269	E/Colour	176Ft.	

TECHNICOLOR USE ONLY.

SPECIAL INSTRUCTIONS.

Original Print (Clippings Enclosed) for both scenes, fade out and fade in. Please match inter-negative as close as possible since both opticals will not run the full length of the scene.

ST.213A.

A standard Technicolor Laboratory optical specification layout. Here, the order specifies information required for two fades—a 4 ft. fade-out, and a 3 ft. fade-in. Note the "boxed" zero frame and the fact that Technicolor require only "Fade Full Out", or "Start Fade In" frames, plus the length of the fade.

163

Information must be provided by the editor so that the negative can be located, a fine grain duplicating positive made, and the correct section of the scene duped incorporating the required effect, if the entire scene is not needed. A new dupe negative can then be made and a print provided for the editor. Again, he will have to visually match the action before cutting in the new print in synchronism.

Library negative

If a film library stock shot is to be used in the final film, a new dupe negative is made for eventual negative cutting. Naturally, the stock film library always want to retain their original negative for future use, and so a duplicate must be made from the fine grain print which they supply. Once again, a new print is made from this dupe negative, key numbers being common to both to enable negative cutting to take place.

There may be times when, in fairly desperate circumstances, a normal lens stock shot may have to be included in a CinemaScope film if there is no suitable alternative. Here, the film library provide a squeezed fine grain print so that the dupe negative made from it can be included with the similar cut negative for the complete film. Squeezing an image so that it still occupies the same overall negative frame area as the original requires a slight enlargement of the image. This is done when the squeezed fine grain print is made. This results in a slight loss of picture area at the edges, and rather more loss at top and bottom of the frame.

The framing of the anamorphized enlargement can be adjusted to favour top or bottom of the picture to avoid poor composition of the enlarged shot and loss of important parts of action. The editor must specify what he wants for such "panning and scanning" work.

Planning a montage

More complicated dissolve sequences (perhaps a pictorial montage of shots in which constantly changing images are superimposed throughout) take a lot of patient planning and imagination if the final result is to be effective. Trying to commit such detailed information to paper with no fear of misunderstanding is quite complicated. Each section of film in such a montage fades in, is held for a required footage and then fades out, during which time other sections will be fading in and out. The whole superimposed

MONTAGE LAYOUT FOR "DARK OF THE SUN"

FOOTAGE	SLATE	SLATE	SLATE	SLATE	SLATE
0	START DUPE AT KEY NUMBER A1X 489132				
8		A3X 216581			
14	SLATE 429-1 TRAIN PASSING (DAY)	A3X 216587			
18	A1X 489150	SLATE 196-3 C.S. MAN'S FACE			
20		AT WINDOW (DAY)	A12X 643721		
24					
26	A1X 489156		A12X 643727		
32			SLATE 254-2 C.S. ENGINE WHEELS AT SPEED (DAY)	A6X 294268	
38				A6X 294276	
42			A12X 643743	SLATE 500-2 NEWSPAPER HEADLINE	
48			A12X 643749		
52				A6X 294284	
54			A12X 643755		
56				A6X 294292	A1X 490250
58			A12X 643761 SLATE 254-2 C.S. ENGINE WHEELS (NIGHT EFFECT PLEASE)		
62					A1X 490256
66			A12X 643767		SLATE 453-1 TRAIN PASSING (NIGHT)
70		A3X 214643	A12X 643771		
76					
82		A3X 214649			END DUPE AT A1X 490306

This type of layout is very clear to the optical department at the laboratory if set out on lined paper, each line and space representing one foot of film. Confusion is less likely with this style as compared with a written order form because the length and relationship of the components is very obvious, as is the way they are to fade in and out when superimposed.

165

effect is dependent on timings and combinations. The final result depends too, on the strength of the exposure of each section in relation to the other as superimposition takes place, but this is often a matter of trial and error during the optical assembly of the montage.

Timing the shots for positioning and relative duration is more simply handled if the whole plan is drawn up on paper with a series of columns, each column representing a section of film involved. Each section of film is marked as fading in or fading out in relation to progressive footage, and in relation to each other. By drawing the appropriate converging fade lines and shading in the areas occupied by each section of film, it is easier to visualize the eventual effect when planning the montage.

Afterwards, slate number and key number information, together with any special instructions regarding, for example, skip-frame work or "flopping over", can be written in against each section.

Inevitably, there are times when the planned montage doesn't reach the level of expectation and must be replanned and reshot. Naturally this is expensive and may even hold up negative cutting.

Matte shot orders

We have seen earlier that with travelling matte shots, painted and split matte shots the editor must select and synchronize the components to be made into one composite negative for the final print. Split matte shots may be complex, involving multiple split work, with several sections of film needing to be made into one composite. However complex the editor must give very clear information to the lab technicians so that they know exactly how each component is to be synchronized relative to another.

Foreground/Background Relationship

Establishing the relationships of angles and synchronism of action is the editor's responsibility. Where the travelling matte system is used, he matches the angles of foreground and background film with great care. Where moving vehicles are involved, speed of movement in each section of background is chosen to maintain consistency throughout a sequence. When necessary, the matte technician can use further optical controls when producing the final composite, speeding up or reversing the direction of the background when there is a limited choice of film. Each cut is

166

matched and synchronized individually with its background so that the best overall result and progression is achieved.

A typical order for one travelling matte composite would be:

To: Technicolor Ltd. *Dark of the Sun.*

Please make composite T/M as follows, and provide one print from the final composite negative.

Foreground: Slate 482–1. Night Interior Car.
                              Full Front angle. 2-Shot.
                              Section required: A12X 194891 to 911.

Background: Slate 2001–1. Exterior country road.
                              Full Back angle.

Synchronize foreground section, above with:
                        A4X 284125 to 165.

Special Instruction: The background has been shot for day— please dupe for night effect. Background should also be "skip-framed" (every other frame) for double speed.

In this example a 20-ft. section of foreground is married to a 40-ft. "skip-frame" section of background film. The type of background was suitable but was shot for day and was also too slow. This is now corrected when making the matte. Once again, a new negative is made and a new print allows the editor to check the quality and accuracy of mechanics before cutting it into his work print ready for negative cutting.

Split matte shots require similar synchronizing information. Painted matte shots, however, only need an identification of the original scene and the key number section required. The painting is then incorporated with that section of the original shot and a new dupe negative produced, no synchronism being involved.

Trade marks and titles

If a trade mark is mandatory, major film laboratories normally keep a fine grain print of the current one in use by a particular company, ready to make dupe negatives, as required. They make a dupe negative, for the editor and provide a print from this for his work print. The new negative is then filed with the remainder of his production film in readiness for cutting.

The positioning, nature and style of main titles is a question of policy related to the particular film. Possibly there will be a very specialized approach to the problem, the entire title negative being provided by an organization operating independently of the editor. If so, the editor is provided, at the very earliest opportunity, with a blank guide film so that he knows not only the exact overall length of the final title sequence but also the positioning of certain individual "key" titles such as the main title card itself. He needs to know this so that he can set the length of the reel concerned and provide details for the music composer. Blank guide film is necessary for all proposed titles; intermission title, end title, cast roller, where applicable, to set the reel length and allow for music.

Titles, particularly main and end titles may be superimposed on pictorial sequences. In this case the editor is given an accurate list of title cards so that he knows the order of appearance and the content of each separate title. Now he can plan the duration and position of each card in relation to the photographic background, and if background and titles must dissolve or cut on and off, and so on. Title cards are painted on glass or card and photographed as individual components. A short length of negative is made for each card. The editor orders fine grain prints of each title background in readiness for the optical preparation of the composite title sequence.

In the case of a complicated and lengthy title sequence with many different pictorial backgrounds, the most simple method of ordering the composite would be to assemble a reprint of the entire pictorial sequence. If the backgrounds are to dissolve one to the other, conventional dissolve lines of appropriate length can be drawn, in the usual way. The picture can also be marked to indicate the start frame and end frame of each separate title card, again drawing conventional fade lines if the titles are to fade in and out. This film would then be sent to the laboratory so that they can assemble the picture fine grain prints in the same way, cutting them together if there are no pictorial dissolves, or marking them with the dissolve information if required. Title positions can also be indicated on the fine grain prints and the entire operation will be much simpler than a complicated order written on paper.

An alternative method would be to use the same system as suggested for indicating a pictorial montage sequence, columns being prepared for background film and columns for titles. Fades and dissolves can then be indicated in relation to a progressive footage in each column, as described earlier.

A visual check of title/background relationship should be made in the projection room before ordering a final composite negative.

Two rolls are assembled. One contains all the pictorial background film. The other contains a print of each title, synchronously positioned in the roll in relation to the background, any spaces between individual titles filled with *black* opaque leader film. Leaders with synchronous start marks are spliced to the head of each reel and they are simultaneously screened from two projectors. Obviously there will be no picture dissolves or title fades (if these are contemplated) but it will give an impression of the planned result.

All such work involving special optically prepared negatives must be put in hand as soon as possible so that picture negative cutting can be carried out without delay. Straightforward work to give a speeded up effect or change of direction in a single straight cut are normally ordered during the course of the editor's assembly. But those shots or sequences needing an overall approval of the cut before orders can be safely placed are now given the utmost priority.

The travelling matte process takes considerable time and, although problems of unsteadiness and unsatisfactory matte assembly can often be overcome, there is sometimes no alternative than to recut a sequence to remove a bad shot. With reels set in length, multiple reels of sound effects being built, and music being composed, or perhaps already recorded, the apparently simple task of making such a recut in picture can cause widespread complications.

9

SOUND EDITING

WHILE rough assembling sequences at the time of shooting, the film editor builds a single sound track alongside the pictorial sequences. By the time the fine cut stage is reached, he has a number of finalized picture reels and a similar number of sound reels. This single sound track contains many temporary sounds, used by the film editor to convey the impression of a mixed overall effect as far as possible. In some areas the recording is very incomplete. Scenes shot in the studio normally have excellent sound quality. Though all dialogue and movement sounds are present, they must be augmented. Additional "off-screen" sound effects complete the atmosphere of the setting and lend realism to the scene. But, as yet, the film editor has been limited by using only a single sound track.

Role of the sound editor

Dialogue is the concern of the film editor, or of the dialogue editor if one has been employed.

Sound effects are the province of the sound editor. Before he is ready to present all the effects sounds at the final mixing session there are many jobs for him to do.

The sound editor examines each completed reel and decides which sound effects are satisfactory and which require replacement. He then plans replacements to give the best result. He provides some sound effects synchronized with picture, although this is no problem as he can see what is needed. His true talent, however, is seen as he creates those "off-screen" effects which are *not* seen.

The real art of the good sound editor is to create an effect that adds realism to a scene without being an intrusion.

In theory, there need be no limit to the number of synchronized sound reels he can build for any one reel of picture. In practice, he keeps them to a manageable number. Individual sounds are separated to allow the sound engineers who do the final mixing sufficient individual control to achieve the best overall balance of sound.

The sound editor must remember that there are other sound tracks, dialogue and music, all to be blended with his. So he avoids placing wildly noisy sound effects during the course of a delicate dialogue scene.

If a dialogue editor has been employed to take care of post-synchronizing requirements during the course of the production, the sound editor may not be needed until the "fine-cut" stage. But this would depend on the particular production. Normally, on feature films he is employed at about the half-way stage while shooting is still in progress. If so, he can familiarize himself with the production and perhaps start checking and filing any production sound effects which have already been recorded. If the film unit is to go on an exterior location he makes arrangement with the production sound mixer to record any sounds in the exterior sequence which would otherwise be difficult to reproduce. When a large crowd sequence is shot, he tries to persuade the director to shoot some crowd sound effects before the people are finally dismissed.

Temporary sound pre-mixes

During production the sound editor can take an edited sequence and augment the single sound track with temporary additions to provide a new and more satisfactory single sound track. He compiles for this purpose, a small number of synchronized and separated sounds which can be mixed together in a sound theatre. If looped dialogue recordings are used in the editor's work print, sequences are cold and lifeless. An exterior looped scene, in particular, loses all its vitality. Even one overall background atmosphere sound added to such a dialogue scene gives it temporary life. This is of great help during the screenings which take place before the final sound dubbing. Other sequences, too, may benefit from such temporary "pre-mixing" of sound, for use in the work print. Scenes photographed in mock-up sets on the studio stage—cars, aeroplanes, for example—are better for these early screenings if a temporary background effects track is "dubbed in". This sometimes causes a problem when cutting changes involve looped dialogue not incorporating the temporary background.

172

This is a minor problem. A new pre-mix for the altered section can easily be made.

Although familiar with the production and the types of sound effect he will eventually require, the sound editor cannot begin the physical preparation for final sound mixing until he has complete and finalized work print picture dupes from the film editor. While dissolves, fades, matte shots and titles are being co-ordinated and ordered, sound tracks can be simultaneously built for each reel of picture.

Sound equipment for track mixing

The aim of the sound department is to produce a single strip master dubbed sound track, correctly balanced for each reel of picture. This is combined with the cut picture negative at the laboratory to produce the exhibition prints.

By a series of "pre-mixes", the many dialogue, effects and music tracks are gradually grouped together. Thus, the final result can be mixed from a relatively small number of pre-grouped sound components.

The sound engineers work in a projection room equipped to project the picture on to a screen while many synchronous sound reels are simultaneously running on sound reproducers. To achieve the correct balance of overall sound, they have individual volume and tone controls for each sound reel. These are arranged on a special console. Each sound machine sends out the individual signals contained in the assembled sound tracks. After rebalancing, that is matching them with one another for loudness and quality, they are transmitted through the console to the single film roll on the recording machine.

Each machine, or "re-recorder", handles one reel of sound film at a time. There are therefore several re-recorders, and they can be in synchronism with each other and with the picture projector. The number of these re-recorders in use at any one time is governed by handling capacity of the mixing console. They are designed to reproduce either magnetic or photographic sound and, when of the magnetic type they can be converted to reproduce single, three-track or six-track multiple recordings.

The *recording* machine receives signals as they are finally balanced by the sound mixing engineers. It can be a film or tape recording machine, fitted with single or multiple recording heads, and there are magnetic and photographic film versions for whichever may be required.

Dubbing chart

The technicians in the sound department carrying out this mixing and balancing are relatively unfamiliar with the film when they start work on the first reel. They have one further basic aid, therefore, to help them with this problem. So that they know how the three main groups of dialogue, effects, and music are separated, and how all the individual sound tracks have been spaced in each reel to synchronize with the picture, the sound mixers are provided with a chart to guide them. This dubbing chart tells them not only what sound is in which effects reel, but also indicates the exact footage within the reel where each individual sound effect, dialogue, or music track begins and ends. The picture projector has a built in footage indicator and a progressive footage is visible below the screen area whenever a reel is projected. Using the chart information, the footages and the screen image, the technician can keep complete control during the sound mixing.

Basic requirements in the sound dubbing theatre are:

1. A projector to show the picture, coupled to a visual progressive footage indicator.
2. A number of re-recording machines to reproduce the sound from all the synchronous sound reels interlocked with the projector.
3. A sound film recording machine for either magnetic or photographic sound systems.
4. A mixing console, connected to re-recorders and recorder, so that all the separate sound tracks can be heard and balanced on to a newly recorded single sound track.

In addition to these basic requirements, it is a great advantage if the sound dubbing theatre is equipped with a forward and reverse mechanism operating the projector and interlocked re-recorders. As yet, few are so fitted. When dubbing, sections of reels can be rehearsed again and again without all reels having to be rewound independently and reset on their common start marks. Reversing all machines in use in inter-lock will obviously save much time. Where available, this system is known as "rock and roll" dubbing.

Preparing for final dubbing

The sound editor can now start his basic preparation in the cutting room. He examines each reel of picture and sound on his viewing machine, noting which of the sounds are basically usable and the unsatisfactory sounds which he will eventually replace. At the same time, he notes any areas not covered by production sound effects—the wild tracks recorded by the production sound mixer—so that he is aware of what is basically missing.

From this information, bearing in mind the additional "off-screen" atmosphere sounds he will want to use, his plan follows two courses:

1. To try to locate some of the required sounds at the various sound effects libraries, where many thousands of feet of varied effects are filed.
2. To arrange to make recordings of effects that cannot be found in the sound library. These may be sub-divided into two further sections:

   (a) Sound effects he can record "wild" as they are independent of picture synchronism, e.g. general overall sounds and background atmosphere effects, also anything "off-screen".
   (b) To record those sounds which *are* dependent on synchronism with picture, e.g. footsteps, movements, and on-scene effects which have been lost, for example, when a dialogue scene was post-synchronized.

Having exhausted the resources of all sound film libraries, the sound editor has a sound crew ready to make both "wild" and synchronized recordings. Exterior recordings may need vehicles for specific sound effects.

The sound editor is present on recording expeditions to direct the recordings and ensure that they are all made to his noted requirements. Wild interior recordings are done in the sound studio.

Post synchronized sound effects

When dealing with those sound effects which must synchronize with picture, the sound editor faces a different problem. Just as post-synchronized dialogue scenes require picture loops as a visual guide, so do post-synchronized sound effects. In this case though, only a picture loop is normally required. The value of more than one picture dupe print on each reel on the larger production now becomes apparent. The sound editor prepares all the picture loops needed for the recording session by cutting them section by section, out of one of the picture dupes.

Bearing in mind the capacity limitation imposed by the projection machine, he makes fairly long loops of picture—as long as synchronizing does not become too complicated. As with dialogue scenes, loops are spliced to leaders into which a "sync plop" has been inserted. They are given numbers as they are prepared. A list is prepared describing the sounds required on each loop, as several recording operations may be required to complete a loop. A virgin magnetic recording loop is made for each number and synchronized to length. This looping system is used by the sound editor for easy playback when checking recordings.

Effect props

Many props are required in the recording studio to recreate suitable sounds. Bottles, glasses, cutlery, doors, telephone, typewriter, water tank, etc., are only a few examples of quite a formidable list of items the sound editor must get together. Some synchronizing sound studios are designed purely for effects shooting. Strips of permanently laid flooring of various types such as wood, concrete, gravel and sand are an important feature. Turf can be imported as necessary. Various door mountings, bells, telephones and water tank are among the items always available.

Effects session

When recording takes place to synchronize with the projected picture loop, the sound editor sits with the sound technician in a monitor room so that he can judge sound quality and the degree of synchronism achieved. He can call for playback as soon as he is satisfied with the overall result, and for another recording if the playback check doesn't satisfy him. Helping him recreate these sounds, walking up and down, opening doors, rustling bushes and foliage, reproducing fight noises, are people who specialize in such work and can do all these things while watching the action on the screen.

With a large and complicated film, effects recording sessions in the studio take many days of effort and it is often a dirty and unpleasant task for all concerned. Nevertheless, quest for good sound quality and synchronism must go on as this will save much time when fitting the tracks to picture.

Further post-sync effects are needed if the film is to be issued in a foreign language version. All footsteps, movements and other

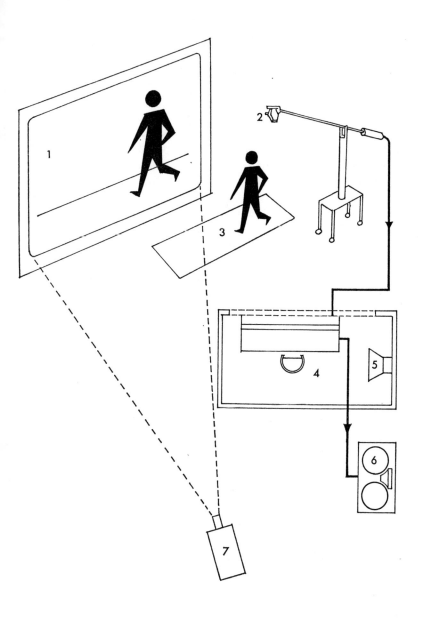

Post-synchronizing footsteps in the effects theatre. (I) Screen. (2) Recording micro-phone. (3) Various surfaces, as required. (4) Sound recordist in monitor room. (5) Monitor speaker. (6) Recording machine, carrying a virgin loop of magnetic film. (7) Projector, running the picture loop.

sound effects recorded with the original dialogue will be lost if they cannot be separated from it. Such sounds must be made in anticipation of foreign language dubbing.

Stripping tracks

While this effects session is taking place, the film or dialogue editor prepares sound tracks of dialogue scenes, separating dialogue from basic effects in the operation known as "stripping tracks". Each reel is taken in turn and the single working sound track split into two synchronous reels in the film synchronizer, alongside the picture. Blank spacing film is inserted into each reel where separation of sound takes place to maintain overall synchronism of each sound track to picture. One reel contains dialogue only. The other has all the footsteps, movements and pure sound effects and is called the "sync effects track". This reel is handed to the sound editor and forms the basis of his effects track assemblies.

The dialogue track which has been stripped in this manner must now be divided and sub-divided into a further number of synchronous reels alongside the picture, if there is a mixture of original and post-synchronized dialogue recordings. Original dialogue is normally kept on one reel and called, "Dialogue 1". Post-synchronized dialogue is further divided so that individual artists in a "busy" dialogue scene occupy separate dialogue reels. Thus balancing the final dialogue (whose component parts were recorded at different times) will be much easier for the sound mixers. Separate dialogue tracks provide complete control for the final mix. These additional dialogue reels are called "Dialogue 2", "Dialogue 3", and so on.

At the time of track-stripping, some dialogue scenes may have only recently been post-synchronized. The original unacceptable sound may still be in the work track. If so, the NG original dialogue can either be stripped right out of the reel and filed as the new recordings are cut into the second or third dialogue tracks, or it can be "flipped over" where it is, so that the reverse side is uppermost, and left in the reel. Flipping unwanted tracks such as these does two very helpful things:

Firstly, it presents the hard and shiny reverse side of the film to the sound reproducing head so that what had been sound track is now blank spacing.

Secondly, if at any time a comparison is needed between original and post-synchronized dialogue on this scene, there is no need to search for a piece of stripped track in the filing system and put it back into the reel. By flipping it in the reel back to its original side, the dialogue can be heard in sync, immediately, and compared with the looped sequence.

All the dialogue is split, reel by reel. Any dialogue needing specific treatment, e.g. telephone or loud speaker effect, echo and reverberation, is separated from dialogue nearby so that once the electronic control is set to create the desired effect, the sound tracks concerned will be automatically treated.

Dubbing charts are prepared for each separate reel of dialogue, indicating the contents of each reel and the footages at which each section starts and ends. This is particularly important in the case of post-synchronized dialogue tracks. Where sections of looped dialogue occur it is important that the name of the character be also included on the chart and in the appropriate area to assist character identification by the sound mixers as the reel is being screened.

UK and USA track numbers

It is interesting to note the sound track numbering methods used in Britain and the USA. The British method names the three main sound groups as dialogue, effects and music. As they become separated within their individual group, the additional tracks are called "dialogue 1", "dialogue 2", "effects 1", "effects 2", "music 1", "music 2", and so on, according to the quantity involved. In the USA, the same three basic sound groups are known as the "A", "B", and "C" strips, any sub-division of tracks within each group known as, "A-1", "A-2", "B-1", "B-2", "C-1", "C-2", and so on. The American editor speaking of his "C-Strip", will be referring to his music track.

Checking sync

Preparation and separation of dialogue tracks is a fairly straight-forward operation depending on the quantity of looped dialogue in the film. Time taken when tracks are being built, to check synchronism of looped dialogue scenes is time well spent. Lip-sync always seems to be suspect when looped sequences are seen over and over again as final mixing takes place. Doubtful synchronizing can be the cause of much wasted time in the sound mixing theatre, as an error of one frame in sync can make a "border-line" looped scene completely unacceptable. Careful checking beforehand will avoid this irritation and expense and the skilled dialogue editor can remove a sprocket of film here or insert two sprockets there, between individual words, so that synchronization with picture is perfect, or as near perfect as possible.

With dialogue, just as with sound effects, there may be a need for additional lines spoken "off-screen". Augmented vocal effects, shouts and orders, can greatly improve the atmosphere of a scene and give added reality. Such possibilities must always be borne in mind and wild dialogue recordings planned in advance to cover all eventualities.

Building effects tracks

The building of sound effects reels calls for a similar technique. All tracks are separated, where necessary, for future balancing. The sound editor is sometimes faced with a mammoth task when he starts to build his many sound reels. Yet, perhaps, there are many more opportunities for originality with sound effects than is realized, particularly with unseen but very imaginative sounds.

The worst problem facing the sound editor as he begins may be the time factor. As with every other phase of production, there is inevitably a dead-line for the sound dubbing session. Sound dubbing theatre reservations are made some time in advance and related to the finishing schedule.

The film laboratory are consulted so that they can plan picture negative cutting to ensure completion in time for combined printing with the final sound track. These schedules are planned well ahead by editorial, sound and production departments, in consultation with the film laboratory.

In planning his effects the sound editor must be as flexible in his outlook as possible. Once he starts, as each reel is before him on his bench, a new thought and a new idea may occur to him, possibly involving a further search for the appropriate sound film. He would never be able to completely pre-plan the track-building operation, other than in a basic form. Nevertheless, on the basis of this plan he starts to assemble the various components of sound, reel by reel, guided by his original notes.

Basic sounds

He tries to build the obvious sounds first, going through all the picture reels and fitting them in, rather than trying to complete each reel as he comes to it. He examines the reels of sync effects stripped from the basic dialogue tracks, rejecting those he considers unsuitable, either by stripping them out entirely, or by flipping them over within the reel so that they become blank spacing. He proceeds until left with all salvable sounds from the original work track. These, too, may have to be separated into individual reels for mixing control, particularly if there are picture dissolves, so that the sound from one can overlap and mix through to the following scene.

Next, he takes each picture reel and synchronously builds all the sound effects which he specifically recorded, spacing out the individual sounds with blank film to keep the overall synchronism. Picture sections which were removed for effects looping are reassembled into complete reels as he builds these tracks, using the sync plop which was cut into the loop leaders as his synchronizing guide. Footsteps and movements are thus built into synchronized effects reels for each reel of picture. Charts with details of sound sections, positions in the reels, and footages are also prepared.

When this basic work has been completed he looks at each reel individually to see what not-so-obvious sounds are now required.

Pre-mixing requirements

While building the tracks the sound editor thinks ahead to the actual mixing operation, as his synchronized reels must be built in accordance with physical limitations in the dubbing theatre. The dubbing technicians will divide the final mixing operation into the three main sound groups—dialogue, effects and music. But the total number of synchronized sound tracks for any one picture reel, in any one main group, may be more than they can handle at one time. This will certainly be the situation with effects, and very often the case with dialogue tracks on "busy" reels. To achieve a first-class overall sound balance they gradually condense the number of component tracks for the main groups in each reel, until left with a small enough number to be mixed simultaneously. This gradual reduction of synchronized sound reels is called "pre-mixing".

A pre-mix example

The sound editor groups the sound tracks in every reel, anticipating pre-mixes, so that the minimum number of sound reels need be run to make a combined pre-mix, otherwise the advantages of pre-mixing are lost.

For example, a reel involving a battle sequence may have, in all, 20 synchronized reels of effects, apart from dialogue and music. Probably one of the busiest items in the battle sequence would be the gunshots and it would be very easy for the sound editor to "spread" all the synchronized gunshots throughout the 20 effects reels, using any space available in each reel. Pre-mixing, however, will obviously be necessary and one of the premixes should be planned for such a quantity of gunshots. A pre-mix can reduce all these gunshots, correctly balanced to picture, on to one piece of sound film and free the sound mixer from concentrated attention on this section of the reel in later mixing stages. Knowing this to be necessary, the sound editor groups the gunshot tracks accordingly, not intermingling them with different types of sound effect. He may even build them as a completely isolated assembly separated from the main sound effects, to be pre-mixed in one advance operation to provide him with a single combined gunshot track that can be cut into one of his effects reels.

Second start pre-mixing

To take this a stage further, let us suppose that the battle sequence was situated at the end of a reel, perhaps the last 200 ft. It would be foolish and time-wasting to start mixing at the front of the reel, balancing the sounds perfectly up to this point, only to make many errors in mixing the last 200 ft. of battle noise because of its complexity. In this case, the sound editor plans to pre-mix the entire battle section before the complete mixing of the reel is attempted. He builds all the battle sounds on separate reels, each synchronized with a start mark inside the picture reel, 20 ft. or so before the start of the battle. These are pre-mixed in sections or groups, picture and tracks starting from this "second start mark", until a satisfactory mix is made of the entire battle scene on one piece of sound film. This new film can be inserted into any vacant space on an available synchronized sound reel for that particular picture or, alternatively, a new sound reel may be built to accommodate it. The individual tracks from which it was made can now be forgotten. As balance has already been achieved, the sound mixer, too, can virtually forget this pre-mixed section when sound tracks are mixed with it to complete the reel.

Some sounds need special additional treatment at the time of mixing. An echo effect, for example, may be required. These tracks, too, are grouped together, even if pre-mixing is not contemplated, so that that particular area of sound can be treated without affecting other nearby sounds.

Sounds which have been prepared specifically for foreign versions, i.e. those replacements of original sound not salvable from beneath dialogue, are completely separated from all other sound tracks, since they will not be required until a later stage.

Multi-track mixing requirements

The method of sound track building discussed so far presupposes that the eventual sound mix is to be a single channel monophonic sound track. It may be, however, that a multiple channel sound release print is contemplated, in which case either four-track or six-track final mixes will be required in final dubbing. Here, the finally dubbed sounds must appear to come from a particular source. Since the projection screens for such productions are large, sounds must seem to originate from the screen area as dictated by dialogue or action, i.e. from the left, centre or right of the screen area. Other sounds may have to come from the body of the theatre, through the special speakers which surround the audience. Certain effects may have to appear to "travel" from the screen area to the rear of the theatre, as, for example, in the case of an aeroplane which passes overhead.

Sound effects that must appear to move across the screen or into the auditorium can obviously not be intermingled with sounds coming from a static source. The sound editor must plan his tracks with this in mind, letting the action of the picture dictate the requirements.

Effects loops

One further "stand-by" sound effect which the sound editor usually prepares on every film is the continuous sound loop. Very long scenes involving a constant background sound atmosphere, possibly spreading over several picture reels, can sometimes be filled with a series of sound loop alternatives. Country atmosphere, birds, surf and river noise are examples.

These loops should be regarded strictly as "emergency fill" sounds, never to be used in place of the properly built sound track. The loops must not contain any predominant or characteristic sound that would repeat regularly. Such repetition would be obvious and irritating.

Some sound studios provide an automatic continuous tape

system which, at the touch of a button, makes available a variety of background effects. Usually contained in cassette form, tapes suitable to the nature of the film can be pre-loaded into a specially designed sound reproducing machine, linked to the sound console.

It is not often realized how complicated and time-consuming the work of the sound editor can be. Basic and obvious sound effects present very little problem, apart from finding the correct sound. Augmented sounds are a different matter and call for intelligence and imagination. In building many individual sound reels and keeping them synchronized to picture, the sound editor must go through the same reel time and again, as he prepares the tracks. Meanwhile he must always bear in mind the need to separate sounds, where required, for the various situations. Carefully prepared and detailed dubbing cue charts are *essential* to the sound mixers, and these, too, take many hours of painstaking preparation. In this respect it is worth noting that the European sound editor prepares charts in much greater detail than his American counterpart, much to the regret of the American sound mixer.

Although one cannot generalize, there are seldom fewer than 6 or 8 synchronized effects reels for each reel of picture, apart from dialogue and music, even on a simple feature film. Often there are 20 or more, apart from small sections specially prepared for independent pre-mixing. Dialogue and music reels are prepared independently, and so the number of components to be finally reduced to one sound track can be formidable.

10

MUSIC EDITING

FILM producers are often heard to say that the most difficult character to cast for the film is the man to compose the music. This can be very true. Making the choice is in many ways something of a gamble, particularly if a relatively unknown composer is used, or perhaps someone who has a reputation in the musical field but has not had the opportunity to relate his talent to film-making.

In other areas of the film a producer does have a reasonable amount of control. Character roles are sometimes re-cast, directors and senior technicians changed after the production has been under way for a short time, not necessarily because of insufficient talent but perhaps because the talent was unsuitable. Faced with a long shooting schedule, the producer may have to make such unpleasant decisions quickly before it develops into a larger problem.

Choice of composer

Where the composer is concerned, the producer has a slightly different problem and he is always aware of this. His choice may be based on a reputation. Perhaps he saw some similar film subject and liked the scored music. Or, in the case of the unknown composer the choice may be just a reasonably calculated hunch. He listens to proposed themes played on a piano and there may be many discussions about the music. He may even go to the expense of test recordings made with a small group of musicians. But he must wait several weeks before large groups of instrumentalists can be gathered together for the music session. Then, for the first time, he can hear the fully orchestrated score and listen to it as it is recorded *in relation to the picture*. It is extremely difficult for a producer to explain in detail to any composer exactly how he envisages the music. Hearing it properly for the first time he may

185

now feel that the score does not come up to expectation. It may even be absolutely wrong for the film. With a tight production schedule, rejecting the musical score at a late stage is a very costly affair.

Types of film music

Film music can be divided into two main groups, each with its particular function. The pure musical sequence and the featured visual music section of any scene perform an obvious function. But scored music for background use is rather a different problem. Not only must it be written with great thought and skill but also the areas of the film which are to be enhanced with such music must be chosen with some care. Unlike the early sound films where it was thought very necessary to add background music of almost any type right through, the present approach is more thoughtful. Music is used to create an atmosphere which would otherwise be impossible. And it is used only where completely effective. Just as the sound editor assembles his sound effects to create an almost musical effect in some sequences, so the music composer creates the instrumental background, to become at times an additional sound effect in itself. Often, it is an augmented effect blending with a dialogue scene so that one is almost unaware of its musical presence yet, adding so much to the value of the scene.

Viewing the cut

The day will come, however, when the producer must make his choice, playing it safe and going along with a reputation, or taking a chance and relying on a hunch. Wherever possible, the decision should be made before the end of shooting so that with many film assemblies available, even in rough form, the composer can be brought into the atmosphere of the film by attending some of the earlier screenings. At the fine cut stage detailed examination of the film can be made with specific reference to the positioning and form that the music should take. When this time comes, the composer may prefer to have one screening of the complete film, alone, not even consciously thinking of where and how it should be musically treated, but rather to absorb the general feeling and atmosphere of the story. This is a matter of personal choice, but he would never be refused such an opportunity.

It will be of enormous help to the composer at this time if he is provided by the editorial department with a "one-line continuity".

186

As the name suggests, this gives a reel by reel breakdown of sequences with a very brief outline of key points. It serves as a reminder of the order of events to someone who has only seen a film once or twice. Not only will the composer benefit, but also the entire editorial department during the last stages of cutting and dubbing. Sound editors and assistants can refer to it and see at a glance the contents of each reel.

Cueing the film for music

Producer, director if still available, editor and composer can then make a detailed examination of musical requirements, taking each reel and screening it as many times as necessary. Each sequence is examined individually, bearing in mind the desired overall effect, and the task of "cueing" the film for music may well be spread over several days.

Inexperienced editors may think that the "fine-cut" is the end of picture editing on the project and that everything is finalized. It is most likely that the music "cueing" session will prove him to be sadly wrong! Working so close to the film for so long, trying to remain objective about it is a problem difficult for the producer, director or editor to combat. Now, someone with a completely fresh and open mind may, perhaps, be finding areas of confusion or scenes which take far too long to make their point. So apart from opinions expressed about the music there may be strong arguments in favour of some recutting, here and there. This should be expected and welcomed. Unfortunately, making changes at this stage is far less simple than before the picture dupes were made and the sound editor unleashed to his task. But these problems must not be allowed to influence decisions to make changes. The editor would be well advised to keep sound and dialogue editors informed of all changes, however minor, if they are to be expected to keep their sound tracks synchronized to the final version of the picture.

Perhaps the most obvious change is when music positioning is planned in detail and it is discovered that music sections now being proposed will carry over from one reel to the next. Where "A" and "B" reels are joined for release, it presents no problem since this can be taken care of in dubbing the final sound track, as we shall see. If music occurs in the changeover from "B" to "A" reel, however, it must either be planned to accommodate the changeover by composing with this in mind or the changeover point must be altered if the music is to be unbroken. This can present a major problem and anything that can be done to anticipate this should be borne in mind when reels are made up into final form.

Selecting music cues

When the composer has seen the completed film, he now begins a detailed breakdown. Reels are screened one at a time, and it is decided *exactly* where to start each separate section of music and *exactly* where to finish. The possibility of employing a specialist music editor has to be mentioned at this point since, although not often used on European feature films of the non-musical type, they are invariably employed on the American feature film. American editorial activity in feature film making is much more depart- mentalized than in Europe and is probably based on the enor- mous annual output of the typical film factory of the "thirties".

A television feature series is a different matter. The music editor engaged on those productions uses the same basic themes week after week and relates them to each picture episode. In consulta- tion with the series composer he skilfully arranges and edits music for each episode as though it had been scored for it. This is a specialized task.

Whether carried out by the film editor or a feature music editor, the routines and techniques are the same. Reel by reel the examina- tion continues, music cues being noted and the general type of musical requirement discussed for each cue. Dramatic and humo- rous aspects of scenes may call for musical punctuation and there is often an opportunity to improve weakness evident in the original shooting. No matter how many times directors and producers comfort themselves with the thought that the music will "save" the sequence, or the picture, this is never likely and they are really giving themselves false hope. Music can *add* greatly to a film—this is why it is used—but, as with augmented off-screen sound effects, background music will do no more than is intended. That is to create an additional atmosphere, impossible to achieve in any other way. Film music is never the saviour of any film.

Composer's cue sheet

Each proposed "cue" is given a number as a means of reference throughout the composing period and the eventual scoring session on the music recording stage. A standard method is to use a number

'DARK OF THE SUN'

MUSIC MEASUREMENTS

REEL 1		FEET	MINS.	SECS.
	Curry has just said to Ruffo "One day remind me to load this thing"			
1M2	Start Music on C.S. UN. Official as he suddenly turns round in reaction to Curry's dialogue	0		0
	Cut to M.S. As Ruffo and Curry leave through airport gate	2½		1¾
	Cut to M.S. as they push their way through the milling crowds	6		4
	Ruffo salutes soldier who is waiting by open car door	9½		6½
	They get into back of car	12		8
	Car door slams shut, at:-	15½		10½
	Curry looks closely at bullet holes in side window	18		12
	Cut to M.S. Curry and Ruffo both looking out of side windows	19		12⅔
	Cut to M.S. Car pulling away	21½		14⅓
	As car passes camera, at:-	26½		17⅔
	Camera starts to pan up to poster on wall	27½		18⅓
	End of Pan up to wall reveals President Ubi looking down from posters	30		20
	Cut to M.S. Curry standing up "alright Sir, here are my provisions. I do not want to get shot at by United Nations Ground and Airforces. General Moses and the worst of the Simbas are around that area and I'll have enough trouble getting through them. So if you can give me a letter telling ......"	346	3	50⅔
	Cut to M.S. Ubi listening to Curry "The United Nn. to let this train go unmolested to Port Reprieve and back"	367	4	4⅔
	Cut to M.S. Curry "That's number one. Number two, I want a letter giving me command of Striker Blue Force and an Open Order to choose my own Officers and men ends	372½	4	15⅔
	ends	383½	4	15⅔
	End Music on End of Reel 1	385	4	16⅔

Section of detailed information prepared for the music composer on one music cue, in this case the second cue in Reel 1. The first one would have been the Main Title music. Progressive footage is not really required by the composer—he works to minutes and seconds—but is written in so that the overall lengths can be extracted for the recordist at the music session. (See also page 193.)

to indicate the reel concerned and also the total number of cues in each reel. The designation "1M1", for example, would refer to the first music section in Reel I; "2M5", the fifth section in reel two, and so on.

Music measurements

Although the composer may have various themes clearly established in his mind, having viewed the picture many times in recent weeks, he cannot start detailed composition until he has a very comprehensive breakdown of the action and dialogue in every proposed music cue.

Each piece of action and every line of dialogue is measured with progressive timings from the zero point at the beginning of the cue, cut by cut. Included with this is a description of the action, and any key points of action or visual effect in each cut are also noted.

The musical treatment for each scene varies according to the demands of the scene itself. If a scene in a restaurant is to be treated with music which is meant to come from an actual orchestra or piano in the scene then a continuous piece of music is called for. Just a few key cutting or dialogue points may be sufficient. If the scoring is designed to augment a dialogue or an action scene with musical effect, however, every detail of timing is needed.

From this information the composer can weave a pattern of music that will never interfere with dialogue, yet accent it when necessary, and follow the action of a scene so that it becomes an integral part of the total effect. Every possible detail must be given so that the composer is free to place the musical accents where he feels they will create the best effect.

To produce such detailed information, the editor's viewing machine is used. The viewing table with its big screen and its ability to handle large reels, is ideal for the task. The Moviola, when

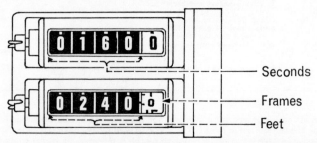

Music measurements are made using interlocked counters on the Moviola. The top counter registers seconds and tenths and the lower counter registers feet and frames.

fitted with take-up reels and a seconds counting indicator, can also be used. Each cue is separately detailed and the typewritten information sent to the composer as quickly as possible, probably a few sections at a time, so that he can start writing. Sometimes he works near the cutting room so that he can re-view a reel or a sequence while writing. But, generally, he vanishes to his private workroom and is not heard of again until the time comes to record the music, unless he has reason to check something.

Recording session

The orchestra is assembled in a specially equipped studio or music stage. All the background music is played and recorded in synchronism with the projected picture. The night club or restaurant background, if not involving visual synchronizing, will possibly be recorded "wild" to an overall timing.

As with post-synchronized dialogue and effects, film required at the music session must be prepared so that synchronized recordings and playbacks can be made. Start marks are needed ahead of each music cue on the projected picture allowing sufficient "run-up" footage not only to give the projector and recorder enough time to reach correct speed, but also to guide the conductor to the start of the music cue. As the music has been written to fit very detailed timing information, the conductor needs an easily

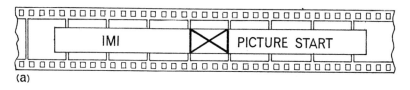

(a)

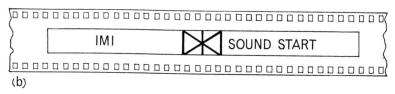

(b)

Film for the music session showing synchronous tape start marks and the information written on tape positioned within the reels of picture and sound as required for the music session. (a) Picture start is positioned on the emulsion surface. (b) Sound start positioned on the cell surface to avoid contact with the reproducing head. The exact "run-up" length must be allowed after the tape.

191

visible timing indicator. This indicates zero after the run-up and then the progressive timing throughout the section while recording takes place.

The run-up time may vary from studio to studio and the editor must check this in advance. Eighteen feet, or 12 sec., is the usual standard with 35 mm film. Start mark information can then be written on thin tape placed on the picture work print and guide

	REEL	SECTION	FOOTAGE TO BE SCORED BEGINS	ENDS	TAKES PRINTED	SEL TAKE	REMARKS
RELEASE_____ CUTTER_____ PROD_____							
PREVIEW_____ PLAYBACK_____ DATE_____							
	ONE	1M1	0	245	1; 2	②	
		1M2	395	515	1, 3, 5.	③	DIALOGUE and CLICK TRACK REQUIRED
		1M3	795	845	2, 6.	②, ⑥	DIALOGUE
	TWO	2M1	40	450		⑤	DIALOGUE and CLICK TRACK
		2M2	710	800		⑤	CLICK TRACK ONLY.
						↓	
						↓	
	TEN.	10M1	30	345	2, 4.	④	DIALOGUE + CLICK TRACK
			510	720	3, 4.	③④	DIALOGUE

Information for the music recording session. The list indicates how many music sections have to be recorded in each reel, how long the section is and where the section start marks can be found (i.e. "footage begins"). It also tells the projectionist how many sound tracks are required with each section of picture.

sound to be used. The projectionist's start frame is marked "X" so that when he threads up he knows where to position the film to allow for the run-up.

There was a time when the work print was broken down into sections before the music session (one section of picture for each separate music cue) and then placed in order of recording in the projection booth. Certainly it was easy for the projectionist to locate the required film but it was very unsatisfactory in other ways.

There are times when, even at the last moment, a music cue is adjusted on the music recording stage, starting earlier, finishing

192

later, with the composer making some quick adjustments to his score. So it is much better to have the complete reels of work print available in case of adjustments.

Tape start marks are incorporated for each cue. White tape can easily be located by the projectionist. The projectionist is also provided with a list of all music cues, showing the number in each reel and the distance into the reel for each tape startmark.

Visual timing

Various systems are used for visual timing. Each studio seems to have a different one. Some use automatic rotating numerals which indicate progressive time in seconds only however long the cue. Others indicate minutes and seconds if the section runs for longer than a full minute. There are those who use a projected timing film interlocked with the picture projector. Again, the system in use must be checked in advance as it has a bearing on how the detailed measurement sheets are to be prepared. There would be little point, for example, in timing music cues longer than a minute in minutes plus seconds if the timing indicator in the studio shows seconds only.

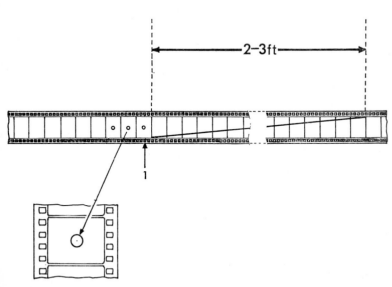

A "streamer" cue line drawn or scribed on the picture work print to lead the conductor to a specific point of action. Usually two to three feet in length, two or three frames are punched (I) at the end of the line as a definite visual indication of the sync point concerned.

The composer usually marks key points in his score with the timings taken from the typed information on the editor's sheets. If the wrong method were used, there could be complete confusion on the music stage. The conductor may have "1:02" marked on his score, for example. If he looks to the visual indicator at this point during the recording and sees "62" he will be completely lost.

The conductor's requirements must be remembered, also. Apart from timing indication the conductor may want several cue lines, or "streamers", drawn on to the picture. These would be guides not only to the start of a section but also to key picture cuts throughout the sequence. They are a great help in controlling the orchestra to attain good synchronism. These too must be established before the session so that the film can be properly prepared. A diagonal line ending on the key point frame can be permanently scribed on the film emulsion or, alternatively, marked with wax pencil.

Audible timing

Apart from visual aids, the conductor may need audible guides, again to help him synchronize the recording to picture. He will probably want to hear the dialogue track when he is recording music for background to dialogue scene.

A dialogue track is usually made available to him on every music cue, the track being run on a re-recording machine in synchronism with picture and transmitted to a head-set worn by the conductor. Preparation is purely a matter of putting a tape start on the work track corresponding with the picture start and indicating to the projectionist that the track must be run with that particular picture section. The conductor not only listens to the dialogue as the music is recorded, but it can also be incorporated into the playback where necessary as a check on the proposed final mixed result.

Controlling the musicians, watching the picture and timing indicator and listening to the dialogue in his head-set, keeps the conductor fully occupied. On a long and intricate music section he may have to maintain a tempo planned by the composer so that the music is constantly matched to the visual action as planned. There may be a point well into the sequence where he must be in rhythm with a specific piece of action. He could here use a metronome, if it were not for the many sensitive microphones surrounding him. Instead, a regular beat is transmitted into his head-set. The timing and rhythm of the beats depends on the requirements of the music section—it may be a constant beat, e.g. one per $\frac{1}{2}$-sec., one per sec., or one per $\frac{2}{3}$ of a sec. But, on the other hand, variations may be needed from section to section within the total length of the music cue. For a regular and constant beat, some studios have an automatic device to produce this over a wide range of rhythms, and the sounds produced are transmitted to his head-set. There are very few of these available however and in any case if a varying tempo is needed the machine is unsuitable.

Compiling click-tracks

Where such a guide is required, the editor can prepare the appropriate rhythm or rhythms by making up what is generally known as a "click-track"—a sound track which when transmitted to the conductor's head-set will reproduce the correctly spaced and timed clicks. Magnetic or photographic sound tracks are used for this purpose.

A form of click can be produced on magnetic by taking blank film and inserting one frame of 1,000 cycle frequency "tone" sound wherever each click is to be heard. The short length of tone passing very quickly over the sound reproducing head is heard as a sharp noise. The editor calculates the frequency of the clicks according to the composer's requirements. The changes in rhythm, the total number of clicks, and how they are to be spaced in the roll of blank film must be worked out mathematically.

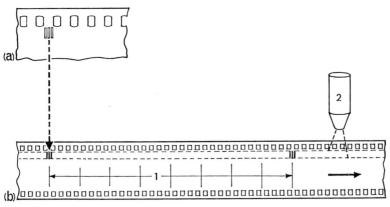

Click tracks. A section of 35 mm blank leader film with punched out areas. These will reproduce "clicks" on a photographic sound system. (a) Enlarged detail of the punched out film. (b) (I) Punch marks at eight-frame intervals (every I/3rd sec.) (2) Photographic sound system exciter lamp.

Making the click track for a photographic (optical) sound system is much simpler, requiring no cutting in of "tone" sound as with magnetic film. The photographic sound reproducing system works by a photo-cell reacting to variations in light striking it. The variations are produced by a varying density film passing through a concentrated light beam directed at the photo-cell.

Any blank film passed through such a system causes no reaction at all and there is no sound. If, however, a hole is punched in the area of the blank film which passes under the concentrated light, the light passes through to the photo-cell causing a very sharp noise. Marks for the correct spaces are first made on the length of blank film where all the clicks are to occur. The film is then wound through and a small hole punched over each mark with a ticket punch, or similar device. Positioning such a punched mark is obviously much quicker than making two splices for each click in the magnetic system. The method is therefore more practical.

The main problem with click tracks is in establishing the rhythm of the clicks, their variance in tempo, and the duration of each rhythmic passage. The editor has the guidance of the music composer, who obviously knows what he has in mind. These clicks *must* be very accurately spaced. Punch holes fractionally misplaced would cause an impossible situation for the conductor, who is trying to establish a strict tempo. Clicks which "wander" in rhythm are worse than no audible guide at all. This also applies to the point where the tempo changes—the change of rhythm must be accurately marked before the click punch is made.

Stock click-track masters

For producing regular tempo click tracks, music editors keep a series of fairly short film loops, each one punched with clicks of a different but constant tempo. Obtaining the footage they need for a constant tempo click track thus becomes a simple matter of selecting the appropriate loop and sending it to the sound transfer department. There they will run the loop on a photographic sound re-recorder and transfer the clicks on to a roll of *magnetic* sound film, to the length required. No film processing is necessary, the magnetic click track being immediately available for use when synchronized with picture.

Synchronizing the click track to the appropriate picture and dialogue track, ready for use on the recording stage, is simply a matter of aligning all three in the film synchronizer so that the first

196

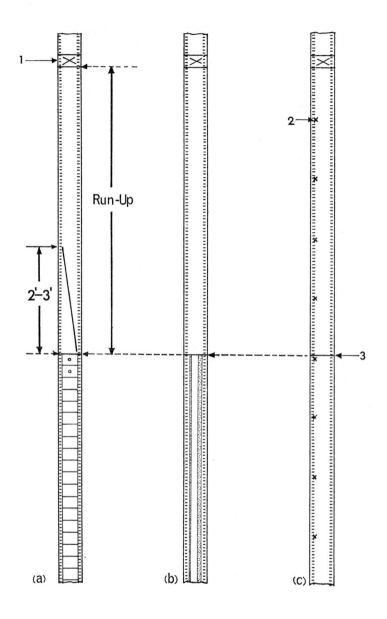

Detail from reels of working film for the music session. (a) Picture work print marked with "streamer" to the start of the music section. (b) Magnetic working dialogue track. (c) Click track for photographic sound reproduction. (1) Synchronous start marks at exactly the required run-up distance. (2) Click punch holes. In this case, 4 lead-in clicks on the run-up leader. Click No. 5 is right at the start of the proposed music recording. (3) The start of the proposed music section.

click appears in its correct relationship to picture. A leader is added to the click track and a start mark inserted level with picture and dialogue start marks.

Lead-in clicks

To give the conductor advance warning of the click tempo when a music section is about to be recorded, and to lead him directly to the first click at the beginning of the music, "lead-clicks" in the appropriate rhythm are included in the run-up film, after the start mark. The composer chooses the number of lead-in clicks required and this information is marked on his score so that the conductor knows what to expect. "Four free clicks", marked at the head of the score tells the conductor that his down beat to start the orchestra must be made as he hears click number five. "Eight free clicks", starts the conductor on click number nine.

The composer indicates his requirements to the editor in the same way. An "eight frame click track with four free", tells the editor to make up a synchronized track with the first click level with the first picture frame at the start of the music section, followed by clicks at eight-frame intervals throughout the section, and four "lead-in" clicks at eight frame intervals before click number one.

Often, the drummer of the orchestra is given a head-set so that he can listen to the prepared clicks. By his synchronized percussive performance he can help the orchestra maintain a set rhythm.

Here is a summary of preparations made in advance of the music session which are all editorial duties:

1. "Cue" the film for music—i.e., choose the areas for music and where each music section starts and finishes; this involves the producer, director, composer and editor.
2. Number each music section for future identification and measure each one in detail, cut by cut, line by line of dialogue, timing and noting also any details of action. Use a progressive timing, starting at zero on the first frame of picture in each section.
3. Establish the projector and recorder run-up time required (for the studio to be used) and, allowing this footage, put tapes with section number and start mark both on picture and dialogue track.
4. Prepare click tracks, if needed, and synchronize to picture and dialogue, all with common start marks.

198

5. Prepare a list showing the numbers of music sections, reel by reel; the position of each section within the reel; whether dialogue and/or click track should be run with picture; the overall length of each music section.

Progress list

As recordings are often made out of continuity, large orchestral sections being done in one session, small groups in another, a list is useful for checking progress and making sure that every section is, in fact, recorded. It also helps the sound recorder operator as he can ensure that there is enough film on the current roll to record a music section.

Recording and playback

Recordings are done on 35 mm magnetic film in feature recording sessions at studios, perhaps with a protective $\frac{1}{4}$- or $\frac{1}{2}$-in. tape machine running simultaneously. Multiple recording heads give three-track or six-track stereo recordings with groups of instruments reasonably separated in the recording so that further minor rebalancing of the overall orchestral effect is still possible when the final dubbed sound track is made.

Once again, these are master recordings. Transfers of the selected takes are prepared for editorial track-laying. Alternatively, the master recording is used for track-laying and the transfer kept as protection.

Sync marks on recordings

So that recorded takes can be played back with picture immediately, the recording technician marks his master sound film with a tape start mark as soon as the picture projector has been threaded and interlocked with his machine. Playbacks from this start mark remain synchronized with picture. So do the cutting transfers of selected takes if corresponding start marks are taped on to the transfer film when taken from the master recording.

Recording session

Knowing the total length of music to be recorded for the entire film, the composer specifies the number of sessions, each session normally being 3 hrs. Highly skilled session musicians and the very complex recording set-up needed are very expensive. Careful

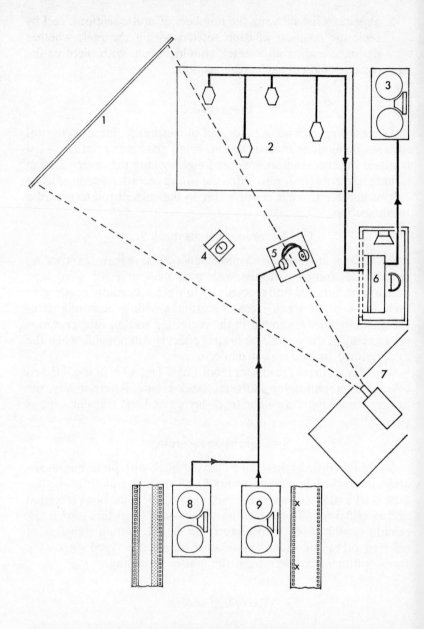

The music recording stage. (1) Projection screen. (2) Many microphones suspended over the orchestra. (3) Magnetic sound recording machine. (4) Visual timing indicator for the conductor. (5) The conductor. (6) Sound mixing position in the monitor room. (7) The film projector. (8) Re-recording machine reproducing the working dialogue track. (9) Re-recording machine (photographic system) reproducing the click track.

budgeting is needed. Ten minutes wasted in a 3-hr session is very serious. The editor and his assistant must ensure that all film is available, start marks correctly positioned and identified and click tracks clearly marked with the music section number so that film can be quickly and easily identified without delay. Picture "streamer" cues must be accurately marked where needed and marked only where they have been requested, to avoid any confusion.

The first section to be recorded on a major feature film will probably take some time. The orchestra must be rehearsed until they produce the sound the composer is seeking.

The music mixer balances and re-balances the sound received from many microphones until both he and the composer are satisfied with the result as they check it through the monitor speakers.

Eventually, the rehearsals will continue with projected picture, with dialogue, click track or whatever is needed being transmitted to the conductor. This is the first real check of the film measurements from which the composer has worked. Any error made at the time of measuring would obviously be a major disaster at this stage. So it can be seen how carefully these detailed measurements must be made.

Checking takes for inter-cutting

Ideally, there should be one perfect recording of each music section but, as with the shooting of the film itself, this is seldom so and many attempts may be made, perhaps none being completely perfect. The best sections of various takes may have to be intercut or perhaps mixed from one to another. As it is unlikely that he will do any intercutting before the sessions are over, the editor must make careful notes about this at the music session.

A large complicated music section may require an immediate intercut check before accepting the section as finished. But, while this is being done in the cutting room, rehearsals begin for the next section to be recorded. If the editor cannot be on the recording stage the whole time he must leave his assistant in charge of note-taking so that records are still carefully kept for future use.

Editors who can read musical scores have a great advantage during these recording sessions. It is simple for them to refer to intercutting points on the score when discussing the merits of various takes with the composer. When the time comes for track-building they can be certain that the correct sections of different takes are used.

201

Sweeteners

Inevitably, there are changes and minor re-orchestrations made throughout the music rehearsals and recordings. Often, after a play-back of a very good take, a suggestion is made to add a group of instruments, brass, or percussion to emphasize a point of action. If this is done the original take would not be discarded. The additional instruments are recorded separately, perhaps "wild" and the editor knows where they should be synchronized to the original take when building music tracks for final mixing. Such sweeteners can also be recorded synchronously and as the conductor is leading the orchestra he listens to the otherwise acceptable take on his head-set, to ensure that the section of the orchestra is brought in at the right time and for the required number of seconds. A sync start mark would be put on the master sound recording and later transferred to the cutting print. The task of track laying is thus made very simple for the editor who builds the final music tracks.

Editors' recording session duties

The responsibilities of the film editor and assistant at music recording sessions are:

1. To ensure that all picture and guide sound film is available on the session, correctly marked with section start marks and listed for ease of location.
2. To check off each section as it is recorded so that no music cue is forgotten.
3. To be always in attendance, making notes for any subsequent intercutting or cross-fading between takes or to make immediate intercuts so that they can be checked before the session finishes.

Building music tracks

Usually, the music tracks which are now ready for building into reels complete the three main sound groups required. Dialogue and effects tracks were probably built while the music was being composed and recorded. Even if the complicated and lengthy task of effects track-laying is not complete in every reel, several reels, at least, will be ready to be blended with dialogue and music as soon as the music sessions are finished. Often, final sound dubbing starts on the day following the last music session.

202

The editor must ensure that the transferred music tracks are delivered to the cutting room with all speed so that dubbing can proceed right away. Such transfers are usually made at the end of each music session, so there is normally little excuse for delay in music track building.

Ideally, final dubbing should be done in reel order, starting with reel one and proceeding in sequence as each reel is completed. By working this way the sound can be balanced more positively from reel to reel. This is not always possible. But it should be the aim, music tracks being laid and built accordingly.

Music track-laying is normally a quick and straightforward operation. Where single takes only, have been printed for an entire reel, track-building starts with a leader synchronized to the picture reel. Blank film is inserted where necessary, and the music tracks are laid in with their start marks matching those which were originally taped on the picture reel and used in the music sessions. Announcements and run-up footage removed, the track is spliced to the blank spacing film and wound through the film synchronizer. If the music was correctly synchronized to picture at the time of recording, nothing further is needed. Dubbing charts are prepared to show the position and footages of each music section in the reel for the convenience of the sound mixers.

Final sync adjustments

Often, of course, slight synchronizing adjustments may be needed between music and picture. Perhaps more than one take may have to be laid, calling for several synchronous music tracks that can be mixed from one to the other using the best sections of each take when final dubbing is being done. A synchronizing adjustment may mean that the entire music take has to be re-positioned in relation to picture, or that minor music track cutting adjustments must be made to correct the synchronism. Either way, the picture and music track must be viewed in the cutting room, establishing a new music/picture relationship—finding areas within the music track where any necessary editing can be performed. This may be a problem for the editor, if the correct equipment is not available, particularly when using multiple channel recordings. Although there is bound to be some "spill" from one channel to the other, editorial viewing equipment is unlikely to be able to "scan" all channels simultaneously. With a fixed-position reproducing head on his viewer the editor may not, from one single channel, be able to locate the sound information which he requires for editing and re-synchronizing.

Three-track reproducing heads obviously, in part, answer this problem. But, if they are not available on the viewing machine in use, a reproducing head movable across the entire film width would help considerably. The group of instruments playing the main melody at any time within the whole music section can now be located.

Re-synchronizing is done in the way that all visual synchronizing is done on the viewing machine, moving picture and sound relationship until the result is correct. The editor must find a cutting point so that the adjustment is made without mistiming or musical jar.

Music tracks are gradually built into synchronized reels, using as many separate tracks as necessary to accommodate more than one take of a section, or for mixing from one picture sequence to the next where separately recorded music is to be continuous. Charts indicate where music mixes from a section on one track to another on a separate track, and how each music section should be introduced or finished. A "fade-in" pencil line on the chart at the head of a music section is self-explanatory, as is a similar set of lines at the end of a section. Straight pencil lines drawn horizontally at the beginning of a section indicate that the music should "ride in" at normal recording level and not be faded. In the final sound dubbing operation all these instructions may be changed but an indication of the original intention serves as a guide to the sound mixers in the early stages of rehearsing the reel.

Demagnetizing equipment

Earlier reference was made to problems which can arise when splicing magnetic film, and should perhaps be reviewed here. Track-building calls for many splices between blank film and sound film and also splices within the sound film itself where editing is done.

Tape splicing is invariably used because it is easy to rebuild the piece of sound to its original form, where for example it has been miscut. A re-splice using the tape method causes no "jumping" or "popping" in the sound track reproduction.

Precautions must be taken with magnetic splicing, however. The instrument used to physically cut through the film must be non-magnetized. Periodic checks of scissors, razor blades, and splicing machines themselves should be carried out to be sure that no unwanted signal is being introduced at the edges of the splice. Brass, or other non-magnetic paper clips should be used where film is clipped together before being spliced by an assistant.

If the worst happens and splices do start "popping" in the sound reproducing system there are remedies, although success is not always guaranteed. Most sound departments have a small pencil-shaped demagnetizing device which, when carefully drawn across the affected area on the sound track can remove the signal causing the unwanted noise. Scraping the oxidized film coating into the shape of a small clear triangle at the splice can sometimes help.

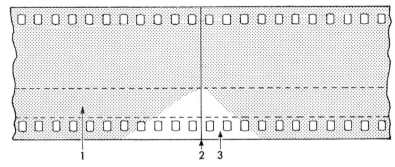

Problems with magnetic sound splices. (1) Approx. area of single-track sound recording on 35 mm magnetic film. (2) The splice. (3) Area of oxidized coating scraped away, removing the offending sound signal. A punch, forming a circular or diamond-shaped hole could also be used.

But, this is only successful with certain scenes since, although the sharp "pop" is removed, another softer noise is usually left in its place.

It should be remembered, also, that visual information required on magnetic film should never be written on the oxidized surface, certainly never in the area of the sound track. This applies, too, to the various start marks placed on magnetic tracks within reels, i.e. second start marks for dubbing, start marks for music sessions both on working tracks and on master and transfer recordings. Tapes or written start marks should be placed on the reverse and non-oxidized side of the magnetic film to avoid any contact with the recording or reproducing sound heads.

11

SOUND DUBBING

THE final sound dubbing operation is one of the last major tasks for the editorial department. Subsequent laboratory processes are largely a matter of routine, as far as the editor is concerned, as long as the routine preparations have been made with sufficient care.

Producing the single master dubbed sound track is generally a complicated and time-consuming task on all except modest productions.

It is interesting to consider that the entire film project started from one single working sound track assembled to picture by the film editor. Sometimes this takes a crude form because of the limitations of working with a single track. It is gradually developed in size and scope in the post-production period. *Dialogue* scenes now have several synchronous sound reels which have been divided so that sounds of varying quality, shot over a considerable period of time and in different recording studios and conditions, can be rebalanced in the easiest way.

At this stage of the proceedings original *sound effects* have been salvaged where possible; recorded when they have been unacceptable or non-existent; and augmented wherever the atmosphere of a scene can be improved. There is now a formidable number of synchronous effects reels to be correctly condensed into the final sound track.

Although they may be smaller in quantity, *music* reels have been built to synchronize with sequences involving featured or background music, again with individual music tracks separated so that a careful mixing and blending of all three main groups of sound is possible.

Once more, the operation is directed towards producing a single sound track, but a very different one from the original.

Checking tracks

If possible, these synchronized sound reels should be checked in a projection room with the picture reel concerned in advance of the dubbing session.

Darkly lit night scenes can cause great difficulty when a sound editor is trying to accurately fit a sound effect to a synchronous action. A minor error of synchronism can be unacceptable when the image is projected on to the big screen in the theatre.

Post-synchronized dialogue scenes, particularly, can never be checked with complete accuracy on a small-screen viewing machine. Careful matching of original to post-synchronized dialogue, word by word, using the reproducing heads on the film synchronizer is, at best, only a guide to correct synchronism.

Music does not generally cause such a problem, although a pre-recorded playback scene can sometimes be troublesome when maintaining correct lip-sync in vocal musical numbers, despite all code-numbering precautions.

Unfortunately there is rarely sufficient time to make all these checks. Inevitably, some reels reach the dubbing theatre without having their individual sound tracks checked against the projected picture image. Any available time should be used for this purpose, particularly with post-synchronized dialogue scenes. Once dubbing is under way adjustments are time-consuming and interrupt the flow of activity in the dubbing theatre.

Some adjustments are bound to be necessary regardless of sync —certainly in the area of sound effects—since many of the sound editor's contributions are seen for the first time during the course of dubbing. They may not coincide with the ideas of producer, director, and film editor, despite many screenings and detailed conferences beforehand. There is no complete answer to these last minute problems but advance operations should be carried out wherever possible to avoid unnecessary delays in sound dubbing.

Finishing schedules

Sound dubbing is planned in accordance with the scheduled finishing date. Sound theatre facilities are reserved for the estimated time necessary to completely dub all reels. A final sound track negative will then be available to the processing laboratory as soon as they have completed picture negative cutting so that the first combined sound and picture "answer print" can be made.

All working picture and prepared sound tracks are assembled for the dubbing theatre session. Picture reels go to the projection booth and synchronous sound reels to the re-recording machine operators. Leaders on each reel carry identifying reel numbers and synchronizing start marks. Sound reels are grouped on racks in dialogue, effects and music tracks for each reel of picture.

Dubbing charts are given to the sound mixers working at the console. On these, footages and individual track positions are clearly indicated in relation to the pictorial content of the reels.

Leader run-up requirements

The amount of leader film needed at the head of each reel of picture and sound depends on the equipment of the particular dubbing theatre in use. Film studio dubbing theatres differ in their requirements as do the specialist sound theatres operating away from studio activities. The facts must be established before any of the sound tracks are built. Normally, the standard Academy leader —12 ft. from synchronizing start mark to the first frame of picture (35 mm film)—is preferred. As the editor used these in making up final work print reels, no special arrangements are necessary. Each sound track is synchronized with its leader start mark level with the 12 ft. start mark on the picture reel.

Some sound dubbing theatres, however, require a run-up leader of 15 ft., or even 18 ft. from the synchronizing start marks so that they can incorporate various sound system tests on to the recording film during the run-up period.

If the 12-ft. start mark is used this amount of leader footage is allowed for when the projectionist pre-sets the visual footage indicator so that as the first frame of picture reaches the screen it reads zero. The counter, which is usually a three-figure indicator, would be pre-set in this case at 988. If the 15-ft. run-up were being used, then it would be pre-set at 985. In either case, after the run-up, the counter will register 000 as the picture begins.

The sync plop

Synchronizing difficulties sometimes arise in projection when so many sound tracks are being run with one reel of picture. A tape start mark for one of the music recordings may have been left on a picture reel leader and would not necessarily provide the required run-up. Here confusion can arise. Also, in spite of many precautions, sound reels are sometimes incorrectly threaded on to the re-recording machines and the start mark not accurately positioned at the sound head. When pre-mixing, the first sound track to be heard may be some distance into the reel. It has to reach this point before it is realized that synchronism has been lost.

To avoid this irritation, it is customary to cut a "sync-plop" into each sound reel leader at a pre-established point just before the picture appears on the screen. Usually a point eight frames before the first frame of picture is chosen. A visible mark (a punched hole) is made on the picture leader to synchronize with this. As long as the machines have been correctly threaded, no matter how many sound reels are being run synchronously, *one* plop is heard in the speakers as the visible mark appears on the screen. A second, isolated plop indicates loss of synchronism through incorrect threading and the machines can be stopped immediately for an investigation.

Because the sync plop is incorporated into all recordings made —from the first pre-mixes right through to the final mixed sound track—it is a useful check for synchronism throughout. Although tape start marks are always synchronous when reels have been correctly threaded, small errors can occur as the electrical load is applied to run up all the machines together. These errors, accumulating throughout the dubbing session can sometimes cause synchronizing problems when the final sound track is produced.

The sync plop serves as the accurate check point at all stages.

Planning the pre-mix

The number of sound technicians working directly at the console depends on the theatre facilities—re-recording machines available and operating positions at the console for example. There should, ideally, be three technicians, one to handle each of the three main sound groups involved—dialogue, effects, and music. Often there are only two people when the dubbing is to be monophonic. One handles dialogue and music and the other handles sound effects. If, however, the final sound track is to be more ambitious—six-track multiple channel, for example—then it is highly likely that, in addition to three men handling the main groups of sound, a fourth will occupy a separate console, "panning" and "swinging" sounds across the wide screen picture.

The sound mixers now examine the dubbing charts for the first reel and can see not only the quantity of sound reels involved but

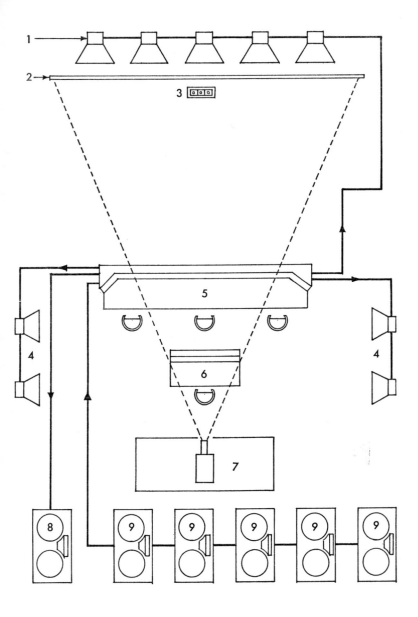

Multiple track re-recording theatre set up for 6-track system. (1) The five main channels for the behind-screen area. (2) Projection screen. (3) Footage indicator. (4) Surround speakers. (5) The main three-position mixing console. (6) The second, single-position console from which travelling sounds will be "panned". (7) The film projector. (8) The master magnetic recording machine. (9) A series of re-recording machines, synchronously reproducing the working sound tracks.

also whether the individual sound tracks have been intelligently presented. They can make this quick assessment because they are specialists in this type of sound recording.

The dubbing operation now follows a distinct pattern, which applies to each reel in turn. Pre-mixes are planned, rehearsed and then recorded on to magnetic film until a final combined mix of all sounds is possible. With the editor and sound editor present, balance of the pre-mix is discussed until a satisfactory recording pattern has been established. The producer or director may not necessarily be present for these preliminaries. They are rather more concerned with the final sound balance, which cannot be attempted until all pre-mixing is complete.

Dialogue pre-mix

Dialogue pre-mixing, where necessary, usually takes place first, particularly, if there is post-synchronized dialogue. This recording is then available as a guide during subsequent pre-mixing. The picture and dialogue sound tracks are put on their respective machines. Each re-recording machine is electronically connected to a mixing position at the console. The controls allow the sound mixer to alter the volume and tone of the dialogue. He can also add echo to the dialogue and he can introduce telephone or loudspeaker effects.

Working with the information supplied in the dubbing chart in conjunction with the visual footage indicator, he goes through several rehearsal screenings until he decides on the necessary balancing treatment. When ready to make the pre-mix, the film recording machine is brought into the sound system, magnetic recording film being threaded at a synchronizing start mark. A single track dialogue pre-mix is now made incorporating all corrections needed for a properly balanced dialogue track.

For future reference, the dubbing chart indicates all the dialogue tracks incorporated in the pre-mix. Each column on the dubbing chart represents one sound track, whether dialogue, effects or music. As pre-mixing takes place, the number of tracks (or columns on the chart) incorporated in a pre-mix is indicated by outlining the number of columns with a coloured felt-tipped pen. Thus, the area enclosed by any one colour represents one pre-mix. These are numbered, "Dialogue Pre-mix A", "B" and so on. Sound mixing is often spread over a period of several weeks and this is a quick way to check on which component tracks have been incorporated in pre-mixes.

212

METRO GOLDWYN MAYER
BRITISH STUDIOS LTD

Sheet No. __1__

DUBBING CUE SHEET

Prod. No. _64_
Reel _8_
English Dubbed Date NOV '67   TITLE "DARK OF THE SUN"   Foreign Dubbed Date _____
P/MIX FX "A"

Sequence _____
Length _872 Ft._

Action Cues	ft.	Dialogue	Track FX 1	Track FX 2	Track FX 3	Track FX 4	Track FX 5	Track FX 6	Track FX 8
			000 CROWD BOARD TRAIN	000 CROWD ON TRAIN	000 GUN RATTLE				ECHO
			8	8	005 HENLEIN Fts				
ECHO 054			BUSGIER F/S ECHO	54 ECHO 054 CLAIRE Fts	54 ECHO 056 KEYS4 CURRY Fts.				
			ALL Fts 64	65	65				
081 END ECHO			81	HERLEINY RUFFO Fts.	SOLDIER IN TRUCK OF TRAIN				
				111	111	111	111		128 F/S BUSGIER
						NATIVE SPEAR RATTLE	NATIVE SPEAR RATTLE	119 GROUP NATIVES RUN R-L. Fts	CURRY4 CHAVE 183
			165			126	126	126	234 BUSGIER FS
			SOLDIERS RUN TO TRAIN	190	144	190	144		233
			ME BOARD TRAIN4 GUNS	SOLDIERS CLIMB INTO TOWER	2 SOLDIERS CLIMB TOWER	MASS NATIVE CHARGE Fts.	SOLDIERS JUMP ONTO TOWER		
			199	199	199		195		
				211 NATIVES SLIDE DOWN BANK	210 NATIVE Fts 4 SPEAR NOISE				
			214 NATIVE Fts	214 RATTLE OF SPEARS 4 Fts	216 NATIVES YELLING. NO	216	216		
			226	226	226				
			235 NATIVES Fts	235 NATIVE Fts	235 SPEAR RATTLE				
			243 240 NATIVE Fts OUT OF TRUCKS	243 240 NATIVE Fts JUMP OUT OF TRUCKS	243 240 SPEAR RATTLE 249	249 SPEAR4 GUN RATTLES	250 BASE PUT DOWN		
			256 252 BODY FALL NATIVES RUN	256 SPEAR RATTLE	256 MORTAR ASSEMBLED 4 NATIVE Fts	251 SPEAR RATTLES	252	400	
			265 264 NATIVES RUN	265 264 SPEAR RATTLE	263	263		END	
			267 266 NATIVES RUN	267 266 SPEAR RATTLE				ECHO	
			269 268 NATIVES RUN	269 268 SPEAR RATTLE					
			273 270 NATIVES RUN	273 270 SPEAR RATTLE	274				
			274	274	274 HENLEIN Fts 278				
			284 SORRIER 4 SOLDIERS GUN 4 Fts	287 WOMAN'S Fts IN TRAIN	288 WOMANS SCREAM NO				
			288	289	291				
			315 NATIVE TROOPS WITH...	315 NATIVE TROOPS ...					

Preliminary sound pre-mixing. A typical dubbing chart giving details of sound effects which have been built into reels for effects pre-mixing. Effects tracks I to 5 inclusive have been incorporated into one single track pre-mix, as now indicated on the chart. It has been called. "Pre-mix, FX 'A'". Note that two individual sounds of a different character in effects track 3 have been deliberately omitted from the pre-mix. They will be moved to another sound reel and included in the final sound mix—volume under independent control.

213

It does not necessarily follow that every dialogue track built for the reel is automatically included in the pre-mix. Augmented dialogue tracks may consist of off-screen shouts and orders, not all of which may be needed in the final sound track. To include them at this stage would be to mix them permanently with the main dialogue. If it were decided to leave them out at a later stage a completely new pre-mix would have to be done with consequent loss of time. Everything incorporated in a pre-mix must be capable of further rebalancing if necessary, as far as such problems can be anticipated. For example if these off-screen shouts and orders were background sounds, yet mixed underneath the foreground dialogue, to lose them would be impossible without making a new mix. To raise or lower the volume of the background shouts would also raise or lower all other sounds mixed with them, and *vice-versa*.

Echo effects

The sound mixer can introduce both echo and reverberation effects electronically. Dialogue is echoed for additional effect in vault-like rooms, tunnels, churches, etc. A bounce effect can be created in dialogue for shouts in mountainous sequences, for example, or for loudspeaker commentaries, by using an oscillator in the sound system.

Staggered sound tracks

Sound tracks can also be specially laid in reels, to create an effect of reverberation, sometimes better than that obtained electronically. Two or three transfers of the same sound can be laid side by side in separate sound reels, "staggered" in relation to each other by a few frames difference in synchronism. They are then run simultaneously for the reverberation effect to be heard. The amount of "stagger" must vary according to the individual requirement and can only be determined by experiment. But a guide to the amount of separation needed can be obtained by staggering the tracks in a film synchronizer fitted with reproducing heads and winding the tracks through by hand. It is sometimes even more effective when a slight electronic echo effect is added to the second or third staggered track only.

Sound editors usually have such an effect pre-mixed in advance of the main dubbing session so that it is already recorded on a single piece of film and built into one of their sound reels.

214

Music pre-mix

Music pre-mixing is not always necessary. This is because there are rarely a number of music tracks running simultaneously. In fact, the music mixer tries to avoid it so that fine control over balance is maintained for the final sound mix. There may be times, however, when it is unavoidable—particularly if six-track music is involved. There is a sheer physical difficulty in mixing from one six-track music reel to another of the same type. As each channel of six-track sound is connected to a separate volume control it involves a most complicated operation for the hands.

In music sessions involving vocal numbers with an orchestral backing, it is usual to position the vocalist in a separate recording room, glass-fronted so that visual contact is maintained with the conductor. He hears the orchestral performance through a head-set and sings accordingly, but the vocal recording is separated from the orchestral recording electronically. The editor, therefore, receives two sound tracks—orchestral and vocal—and minor balance changes between the two are still possible in final dubbing. But having established any final re-balancing, a pre-mix of the two tracks can be made, purely to reduce the number of music tracks having to be handled on the reel, when dubbing takes place.

Physical mixing problems and a shortage of re-recording machines of the correct type (i.e. multiple heads) for the track concerned are the main reasons for having to pre-mix music tracks.

Effects pre-mix

Effects pre-mixing is without question, the biggest preliminary task in reducing the number of tracks to minimum handling requirements. Effects tracks are spread over many synchronous reels because of the many types involved—background atmosphere tracks, footsteps and movement, individual synchronized effects—all running simultaneously with one sequence. Again, pre-mixing is obviously necessary. Groups of tracks within the effects section are gradually reduced until final mixing with all components is possible.

To do *any* form of pre-mixing (but particularly with sound effects because of their bulk) in a haphazard way purely to reduce the *quantity* of the sound reels involved would be stupid. The dubbing chart must be studied with great care so that the components for pre-mixing are chosen intelligently. Once the pre-mix has

215

been made, with the parallel sounds contained therein balanced, it is set in this way. Later, perhaps when the music tracks are introduced for the final mix and heard for the first time in relation to the whole sound balance, it may be found that some of the effects in the earlier pre-mix are now smothered by music. If too many sound effects have been amalgamated in one pre-mix, without much thought for final mixing, it may now be impossible to raise the level of *one* sound effect since any others pre-mixed with it will also be raised and *they* may be correct at their present level. Generally, it is safer to pre-mix those effects which are well spread through the reel and not overlapped with each other. Such groups as background atmosphere sounds, footsteps and movements, *general* battle noises and *general* fight noises, can well be pre-mixed to reduce the number of reels of sound. "Key" effects are left out for the final mix. Then, with all sound groups being mixed, they can be incorporated at the correct sound level since they are still under *individual* control. As stated before, the sound editor must not fill any blank space in any sound reel with any effect in a careless way. On the contrary. Since he is well aware of the pre-mixing necessity, some of his reels will have many blank areas. This is because he is carefully grouping his effects and not inter-mingling too many different types of sound.

As with all pre-mixes, each group amalgamated in one magnetic recording is identified as "effects pre-mix A, B, C", and so on and dubbing chart entries boxed accordingly.

"Rock and Roll" Projection

Pre-mixing is, of course, often a tedious task involving many rehearsals of a small section of a reel before a take is attempted, and then moving on to yet another pre-mix. Pre-mixing sections *within* a reel, particularly if the section is a very short, yet very busy one, can be time consuming in the mechanics of the operation. After each rehearsal, tracks and picture have to be rewound and re-set on their synchronous start marks before another rehearsal can take place and this always takes longer than the actual rehearsal itself. More dubbing theatres are now being equipped with a forward and reverse mechanism, not only for the picture projector, but also for all the re-recording machines in inter-lock, so that at the end of a rehearsal of such a section within a reel, all sound tracks and picture are reversed back to the start marks, Reversing all machines in inter-lock obviously saves much time, avoiding the otherwise separate operation of rewinding each sound track and re-threading on the start mark. This system is called "rock and roll" dubbing, just as the forward and reverse mechanism in viewing theatres is known as "rock and roll" viewing. As with the viewing facility, however, such a system can cause problems, particularly when producers and directors have difficulty in making decisions. Sometimes the ease of rewinding and "looking once again" at a problem can prolong a pre-mixing session, even the mix of a complete reel, long beyond the normal expectation.

The final mix

Eventually, with tracks sufficiently reduced in number, rehearsals begin for the final balance. Editor and sound mixers will confer as rehearsals continue until the best settings are found on all groups of sound and everything is ready to run in this form for producer and director to hear. No doubt they will ask for further adjustments in balance but when all are satisfied the recording machine is brought into the sound system and a take is attempted. This continues until a satisfactory take has been made, all sounds being correctly balanced.

The great advantage of using magnetic film in all these stages is the convenience of immediate playback. Moreover, abortive pre-mixes and takes can be wiped off, and the film made available for further use.

Naturally, with every generation of sound transfer there is a certain loss in quality. The number of copying stages from original sound to cutting print, to pre-mix, to master dubbed track, to photographic sound track, and so on, can be considerable. So unnecessary pre-mixing should be avoided.

Intermediate three-track dubbing

The first complete sound mix of all the dialogue, music and effects contained in a reel is rarely made on to a single track master recording at this stage. The three main groups, dialogue, effects and music ("A", "B" and "C" strips) are usually recorded in *three separate channels* on one piece of 35 mm magnetic film. This is done electronically from the mixing console. Each channel of the three-track master contains a condensed recording of all mixed sounds of one particular group.

There are several advantages in doing this. Films intended for

217

foreign release are eventually post-synchronized and dubbed in foreign language centres. The foreign dialogue can be mixed in with final effects and music mixes provided from this first dubbing operation. A combined music and effects track can be supplied from the three-track master simply by making a mix of the "B" and "C" channels, leaving out the dialogue or "A" channel, then adding the specially prepared foreign version effects which were not salvable from beneath original dialogue. Sound levels and balance will be exactly the same as in the original dubbed sound track.

Because the three channels are separated, minor re-balancing between them can still be carried out if necessary when making the single track master. Dialogue level can be raised, music or effects lowered. Obviously in doing this, *all* the effects or *all* the dialogue is raised or lowered in volume level, but it is a very useful possibility.

A perfect "take" can be attained at the three-track stage except, for example, that one important sound effect was accidentally left out by the sound mixer. It may have been a difficult reel, a long time having been spent in producing this otherwise perfect mix. But rather than try for another perfect take, the missing effect can be added to the existing take when the single-track master is made. These additions, or "sweeteners", can also incorporate new ideas —something thought of after the three-track mix was made, and not necessarily an accidental omission. The sound editor prepares a separate sweetener track, adding the information to his dubbing chart, so that it is not forgotten at the final stage.

When the three-track mix has been successfully completed on a reel it is usual to move on to the next reel rather than make a single-track master at this stage. Eventually, when all reels have been completed, one operation with each reel produces a magnetic single track master. A photographic sound track may be made simultaneously if the sound theatre can run both types of recording machine at the same time.

So far, sound for four-track and six-track release printing has not been discussed and, at the moment, a single photographic negative is the eventual objective to provide the film laboratory with sound for normal release printing.

Combined print changeovers

Every operation in the cutting room, in the projection room, and in the sound dubbing theatre has been performed with separate picture and sound track, both synchronized level to each other in

218

film synchronizers, viewing machines and projection equipment. Projection rooms handling such separate picture and sound film are specially equipped to do so, with separate machines for each job.

Normal photo-sound release prints, however, are combined picture and sound prints, both printed on to one piece of film in a dual printing operation before processing. The result is a single narrow band of variable area photographic sound track at the edge of the picture image. Such a *combined* track and picture film must be handled by a single machine. But level synchronism of picture and sound is no longer possible. The projection of the pictorial image calls for an intermittent movement at the projection aperture, each picture frame being momentarily held still while projected on to the screen, before a shutter closes and the next frame is drawn into position. This cycle is repeated 24 times per sec. Sound reproduction cannot take place at the projection aperture because the sound track must travel smoothly and at constant speed over the magnetic or optical head. In any case, there is very little space in a projector "gate" and it would be difficult to incorporate a sound reproducing system at this place.

The sound head for reproducing a photographic sound track is positioned in the lower area of the combined film projector. At this distance from the gate the intermittent motion of the film has smoothed out and new tensions can be applied to the film to ensure its constantly even passage. The distance between picture and sound reproducing mechanisms is standard for every type of projector and, in order to have synchronism, the sound track must be printed on to the combined print separated from its synchronous picture frame by exactly this distance. In 35 mm release printing the optical sound on the combined print is advanced by 19½ frames (in practice a 20-frame advancement is usually made). With

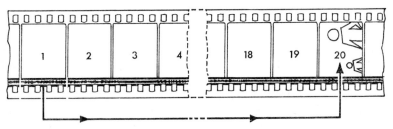

Picture/sound relationship in 35 mm married print with photographic sound track. The sound level with frame No. I is synchronous with picture frame No. 20.

16 mm prints the track is advanced by 26 frames. This is an automatic laboratory printing procedure and, as long as they know the "level sync" relationship between picture negative and sound negative, they can make the required adjustment during the dual-printing operation.

Double reel allowance

If all reels were to be issued to exhibition theatres in the single form now being used for sound dubbing, nothing further need be done but, as we saw in the section dealing with reel to reel change-over allowance, they are first combined printed in single reels, the prints of each pair of consecutive reels being spliced together later to form an "A/B" reel for exhibition.

Taking as an example a 35 mm combined release print, the optical track is advanced by 20 frames when the print is made. Therefore, the first 20 frames of the sound track appear on the Academy leader of the reel, printed just inside the perforations at one side. Naturally, the last 20 frames of picture on the reel will have no adjacent sound track since the track has been advanced by that amount. Making a changeover from this single reel to the next during projection is no problem, the scanning of the sound track being continuous from one reel to the other. If the combined print of each pair of reels were to be physically spliced and joined together, however, the splice would obviously be made on the picture frame line of the outgoing reel and the similar line on the incoming reel. So the end leader on the "A" reel and head leader on the "B" reel would be cut off. As a result, the last 20 frames of the first reel will be blank—but they should, of course, be occupied by the first 20 frames of the second reel which were lost when its head leader was removed.

This problem has to be taken care of when the single track master is made in anticipation of the normal procedure for photographic release printing. An allowance must be made for each pair of reels where a positive splice will eventually be made. The first 20 frames of reel two, for example, must be dubbed on to the end of the reel one sound track and this operation continued throughout the entire film so that the first 20 sound frames of each reel of *even* number is dubbed on to the end of each single reel of *odd* number. These 20 sound frames are not physically removed from the front of the even-number reels, in case it is ever necessary to continuously project combined prints in single-reel form, even though this is unlikely. They are produced by making a magnetic sound transfer

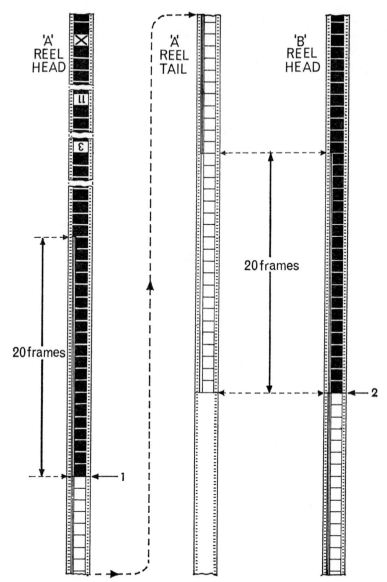

"A" and "B" reels for release. Combined print sound problems when 35 mm "A" and "B" reels are to be spliced together *after* printing. *Left:* "A" reel with standard academy head leader, photographic sound track advanced 20 frames. (1) Picture starts here. *Centre:* End of "A" reel—last 20 frames of sound track blank, but should be occupied with first 20 frames of "B" reel sound track. *Right:* "B" reel leader with sound advanced 20 frames. (2) Splice line at which "A" and "B" reels will be joined. First 20 frames of "B" reel lost unless added to the end of the "A" reel during sound dubbing.

221

of the front of each even-number reel before the single-track master is recorded. The sound editor takes each transfer and adds these 20 frames to the end of one of his sound effects tracks where it will be well clear of any other sound effect, indicating this fact on the dubbing chart. Every "A" (odd-number) reel must consist of its complete sound track, plus the first 20 frames of the following reel.

Single-track dubbing

Now the single-track recording can be made. Picture and three-track master sound are threaded on their machines, together with any additional sound "sweeteners" which have become necessary. In the case of an odd-number reel, this includes the sound effects track which carries the 20-frame extension (the beginning of the following reel). All the sounds are now condensed into one single channel on the recording film with correct overall balance.

Even-number reels, eventually to be the "B" section of doubled-up combined prints, do not require a 20-frame sound extension at the end since at this point in a continuous screening a manual changeover will be made to the next reel.

The single-track master magnetic recording would be marked with a tape start mark at the time of machine-threading but the "sync plop" would also be recorded on to its leader for ease of future sync-checking.

Making the optical sound neg

When all reels are completed, the photographic sound negative is made, if this could not be carried out simultaneously when the magnetic master was made. This is done by making a straight-forward "one-to-one ratio" (normal level sound recording) transfer of sound from magnetic master to photographic sound negative using a transfer sound system and not necessarily through the dubbing console.

The sound negative is produced in an optical sound recording machine. Sound signals are converted into electrical impulses which, by means of light reflected from an oscillating mirror, are transferred on to the negative sound film in a narrow band of varying area.

Subsequent photographic development reveals a negative image from which a positive print can be made.

Undeveloped recording film is loaded in light-tight film maga-

222

zines and unloaded again in a darkroom after the recording has been made. They are then packed for shipment to the processing laboratory.

Optical sound start marks

The tape system for start marks on magnetic film is unsuitable for undeveloped negative film, so a different method is used. When the unexposed film is threaded into the recording machine, the operator punches a small hole in the track area of the film and, using this as the synchronous start mark with the magnetic master film from which the recording is to be made, places this in position at the optical sound head when ready to record the reel. A positive print

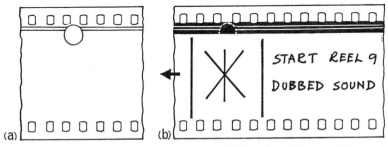

(a) (b)

The negative "punch" synchronizing start mark. (a) Developed photographic sound negative. The hole was punched at the time of transfer from the master magnetic dubbed track and used as the synchronous start mark. (b) The appearance of the punched out area in the positive sound rush print.

made from the developed negative shows this punch mark. It will serve as a temporary synchronizing guide when the rush sound prints are received from the laboratory.

Synchronizing rush sound prints

As with original camera material, processing is usually an overnight operation. Rush prints of the sound track are received in the cutting room some time the next morning. Each reel of negative is given an identifying roll number and filed at the laboratory. Positive prints carry a matching roll number. Also, as with picture negative, matching key numbers appear on the edges of both sound negative and positive print.

As they are received, each reel of sound print is synchronized with its picture reel. The punch start mark is aligned in the film

223

synchronizer level with the picture start mark. As dialogue synchronism is probably the most important factor, the main dialogue track, containing original dialogue used in the first shooting operations, is also placed with its start mark in the synchronizer. The three films are wound forward in the synchronizer to the sync plop in the magnetic dialogue track leader. The now visible plop in the photographic sound print should be level with it. If not exactly level, the sound print position is adjusted and then relocked in the synchronizer, all the film then being rewound back to the start marks. A permanent synchronizing start mark is now made on the sound print, level with the picture standard Academy start mark. It is unlikely that any adjustment at the sync plop will involve moving the sound print more than one or two perforations, either way.

If for some reason the sync plop was left out in transfer, although very unlikely, a further sync check can be made. The three films are wound through the synchronizer, using a magnetic sound reproducing head on the dialogue track film drum, until a sharp sound, such as the beginning of a sharply spoken word, has been located in the magnetic track. The synchronizer is slowly rocked back and forth until the beginning of the sound has been accurately located. A pencil mark is made at this point on the film. The sound modulations on the photographic sound track will be clearly visible and the beginning of the same word will be seen as a strong and mounting variation of area pattern emerging from a previously clear track. If all machine threading has been correct throughout, the beginning of this strong modulation should be exactly level in the synchronizer with the pencil mark made on the magnetic track. If not, the photographic sound print must be re-positioned in the synchronizer so that they are level. Again, only minor corrections should be necessary and the film can be rewound to the start marks, the new print given its start mark level with the picture start.

Checking synchronism is most important. The tape and punch start marks must serve only as a guide and never be accepted as completely accurate. Although all electrically interlocked machines must, theoretically, always run in step with each other there can be an occasion when minor sync fluctuations take place. For instance, the operator might not position the tape start correctly over the reproducing head. Another example involves the "load" applied when starting a large group of machines, all locked with the projector. If not correctly checked before being started, a machine might lag slightly on the start-up causing a minor but important sync alteration.

224

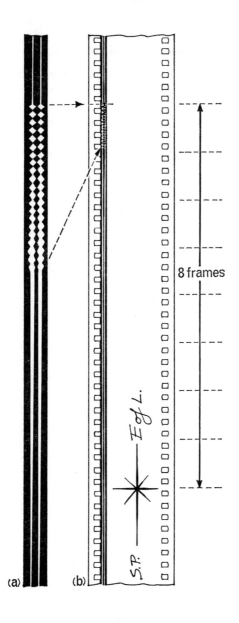

The sync plop transferred from magnetic master to photographic sound track. (a) Enlarged detail of the plop and the sound echo tailing off afterwards. (b) The normal position of the plop in relation to the start of the actual sound track. A line is drawn across the sound film and marked "End of leader" (E of L) and "Start picture" (S.P.). This is the guide to the negative cutter to splice the sound negative leader at this point on the negative.

Visual and audible check

With all reels checked and correctly synchronized, the entire film, picture and separate photographic sound track, can now be screened. Visual synchronism, quality of sound reproduction and especially reel to reel balance can now be checked. The sound department also makes a visual examination of the sound track itself to ensure that negative processing has produced within fairly close tolerances the required density of the track.

Marking sound print for neg cutting

If all is well, the sound print can now be marked as a negative cutting guide for the laboratory. Once again, each reel of picture and photographic sound print is aligned in the film synchronizer at their common start marks. Winding both down to the end of the head picture leader, a line is drawn across the sound film level with the splice on the first picture frame. This is marked, "Start picture —level sync". Both films are then wound right through on the synchronizer until the end of the picture reel has been reached. Another line is drawn across the sound film level with the point at which the last picture frame is spliced to the tail leader. This is marked, "Picture ends—level sync".

If this is a 35 mm film, a 20-frame advancement of sound for combined picture and sound synchronism is necessary. In order that the A and B assembly of release prints allows continuation of the sound track at the end of the A and the beginning of the B reel when they are spliced together, another line is drawn across the sound print at an overall distance of 20 frames after the end of picture. This is where the tail leader must be spliced on the sound negative, and it is marked "20 frames".

This is all that the laboratory normally requires. They match the sound negative by key numbers and join printing leaders to the head and tail of each sound reel as indicated by the lines drawn on the editor's print which is sent to them as a cutting guide. Eventually, at the combined printing of the picture and sound, the sound negative is advanced the required number of frames to attain correct "printing sync".

The picture and sound negative leaders have printing start marks incorporated so that the operation in the laboratory to produce a combined print is routine from here on—any number of prints being produced as long as all negatives are handled with great care.

Inserting dubbed track sections

It has been assumed that the reels of photographic sound were all complete, unblemished, and that everything was perfect.

It could be, however, that screening the sound rush print revealed some defects in the photographic film since, with any photographic emulsion, manufacturing coating defects can occur. Machine damage can also be caused at the laboratory, in spite of rigid routines and precautions, and a reel of sound may have been affected in either way at this final stage.

Suppose, for example, that a coating defect affected the sound track at a point 30 ft. from the start of the reel. A blemish on the negative might have produced a minus-density area in the sound print, resulting in a sharp "crack" in sound reproduction as this point is reached. Or, negative film perforations may perhaps have been damaged beyond repair (and such repairs are sometimes possible by very skilled technicians responsible for negative handling) over a small footage of the reel. If financial resources are being strained, it need not be vital to completely replace the entire negative reel of sound by making a new photographic transfer from the magnetic master recording. A small section, covering the affected area, can be transferred, developed and printed. The print sent to the editor is then checked for density to ensure the continuation of correct processing and, if acceptable, the new section can be cut into the original sound print to eliminate the damage. Synchronizing is simple. As long as the original reel of sound was correctly synchronized, the new section can be visually matched to the old by aligning the very distinctive sound modulations seen on each sound track.

Negative cutting will now involve a little more than splicing head and tail leaders. The editor's work print is used as a cutting guide and the replacement section of negative is inserted in exactly the same way, using the key numbers to ensure accuracy.

Sound negative splice problems

The points at which the negative splices must later be made have to be borne in mind when cutting in a positive replacement section. The negative splice is of the overlapped type and the double splice line when printed would cause a sharp "crack" sound in the theatre reproducing system.

The part of the negative splice which covers the sound track area can be punched out, leaving a small clear triangular space. In the subsequent positive printing it becomes completely black. This will give a fast "fade-in, fade-out" (or dropout) effect in the sound system and although eliminating the "crack", will still result in a slight noise.

It is far better to choose a point for each splice in the negative where sound modulation is very strong. Splices made in these areas are so buried in the strong modulation that they pass unnoticed in the strength of the reproduction and no punching of the negative splice is necessary.

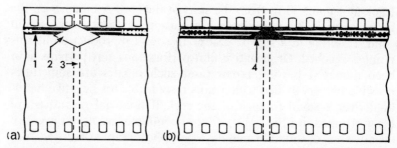

"Punching" a photographic sound negative splice. (a) A diamond-shaped hole is punched out of the sound negative at the splice line. (1) Sound track. (2) Punched hole. (3) Negative splice. (b) Subsequent positive print with black opaque triangle in the track area hiding the splice line.

Editorial procedure on receipt of the final photographic sound daily rushes can be summarized, thus:

1. Identify each reel of sound print with its matching negative roll number as indicated on a Laboratory Report.
2. Using the punch start mark as a guide and, checking the visual sync plop transferred through all the dubbing operation, make a final sync check by matching the photographic sound against an original dialogue track in the film synchronizer.
3. With the film still in the synchronizer, wind back to the picture start mark and make a synchronous start mark on the new sound track.
4. Screen the entire film for a check on visual synchronism, overall sound quality and reel-to-reel balance.
5. Hand the sound print to the department responsible for checking sound track density, proving the correct development of the sound negative film.
6. Make any new section of sound negative to eliminate any

blemish or damage incurred in the original. Visually synchronize the new print and cut in, splicing at a point of full sound modulation if possible.

7. Mark the "level sync" lines level with start and end of picture frames and allow an additional 20 frames at the end of the sound (for 35 mm film).

8. Send the positive sound reels, identified with reel number and negative roll number to the laboratory for negative cutting and leader splicing.

The laboratory now have the sound facility for making any number of release prints, although we have not yet examined the preparation of the picture negative.

Allowance has been made for the doubling-up of "A" and "B" reels, after combined prints have been made, by incorporating the first 20 sound frames of every "B" reel at the end of every "A" reel of sound negative. There are times when this last operation is not required, but the laboratory handling the film will give the decision. They may, for example, double-up the picture and sound *negative* of the single "A" and "B" reels before any prints are made. There will, in that case, be no loss of sound track between the "A" and "B" reels as the prints are made after the single negative reels are spliced together. Each single reel of sound track is then prepared without any 20-frame allowance for doubling-up combined prints. This situation is usually met where colour release prints are to be made by the dye-transfer process which involves no photographic development of the final pictorial image (see page 256).

Four, and six-track systems

Until now, we have assumed that the commercial release of the film is to be with normal combined picture and photographic sound prints.

When shown in exhibition theatres, the sound track on such prints is reproduced through a single-channel sound system—mono sound.

No matter how many loudspeakers, or horns, there are behind the screen (and in most theatres there are several) the sound is evenly balanced in each.

Multiple channel sound is designed to add realism to the very large screen image produced by modern wide screen processes. Here, the sound not only follows the visual movements across the

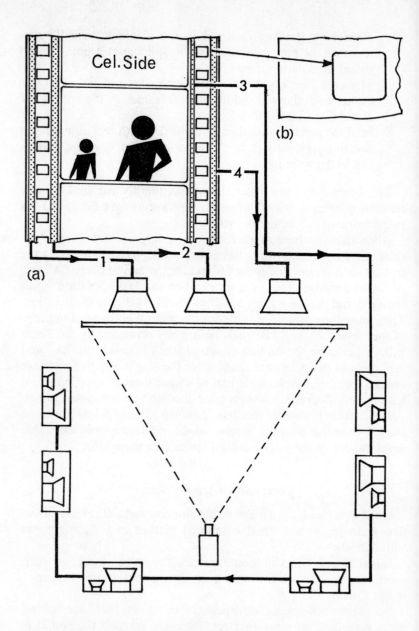

Striped release prints. (a) 35 mm combined 4-track magnetic stripe release print. (b) Special film perforation to allow more space for the magnetic sound stripes. (1) Left channel. (2) Centre channel. (3) Ambient (surround) channel. Note the narrower stripe. (4) Right channel.

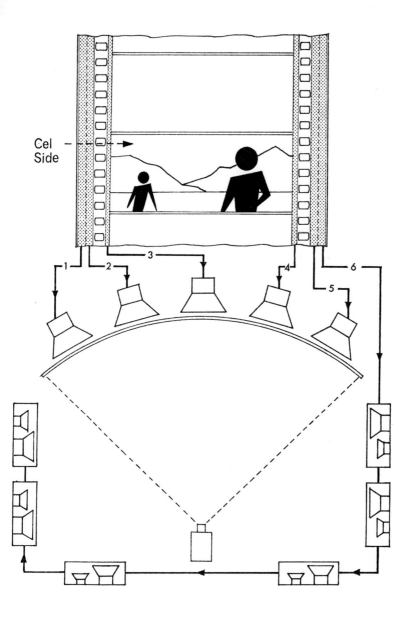

Cel Side

70 mm combined 6-track magnetic stripe release print. (1) Outer left channel. (2) Inner left channel. (3) Centre channel. (4) Inner right channel. (5) Right channel. (6) Ambient (surround) channel. Note that there are five film perforations per picture frame.

screen but additional sounds are spread throughout the theatre by the use of ambient, or surround speakers strategically placed at the sides and to the rear of the audience. Audience participation thus becomes more real and exciting.

Two magnetic sound systems are currently in use in exhibition theatres, the four-track and the six-track.

The four-track system is designed so that sound can be distributed between three horns positioned across the screen area, each horn reproducing sound from a separate track, or channel. The fourth channel is devoted to the ambient speakers which create additional effect. The four channels are called left, centre, right and ambient.

The six-track system is exactly the same in principle, except that five channels are devoted to the screen area—left; inner-left; centre; inner-right; right—giving much more directional control over the sounds to be moved across the screen as the visual action moves. The sixth channel provides the ambient sound.

Four channel systems are usual on the CinemaScope type of release print. Six channels are considered necessary for the bigger screen image provided by 70 mm and Cinerama release prints.

Sound stripes

No development process is involved to "marry" the sound track to the picture print when a multiple channel release print is made. Invariably, the four or six channels are carried on individual magnetic stripes which are specially coated on to the finished picture print.

Picture negative cutting is carried out in the usual way, academy head and tail leaders being cut on to each reel as it is assembled for printing. This procedure is described in the following chapter. The doubling-up of individual reels may take a different form from that of the normal 35 mm release print, certainly if the release is to be in 70 mm.

Mute prints are made from the single reels of cut picture negative checked for density and correct grading of print and then sometimes two, three and even four single consecutive reels are spliced together in positive form, depending on their individual size. This unit is then run through the magnetic track coating machine. Here four or six stripes of oxidized emulsion are rolled on in narrow bands clear of the perforations and the picture area. The coating is applied to the base, or cell side. All forms of mag-

232

netic sound film coating must be hardened completely before any sound signal can be transferred on to them so the roll of newly striped picture is stored at a controlled temperature for at least 24 hours in a "curing" process. In emergencies, "forced curing" is sometimes necessary, the temperature being raised to reduce the hardening time. The slower 24-hour cure however, produces a more reliable result.

When all reels have been prepared in this way, the film laboratory have completed their part in the process. Putting the signals onto the tracks is a sound transfer operation. For this, a master magnetic sound track is required with the correct number of channels. The original sound dubbing is carried out with this in mind.

In preparing dubbed tracks, pre-mixing is done for the same basic reason—to reduce the number of sound components to a manageable quantity. But in this case they have to incorporate directional movements of sound as required by the movement of action. For this an operator seated at the mixing console operates a "pan pot" to move the sound as he wishes. Ambient sounds are mostly confined to effects and music, and they are planned with great care for the maximum effectiveness.

Sound tracks are built by the editorial department so that sounds can be separated and "panned" in relation to obvious movements of pictorial action. Some specific sound effects may need to move across the screen area, for example, while others, in the same sequence, remain "spread" as a total effect. These two types should not be built into one sound reel.

As with the mono mixing, each reel is correctly balanced in sound. But now the balance must be shared in whatever ratio is required between three, or five, front horn channels and the ambient channel. The resulting magnetic track is known as the six-track (or four-track, whichever the case may be) printing master.

Multi-track sound transfers

As reels of mute pictures have been doubled-up ready for sound transfer, so are the appropriate reels of printing master. The start mark at the head of each unit is matched to the Academy start mark on the picture leader. A sync plop can be incorporated in the end leader of the Printing Master, matching a sync frame on the end leader of the picture unit.

Putting the master sound on to the striped picture now becomes

233

a straightforward transfer operation. The four- or six-channel printing master is run on a re-recording machine with the appropriate number of reproducing heads, and the picture is synchronously run on a recording machine, each of the magnetic stripes receiving the correct channel of sound. Naturally, the "level-sync" start marks are adjusted at this stage by the transfer operator so that the transfer is made in "printing sync".

The standard picture/track relationship for all gauges are as follows:

Photographic combined print

35 mm   Track 20 frames advance.
16 mm   Track 26 frames advance.

Magnetic combined print

35 mm   Track 28 frames retard.
70 mm   23 frames retard.
16 mm   Track 28 frames advance.

Until quite recently, the transfer operator was unable to see a screened picture while making the sound transfer from the printing master, but could only monitor the sound in his head-set as it was being applied to ensure clean quality. At the end of the transfer he could check that the sync plop was heard as the picture sync frame marked on the end leader of the picture reel passed through the recording head. Later magnetic release sound transfer systems incorporate a small screen so that the operator can make frequent visual checks throughout, in addition to monitoring the sound.

Music for road show release

The large "road show" type of production is normally introduced with an overture lasting approximately two to three minutes. After an intermission, entr'acte music introduces Part 2 of the film and, after the final title, there will be "walk-out" music to complete the show. Music prepared to cover these areas is dubbed on to four-track or six-track (whichever is required for release prints) printing masters as separate units, and then spliced on to the main printing masters of the reels concerned. Striped blank picture film of exactly the required length is added to the head of reel 1, the head of the reel which opens Act 2 of the film, and to the end of the final reel, after titles, so that these music sections become a part of the complete print.

234

Although the editorial staff are not directly involved with the magnetic sound transfer operation it is well to know a little of the mechanics involved as it explains some of the routine tasks more clearly.

Multi-track sound masters

Whether the printing master be for a 35 mm picture or 70 mm picture, it is always made on to a fully-coated 35 mm magnetic film roll, the required number of channels being correctly positioned by the appropriate recording heads. The problems of inserting newly dubbed sections into a photographic sound negative reel do not apply here. A new section can be cut into a multi-channel magnetic reel by making the splices carefully and using a tape splicing machine and as long as the joins are correctly "butted", no unwanted clicks are heard as the splice passes the sound head.

If 70 mm release prints are to be made, the sound transfer operation is slightly different from that for 35 mm release prints. The 35 mm picture frame occupies an area within 4 sprocket perforations on the film. On 70 mm film each picture frame is within an area of 5 perforations and its projection speed is 20 per cent faster than that for 35 mm film.

Sound transfer from a 35 mm printing master to a 70 mm release print is, therefore, carried out with the 35 mm re-recording machine running at *its* standard speed, and the 70 mm recording machine running at *its* standard speed. The relative sync is then correct.

Summary of responsibilities

Final sound dubbing is a fairly complicated and time-consuming operation, particularly if multiple channel release is contemplated. But, no matter how simple or elaborate the production may be, the editorial objective is the same—to present the groups of sounds to be balanced for a final sound track in an intelligent way so that sound-mixing problems can be kept to a minimum. Synchronism of all individual tracks must be checked in advance of a dubbing session, wherever time permits, and checks must be maintained throughout the various procedures so that the final sound track, be it mono or multiple channel, is as perfectly synchronized as were the original daily sound rushes at the time of shooting.

Constant watch is maintained on the mechanics of track building so that equipment which can cause splicing problems is frequently checked for unwanted magnetism. Splicers must be kept clean so that joins are evenly matched, correctly aligned and cleanly punched at the perforations.

It sometimes helps if magnetic film cuts are made so that the line of the splice is diagonal, rather than at 90 degrees to the sound track. A very slightly superimposed fade-out, fade-in effect is achieved as a diagonal splice passes the sound reproducing head. This improves the smoothness of sound cutting.

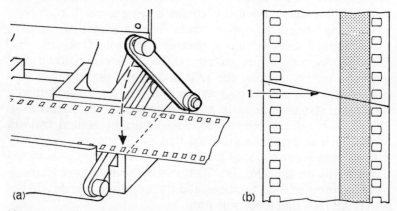

Magnetic sound—diagonal splicing. (a) Tape splicer with additional outside cutting knife which produces a diagonal cutting line. (b) Striped magnetic sound film. (1) The angle of the splice.

Anything which can be done ahead of the main sound dubbing session is well worth while—obvious pre-mixes can be combined to one single track, reducing the amount of time spent at the main session. Time can also be saved by making experiments in advance, so that an unusual sound effect can be reproduced without having to experiment during the valuable time devoted to the main session. Tape recording machines with variable speed control can create strange and often desirable sound effects. Special machines which change the speed of a sound track, yet maintain its pitch frequency by allowing the sound heads to rotate in relation to the tape speed can help the sound editor striving to find an unusual sound effect.

12

PREPARATION FOR PICTURE NEGATIVE CUTTING

IN the interests of clarity, picture negative cutting has only been briefly mentioned in earlier sections. In fact, preparation is carried out as soon as individual reels of the editor's work print are completely assembled, fine cut, and contain all the rush prints of any special optical work. Such optical work would include dissolves, fades, travelling matte shots, or any work which required special picture negatives. If advance preparation is not delayed, the picture negative is usually cut during the final sound mixing period so that both picture and sound negatives are ready for making the first Answer Print.

Those of the editor's picture reels which involve no trick work are ready for negative cutting the moment the fine cut is settled and the content of individual reels finalized. Others will be incomplete until titles and other special negatives are received and approved, titles often being delivered at the last minute. Preparation of picture negative so that it is sorted, reel by reel, ready for cutting should never be delayed, even if the work print reel is still partially incomplete. Sorting negatives is a time-consuming job and the negative department at the laboratory will have to fit it in with work on other productions. So the sooner they can dispose of preliminary work the quicker they can deal with the later stages.

Each reel of positive work print prepared by the film editor contains many individual picture cuts, built into sequences over many weeks, examined and recut as necessary. Each work print reel is mounted in its final form with standard head and tail leaders and, although the problem of projection changeover was taken into account when reels were finalized, each reel is a self-contained unit as far as printing is concerned once the negative has been matched and cut.

Provided that the editor has taken certain elementary precautions during the cutting period, negative cutting is a routine task. The key numbers on the positive work print are matched to the key numbers on the appropriate piece of negative, making physical cuts in exactly the same places as on the positive print. This is done with the greatest care. Negative film is not to be damaged in handling and key numbers must be accurately matched to avoid any mis-cutting of the negative.

Breaking down the negative

The operators at the laboratory cutting room use equipment designed specially for negative handling. They wear clean cotton gloves which protect the materials from moisture on the skin. Film is carefully wound so that rolls remain flat and are not subjected to stress when winding. This prevents dust from causing abrasions when trapped between tightly coiled rolls. Negative cutting is a painstaking task, calling for concentration. If a negative is mis-matched and incorrectly cut, nothing can be done to make it whole again. Any advance work that helps to make the task as straight-forward as possible must be done by both laboratory and film cutting room.

The negative processed daily at the time of shooting is normally filed in complete rolls assembled just as they were printed. Reports are prepared at the time which identify the contents of the roll and its negative filing number. If the editor needs a picture reprint during this period, he merely quotes the roll number, the slate number, and the front and end key number of the take. All this information is recorded in the cutting room master record book as a daily routine.

When shooting has finished, however, although several weeks may elapse before negative cutting will take place, it is customary to make a preliminary breakdown of each roll of negative. Every take is separated from its neighbour into individual rolls and re-filed by slate number and key numbers. Careful records are made to help sort the scenes which will be required before negative is cut. Nothing further can then be done at the laboratory until the editor's work print is received.

Checking the work print

The editor examines each reel of work print, establishing which are complete for negative cutting and which are still incomplete,

238

where titles and trick optical negative have not yet been made. He lists the missing negatives reel by reel. Completed work print reels can be sent to the laboratory for negative cutting but, before doing so, a further examination must be made.

Unintentional positive splices

There must be nothing in the positive work print to cause confusion when the negative is cut. There may be several areas where scenes have been cut and re-cut during assembly as the editor searched for the best pattern. Shots may have been extended and, although a splice may exist in the work print, the negative cutter should not be led to make a cut, only to discover on a closer examination that the scene is, in fact, continuous.

In other scenes, jump-cutting within the same take is deliberate at times to remove unwanted footage. A long panning shot, for example, can be reduced to two straight cuts by splicing together the static front and end sections clear of the pan. Yet the negative key numbers tell the cutter that he is about to cut two pieces of negative from the same slate and he may not realize what has been done. Jump cuts can also be made in static set-up shots, removing excess footage before a piece of violent action, the action itself hiding the jump.

Positive film may have been physically damaged at a late stage of editing. It is pointless to order a reprint just before the negative cutting stage; instead, a section of blank film is cut in to maintain synchronism.

Marks to guide the neg cutter

Any false positive splices must be clearly marked and any deliberate, but otherwise confusing jump cuts within a slate, must carry instructions which leave the negative cutter in no doubt of the editor's intention.

Cut by cut, each positive reel is examined. Each extension of a shot is checked to ensure that the action is continued without any frames having been lost and also to make certain that allowance has been made for the overlapped negative splice where cut-backs have been made in a slate. Ideally, each unintentional positive splice made where a scene has been extended in the positive print should be marked "Don't cut negative". But in practice this is cumbersome and a wax pencil mark clearly and firmly drawn across the splice indicates the same instruction to the negative cutter. The same applies to sections of blank film cut in to replace damaged scenes as long as the damage is contained within the same slate, the splice at each end of the blank film being so marked.

Occasionally, blank film is used where a shot is damaged at the beginning or the end of the cut, or an extension is made without using the film trim required. In either case, an <u>arrowed line</u> is

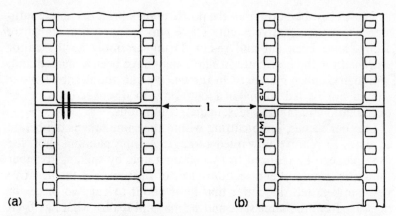

Marking the picture work print for negative cutting. (1) The position of the tape splice. (a) Conventional marks for unintended splice. This is the instruction to the negative cutter *not* to cut negative at this point. (b) A deliberate removal of a section of film *within the same slate* will result in a Jump cut and confuse the negative cutter unless specifically marked as an instruction.

<u>drawn through the blank film</u> with its tip pointing to the splice line where the shot begins or ends in the negative. The words, "Cut for length" are sometimes written on the blank film in addition to the arrowed line.

The splice where a jump cut has been deliberately made must be indicated by "Jump cut", or "Cut negative", clearly written at the splice. Recheck all scenes involving fades and dissolves which do not run the dupe for the full length of the picture cut, to ensure that there are no unintentional "jump cuts" where optical print has been cut to original print in the continuous action of one slate.

Short cuts without key numbers

Although a key number appears on every running foot of film, there are occasions when very short action cuts, perhaps of six to eight frames, entirely miss the section containing the key number. There would be no guide at all as to how the negative is either

240

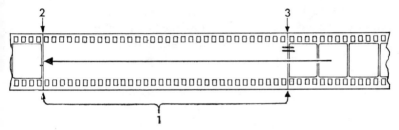

Marking the picture work print for negative cutting. (I) Area of damaged positive print replaced with the correct length of blank film down to the next picture cut. An arrow on the film instructs the negative cutter to continue the picture negative for the length of the blank film as far as the next splice (2). (3) The splice to the blank film is marked conventionally as an instruction not to cut negative here.

located or cut. These cuts should be marked when the sequences are assembled. A frame is identified with the nearest key number, plus or minus the appropriate number of frames, and the slate and take number also indicated. This is best done with a sharp scribing tool so that the information cannot be erased while handling the film.

Pre-graded negative sections

There are other problems with a series of extremely short picture cuts. It is unwise to have too many closely spaced negative splices

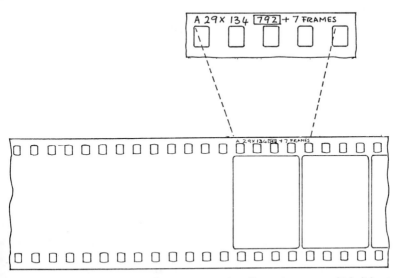

Marking the picture work print for negative cutting. Short picture cut which did not include part of a printed key number. Information to guide the negative cutter is scribed over one picture frame.

241

passing through the printing machine. Their rapid passage and extra overlapped thickness can cause the film to jump off the rollers and damage the negative. Also, the automatic grading mechanism by which each individual picture cut is graded in relation to its adjacent cut requires a minimum amount of film to enable it to operate. Both problems can be solved by duping the negative of the scenes involved before cutting takes place. The complete scenes are assembled in order of appearance in the cut sequence and grading corrections are done *when making the fine grain duping positive*. The complete section containing all the very short cuts can now be assembled in fine grain form by matching the editor's work print and cutting the fine grain positive accordingly. The dupe negative made from this cut fine grain not only has the grading corrections already incorporated but there are no negative splices in the section. A print is then made from the new dupe negative to be inserted in the work print.

This treatment only applies to a series of short cuts adjacent to each other and the film laboratory will advise if it is necessary. It is obviously important, however, to establish this need before negative cutting is started.

Sorting the negative

When each reel has been examined to ensure that all the required work is complete and that there is no possibility of negative cutting confusion, they can be sent to the film laboratory negative department. This is still only a preliminary stage of the operation and can be carried out, even if the actual cutting of negative is to be delayed, perhaps to preview the complete film in work print form with a dubbed sound track beforehand.

The negative department lists the key numbers of each picture cut in the work print reel, identifies the slate and take number by reference to their filing system, and puts the pieces of negative in numbered tins in the order of cutting for each reel.

Cutting the negative

When the order is given for negative cutting to go ahead the negative cutter is given the work print reel and the tins containing all the sorted negative for that reel. Matching the positive and negative in the synchronizer, each scissor cut is made across the centre of the frame preceding or following the eventual splice line. The

242

excess film is removed in the formation of each overlapped splice as negative is joined together into reels. The reel is completed with standard Academy head and tail negative leaders, and it is carefully cleaned and stored ready for printing. Negative cutting is done by specialists who do nothing else but this. They know how to handle the film to avoid marking it and they wind it without causing stress marks. Assistants in positive cutting rooms are well advised to watch this operation so that they can see how film should be handled. The cotton glove is probably the most misused item in positive film cutting rooms. Abrasive dirt which accumulates in a glove can cause expensive damage. Even if a glove is worn film should always be handled at the edges, particularly during rewinding.

As positive work print reels are completed with main and end titles, opticals and matte shots, rush prints from these special negatives are cut in to the appropriate reel and screened for approval before negative cutting is authorized. All remaining editor's picture reels are sent to the laboratory with the authorization to cut negative and supply a fully graded combined picture and sound answer print, using the sound negative which is probably still in preparation at this time in the sound dubbing theatre. Having already basically sorted the picture negative needed for each reel by earlier reference to the work print key numbers, cutting proceeds. As each positive cut is matched to its negative the reel is completed and joined. Negative "part titles" are incorporated in negative leaders so that each print will carry the name of the production and the correct reel number.

Protective masters

Each complete reel of negative must be examined cut by cut to assess grading requirements in order to produce a print properly balanced, both in density and colour. Before handling the valuable negative any further, however, it is customary to make a protective fine grain master positive so that duplication of the negative is possible in the unlikely event that the original negative is accidentally damaged.

Grading assessments

Records are kept during the course of the production showing how the rush prints have been graded. These may serve as a basis on which the grader can work, but much rebalancing is usually needed when complete reels of cut negative are printed. This is not meant to imply that grading exists to correct exposure faults of the cameraman—far from it. Even with correctly exposed individual shots there is always a need for density control and colour filter correction when balancing reels which contain many separate negative cuts.

Often, if the cameraman is available, he screens the work print with the grading technician and makes known his requirements so that final adjustments can be planned and executed.

The answer print

With so many individual cuts in a film several prints are often made before the correct final colour and density balance is achieved. Whatever mechanical aids are used by the grader, and there are several, his experience and judgement are the determining factor in creating the best possible print from the negative at his disposal. The laboratory will perhaps make a silent grading print before the sound track negative is ready, as a further basis for grading assessment. But eventually, when the sound track is available a combined picture and photographic sound print is made. The aim of the laboratory is to present a properly graded and synchronized answer print, acceptable to the production company, on the basis of which all further combined release prints can be produced.

When the answer print is screened, "key" production personnel attend so that any regrading requirements are made clear to laboratory technicians. Rebalanced reprints are made and viewed until everyone is satisfied.

Negative mis-cuts

There are times when negative mis-cuts are revealed for the first time at the answer print screening. Each reel of negative must be checked as soon as it is cut and joined. By running it through the film synchronizer with the work print, each cut is re-examined and the overall length of the reel checked. But a mis-cut is still possible. Negative cutters seldom rely entirely on negative key numbers for matching negative to positive. They always check any visible action as confirmation of the correct matching of key numbers. Unfortunately, original negative key numbers are quite tiny and blurring sometimes occurs. Certain numerals can easily be misread for other similar numerals. The figure 3 may be confused with an 8 for example, and if there is no obvious visible action in the film it is very easy to mis-cut. Checking against the work print when the reel has been completely cut may not reveal the misread number yet the overall length of the reel can still be correct. When the combined answer print is seen on the screen for the first time, loss of synchronism in the cut is revealed if dialogue is involved, and a remedy has to be found.

Occasionally, the mis-cut is well clear of the negative section which should have been used. The correct section is then located in the carefully filed negative trims of the slate concerned and the cut remade. As negative splices have already been made at each end of the incorrect section, the replacement negative must be a frame longer at each end for new overlap negative splices to be made. The restoration must maintain the same overall length to preserve synchronism. It is sometimes possible for a negative join to be successfuly "split" and subsequently remade. But this is always a doubtful procedure and it is much safer to allow a compensating frame at each end of a replacement cut, removing a frame from the preceding and following cut.

If the mis-cut incorporates a section of the negative which should have been used, then the problem is more awkward. The offending cut can be taken out of the reel and joined to its negative trim but this will certainly create a jump of one or two frames. Film is not only lost in making the original splice but more will be lost in making the new one. This is unacceptable. The picture angle itself can perhaps be changed, using a completely new piece of negative and treating any dialogue involved in the cut as an "off-screen" line. But this is unlikely to be completely satisfactory. An unused take of the correct angle may be available, even a take which was never printed. This substitution not only means re-cutting the picture negative but also making a new section of dubbed sound track to incorporate the newly synchronized line of dialogue.

There is always a way of solving the problem but there is obviously no rule which can be laid down for finding a solution.

Checking sound in answer print

Apart from picture grading and balancing, sound quality must also be maintained in combined printing. A representative of the sound department responsible should be present at answer print screenings, even though the rush print of the photographic sound track was checked at the time of receipt. Photographic sound negative is incapable of reproducing the same range of sound frequencies as magnetic recording film but careful checks of laboratory processing control will ensure that quality loss is minimal.

Replacement sections in answer print

During the period of grading and checking to arrive at an acceptable answer print, it does not necessarily follow that complete reels are reprinted each time a grading change is called for. Bearing in mind that the laboratory have probably done considerable advance work by making mute grading points before the sound negative was available, the first answer print submitted at a screening for the production company is normally very close to the final objective. Just minor areas of reels may be troublesome with cut to cut picture balance. So it is customary to make combined reprint sections incorporating adjustments to grading rather than reprint the entire reel concerned. Such section reprints are then matched and cut into the reel concerned, making the splices at the point of an original cut. This work is usually carried out by technicians in the positive assembly room at the laboratory. Section reprinting is, of course, a temporary expedient and if the new grading is acceptable a complete "no-join" fully graded answer print reel is made.

Temporary changeover cues

A word here about projection changeover cues. It is customary, at this stage, to mark only the *positive* combined print with the necessary motor and machine-changeover cues to enable the projectionist to make a smooth and continuous screening of the print. Small circles are scribed on to three or four frames of picture where each cue is to occur, by using a metal frame fitted with perforation register pins which holds film and scribing tool in register as the marks are made. Cues are then scribed in matching positions on each of the frames. Standard positions for 35 mm film are $12\frac{1}{2}$ ft. from the end of the reel for the motor dot, cueing the start of the leader run-up on the second machine, and $1\frac{1}{2}$ ft. from the end for the changeover dot, at which point projection is changed over from one of the machines to the other. The register pins ensures that dots marked at the three or four frame period for each cue are positioned so that they appear in the corner of the screen as one mark and do not "wander" because of haphazard marking. Later, when final approval is given, permanent cues are positioned on the picture negative and become an automatic feature of the printing operation. But it is still inadvisable at this stage as further editorial changes may still be called for.

Audience reaction is sometimes tested by holding a few private screenings with an invited audience, before the film is considered to be in its final form. Changes called for as a result of such screenings involve picture negative recutting, and sound track redubbing may also be necessary. Re-positioning of scenes is not unknown and, if permanent changeover marks have been made on the picture negative considerable damage will result if the last scenes in a reel have to be moved. In any case, negative changeover marks are only needed at the ends of every other reel—the "B" reel, where positive prints are to be doubled-up for exhibition. It has been known for every single reel of negative to be accidentally "punched" with such marks, and this mistake is unforgivable.

Sneak previews

Although less frequent in Europe, public previews have over the years become standard practice in the USA. Audiences are now conditioned to the preview system and, to a great extent, take delight in filling in a questionnaire and acting as temporary film critics. Obviously, the information received from such screenings has to be sifted with great care and, just as audiences have become conditioned to the preview system, so have production companies to its interpretation.

The mechanics of setting up a public preview—the choice of theatres, whether a certificate of censorship has to be obtained in advance, and so on, are not problems for the film editor, although censorship will be examined later. The producer must decide whether the preview is to be held before picture negative cutting, using the editor's work print and a separate dubbed sound track and leaving the original negative intact, or whether to carry out the entire negative cutting operation and produce a clean combined answer print for preview. The decision will usually depend on how confident the producer feels about the shape of the film.

Work print preview

If the work print is to be used, there are two possible modes of operation:

1. Locate a theatre which is suitably equipped with double-headed picture and sound projection (or capable of being temporarily adapted with dummy sound reproducing heads interlocked with the picture projectors). This preview would be with separate picture work print and dubbed sound track. The choice between magnetic or photographic sound print will depend on the equipment available.
2. Use a theatre which has a magnetic sound reproducing system for striped combined prints. In this case, the work print can be sent for striping so that a single track master dubbed sound can be transcribed to the work print.

Separate picture and sound

Both systems are potentially dangerous since, unlike a combined copy, the work print is full of physical splices, any of which may break in spite of advance checks and precautions. If a break does occur in projection when using separate picture and sound, re-synchronizing takes time and depends on having matching code numbers on picture and the newly made sound track. Theatre projectionists are not as familiar with handling separate picture and sound reels as are their studio counterparts. To put the studio projectionists in charge of strange equipment for one screening is not necessarily advisable. The choice of theatres is obviously reduced in view of the special equipment needed and they may not all be adaptable to receive portable dummy sound heads.

Striped work print

Striping the work print and transcribing the master sound removes the problem of loss of synchronism if the film were to break in projection. But the theatre must have the correct magnetic sound reproducing system. Perhaps the most difficult problem is the striping operation itself since, if the many joins in the work print have been made with a tape splicing machine, the magnetic oxide stripe does not always successfully "take" on the tape surface. Therefore, slight sound distortion is apparent as each join goes through the machine.

Furthermore, a certain number of scratches are bound to be present on the picture after many weeks of handling, no matter how careful editorial and projection staff have been at the studio. Unless many regraded reprints are to be made, the shortcomings of an assembled work print just have to be accepted.

Preparing work print for preview

Previews are frequently held with a work print, however, but it is more common to use separate picture and track than the combined magnetic stripe. The latter system is never completely reliable.

Special film code numbering is essential for such a preview. Each reel of picture and sound is synchronously numbered from its start mark to the end of reel. If possible, picture code numbers should not be superimposed on any numbers which already exist on the film—numbers which were printed when daily rush prints were delivered for editing. Using the opposite edge of the film, or positioning the numbers with individual numerals appearing between perforations may be the answer. Anything should be done to avoid confusion between the special preview number and original numbers. If a film break occurs, matching picture and track numbers must be found, marked for the projectionist, and positioned in picture and sound heads so that screening in synchronism can continue with minimum delay.

Naturally, the entire work print must be examined very closely before the screening. Joins made with tape tend to open after a while and make the picture jump on the screen as each splice passes the projection aperture. They must be checked and remade if their strength is in doubt. Pencil lines marked during dubbing must be removed from the film and it is a wise move to hand all picture reels to the laboratory so that they can be given professional cleaning. Code numbering for preview must be done after this event otherwise printed numbers will miraculously vanish. It is well to ensure that tape joins also will not be affected by the cleaning process.

Synchronizing start marks and identifying reel numbers must also be clearly entered at the head of each reel of picture and sound so that no misreading of marks and reel numbers will be possible. One reel of sound, after all, looks very much like another. Change-over cues, too, must be standard and the projectionist should be informed of the type of temporary cue mark being used on the work print. A rehearsal screening in advance of the public show is invaluable to the projectionist.

Previews with separate picture and sound track are, without question, a nerve-wracking experience for the film editor as he sits in the auditorium waiting for the film to break in the machine, and praying that it doesn't.

Post-preview changes

Changes needed as a result of this type of preview present no problem. Picture recuts are made just as they were during the period of fine-cutting as the negative has not yet been touched.

Sound track changes as a result of picture recutting may well involve redubbing a section, even a complete reel, particularly where music is involved in the change. Tracks may have to be rebuilt, and this is where the trained music editor is invaluable, shortening music sections and repeating them where necessary. Whenever possible, this should be done in consultation with the composer. Indiscriminate cutting or "stretching" of music tracks may not necessarily coincide with his musical ideas. He may have a more successful alternative to meet the requirements of the alteration.

Unlike original fine cut changes, when only one sound track was in existence, picture alterations at this stage also involve dialogue, effects, and music tracks. Many pre-mixes and three-track mixes went into the preparation of the final single track master. Each alteration made to the picture must be noted, no matter how small, so that every component sound track and pre-mix can be recut and resynchronized for redubbing purposes. This is often a painstaking chore and editor and sound editor must have complete co-operation so that there are no misunderstandings and nothing forgotten.

If second, and possibly third previews are contemplated, changes are made wherever possible to the existing dubbed sound track between the previews, even though these may be unacceptable in a final version. Magnetic sound cuts are simplified by using a tape splicing machine, but with photographic sound track splices may require a "blooping" treatment to avoid any unnecessary cracks and bangs in the theatre speakers as joins pass the sound reproducing head. A minute gap between two pieces of magnetic film at the splice will cause no interference in reproduction, particularly if a diagonal join is used. But the smallest gap between two pieces of photographic sound causes a violent reaction in the sound system as full strength light from the exciter lamp strikes the photocell. Blacking out the gap parallel to the line of the splice softens the noise but does not eliminate it. A triangular area (see page 228) must be blacked out, parallel to the direction of film travel using opaque fast drying ink. Correctly applied, the quick fade-in, fade-out effect of the black triangle at the join will be unnoticeable in sound reproduction.

Eventually, having assessed preview reactions and acted upon them, the entire cut is finalized and the picture can be sent for negative cutting. Any required section or complete reel redubbing can then take place using a corrected black and white work print dupe and the recut sound tracks.

Preview after neg cutting

If the preview is held *after* negative cutting and combined printing has taken place, a different technique is needed for any changes. Naturally, the great advantage with this type of preview is that any standard projection theatre can be used. No special equipment is needed and the print can be screened just as all exhibition prints are screened. There are few, if any, splices in the combined print and film breakage is as rare as during any normal theatre screening.

Changes as a result of such previews now involve recutting negative. But if more than one preview is to take place and experimental changes are to be tried at second and third previews, there would be little point in making permanent changes in the cut negative until all reactions are assessed. Temporary changes between previews, often crude in execution, are made in the combined print so that further screenings can take place without touching negative film.

Making cuts in combined picture and sound prints obviously presents a problem with the photographic sound track which has been advanced in printing synchronism to meet the requirements of the film projector. Sometimes it is possible to make an elimination where both picture and sound requirements are taken care of, the cut being made so that a jump in sound reproduction is relatively smooth. Often, this is just not possible and the cut is made concentrating on the picture requirement rather than on sound—a jump in sound reproduction being inevitable. Recuts are mainly confined to scene eliminations, although with care, switching the order of sequences is sometimes possible. It may be necessary to "bloop" an area of the photographic sound track, using brush and paint, to diminish the crude effect of such a temporary cut.

Temporary fades

Picture dissolves can obviously not be recreated when dealing with temporary cuts in combined prints, but a very old established method of jumping from one scene to another should not be

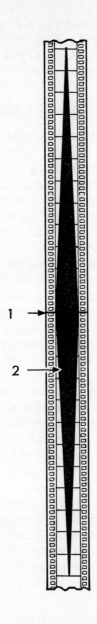

Temporary scene-to-scene transitions for sneak previews. The paper fade. (1) The splice.
(2) Area of "dead-black" tape, or fast-drying ink.

252

ignored. Although audiences are now conditioned to accept "time-cut" transitions from one sequence to another, particularly if sound is intelligently used to smooth, or even "point" the transition, temporary cuts in preview prints can be helped with a device which used to be known as the "paper fade". With self-adhesive tape, or opaque ink, a temporary and otherwise brutal transition from one scene to another can be made by marking editor's conventional fade lines on the print and filling the area between the lines with opaque tape or ink—a 2-ft. fade being quite acceptable. Obviously, this is but a temporary measure in a preview operation and, although "old hat" in conception, the device is very useful and often new to the relatively inexperienced editor.

Multiple track preview

Answer prints with four and six multiple sound tracks may also be made and used for preview purposes, although changes between previews, if more than one is to be held, will be less simple than with the photographic combined print. When final changes are settled, the striped copy need not be a complete loss to the production company as, when the negative has been recut, new sections of reels are printed and striped with the required number of tracks. These sections are cut into the appropriate reels and the entire copy demagnetized so that the sound tracks are "clean" once more. Redubbing takes place, as necessary. A new printing master magnetic track is produced and the copy is sounded once more in its new form.

Negative recutting

When changes are made and approved after the final preview, picture negative must be recut, and also sound negative unless a complete new negative is to be supplied as a result of redubbing. Those changes made, temporarily, in the combined preview print must now be carried out on the editor's work print and all the sound tracks involved. Crude alterations necessary with a combined print are now more carefully made in the work print as the operation is no longer tied to the advanced sound synchronism. Picture changes must allow for overlapped negative splicing, not only the newly made negative splice, but also bearing in mind the amount of film which has already been lost in making original negative joins when reels were first cut.

The editor's revised work print is once again sent to the processing laboratory for negative recutting with any new dissolves incorporated if necessary. The negative cutters at the laboratory know little, if anything, of what has been done as a result of the preview. So, wherever a picture change has been made, a paper in the work print, inserted at the recut, will serve as a guide when negative and positive is rematched in the film synchronizer.

Sound negative recutting is done in the same way, if needed. Recut papers are inserted in the sound work print where cuts can be made without redubbing. Straight cuts are better if made in areas of strong sound modulation or right on the beginning of a sharp noise so that the splice line is not heard in reproduction. Cuts made in clear areas in the sound track mean that the area where the splice line crosses the track must be punched out in the negative, a triangular shaped section of negative being removed to give a black fade out, fade in effect in the positive print (see page 228).

Overlapped negative splices have to be allowed for whether picture or sound negative cutting is to be done, never planning a new join where an old one already exists.

Whether or not previews are held, negative cutting is eventually completed for both picture and sound, the answer print is made in combined form and approved, and release printing can take place, as required for the production.

Duplicate printing facilities

So far, only one picture negative and one sound negative is available for this mass printing. It may in some cases be necessary to provide further printing facilities for large scale distribution, not only to limit the possibility of damage to the existing negatives, but also to allow printing in various territories for the world market. Original language versions may be needed both in the USA and in Europe and printing may be required simultaneously in all areas. Duplicate printing facilities therefore have to be made available.

Duplication of the picture negative is straightforward. Fine grain positive duplicating prints, or inter-positives, are made from the original cut picture negative. Inter-negatives can also be made direct from the original negative without going through the intermediate positive stage. Either system provides another synchronous picture negative which can be used for printing.

Second sound negative

Sound negatives can be duplicated in the same way by means of a photographic copying process but results in a loss of quality in sound reproduction which may not be acceptable. It is far better to make a further optical transcription from the original magnetic sound master. This was made just for the purpose of producing further original sound negatives with no loss of quality, and the operation is simple. A one-to-one ratio transfer is made from magnetic on to photographic negative and no complicated sound theatre set-up is needed.

Combined printing duplicates

Occasionally, combined duplicate negatives are produced to provide additional printing facilities. Release prints are then made without the dual printing operations needed with separate picture and track negatives. For the sake of quality, however, second original sound negatives are usually made and used in conjunction with a separate picture dupe negative.

Release prints may also be made other than from a standard 35 mm picture and photographic sound negative. Reduction prints in 16 mm can be made from a 35 mm negative. Here the sound track is either optically reduced or a special negative made from the original magnetic sound master, according to laboratory requirements.

70 mm enlargement prints

A 35 mm picture negative can also be used to make enlarged prints by using a special printing machine—mute 70 mm reels being printed, then striped and recorded with multiple sound tracks from magnetic printing masters specially made. The film editor has to be on guard when 70 mm enlargement prints are to be made in this way. The very considerable increase in size of the projected image may reveal details in a shot not previously seen on his 35 mm work print. Focus problems, which are borderline irritants in a 35 mm print, may be quite unacceptable in a 70 mm enlarged copy. They have to be watched carefully. Where any such doubt exists, a check 70 mm enlarged rush print should be made from the 35 mm negative before final negative cutting. The expense involved is very small if the print reveals some unacceptable feature in a shot, discovered in time to make a different assembly.

Checking multi-channel release prints

Quantity checking of striped release prints can be something of a problem, particularly with the six-track, 70 mm copy. Photographic sound combined prints can be checked in almost any theatre. But multiple channel magnetic prints call for a specialist projection room with the correct sound system. Each individual print has to be checked, not only for print grading quality, but also to prove that striping and hardening of the magnetic oxide has been successful and no distortion exists on the multiple sound channels.

Mag/optical prints

Although perhaps used less frequently now, dual magnetic and, photographic combined prints are still made (particularly with 35 mm CinemaScope films) so that both multiple and single channel sound theatres can project the prints. A normal married print is made carrying the standard photographic sound track. It is then striped with the required number of magnetic sound tracks, the magnetic printing master sound being transferred in the usual way. One of the stripes partially covers the photographic sound track but reproduction is not greatly impaired. Such a "mag/optical" combined print is usually of the four-track variety and can be played in theatres having single channel photo-sound systems or four-track magnetic systems.

Dye transfer prints

Although the film editor is not directly concerned with printing systems, he should be aware of the dye-transfer method of colour

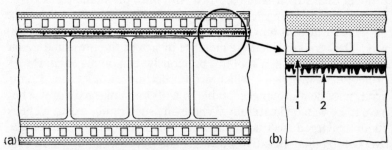

Special striped release prints. (a) The Mag/optical sound print. (b) Enlarged detail with magnetic stripe (1) covering half of the photographic sound track (2). Such a print can be exhibited on either 4-track magnetic or single channel photographic sound systems.

256

release printing, if only to understand the different type of duplicating facilities he may have to order.

In the dye-transfer system, the cut colour negative is not used to directly produce the print. It is used, at the first stage, to manufacture three photographically etched printing moulds, or matrices, each representing a secondary colour combination of the series of scenes in a reel—yellow, cyan, and magenta. Each matrix reel receives an application of its appropriate colour dye and is then brought into contact, in registration, with blank perforated film. After the raised part of each matrix has imparted its dye (the etched part does not make contact) to the same section of blank film the resulting colour combination reproduces the image in original colour form.

When a combined dye transfer print with photographic sound is to be made, the sound track is printed and developed first, the remaining area of the perforated film being left clear and transparent after development. Dye transfers are then made from each matrix and the image is formed in the original colour.

Duplicate negatives are not made to provide additional dye transfer printing facilities. The original cut negative is used to make as many sets of matrices as required, each set consisting of one matrix for each of the dye transfer stages—yellow, cyan and magenta. These are used for simultaneous colour release printing in various world centres just as duplicate negatives are used in other systems.

13

FINAL RESPONSIBILITIES

RESPONSIBILITIES of the editorial department go beyond the approved answer print stage. These are not necessarily the concern of the individual film editor but can be handled by an assistant who has been working on the production.

A number of tasks to be carried out at quite early stages were only briefly mentioned in the preceding chapters when examining the more major problems at that time.

Foreign versions

There may be considerable foreign version requirements for a film. Let us examine these on a major feature where distribution is to be in both 70 mm and 35 mm formats, with multiple and mono sound channels. The responsibility for providing the necessary foreign printing and sound dubbing facilities usually rests with the production company. Delivery of such film is part of a contract existing between producing and distributing companies. The concern of the film editor will be to see that appropriate orders are issued to laboratory and sound department to ensure that contractual obligations are met.

Foreign picture requirements

Picture requirements for foreign versions are fairly straightforward.

Materials must obviously be provided for release printing. These are usually duplicate negatives made from the original cut picture negative (or sets of matrices if dye transfer printing is to take place). These must incorporate all final editorial changes.

A black and white work print picture dupe must also be sent to each foreign dubbing centre, together with an original language dialogue sound track. The track is used for making an accurate translation—the picture for post-synchronizing the foreign language, and eventually for making the final mixed sound track.

Unfortunately, the time factor can become a problem with a major foreign release and often it is impractical to wait for every change to be finalized before sending out work print dupes and dialogue tracks so that translations can begin. Unsatisfactory matte shot composites, and title work, sometimes necessitate last minute editorial changes even though the film up to that time, had been regarded as final. When this situation does arise and foreign work prints have already been sent out, they must obviously be corrected accordingly. A replacement section or a replacement reel is made and shipped to foreign centres so that all versions are synchronous. Such changes are normally very few in number and, if as may be the case, post-synchronizing in the foreign language has already begun, corrections can very quickly be made as long as replacement work print reels are provided. Sometimes, in the last minute rush to make such final editorial changes in the work print, the component sound tracks, the pre-mixes—in fact everything which has to be corrected to allow redubbing to take place—the foreign work print is forgotten. This causes many problems when foreign dubbing does eventually take place with non-synchronous sound facilities.

Foreign sound requirements

Foreign sound materials are a little more demanding in preparation. But it is a routine task as long as the requirements have been anticipated during sound track building, and that sound dubbing was carried out with these facilities in mind. A mixed sound track is provided (synchronized with all final editorial changes) consisting of all music and effects used in the final master dubbed track, minus original language dialogue. As we have seen, a separate working dialogue track is provided as early as possible so that translations and foreign language post-synchronizing can take place without delay.

Music effects (M and E) track

If the "A", "B", "C",—(dialogue, music, effects)—three track preliminary dub was made during the main dubbing operation, each group being channelled separately before the final single track

260

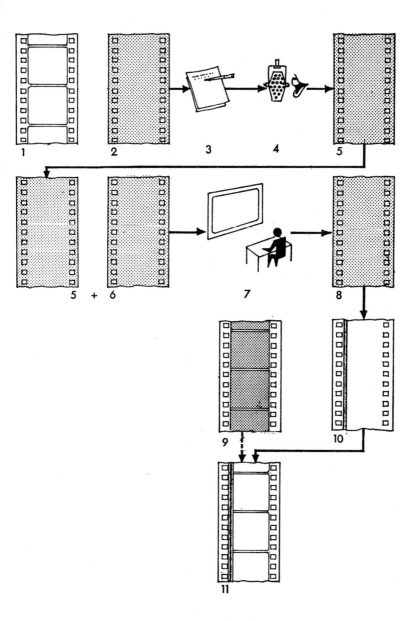

Foreign versions. (1) Picture dupe work print and (2) working dialogue track sent to foreign dubbing centre for dialogue translation (3). (4) Foreign dialogue post-synchronizing to produce (5), foreign synchronized dialogue track. Foreign dialogue track combined with M & E track (6) in foreign dubbing theatre (7). This produces foreign master dubbed sound track on magnetic film (8) which is then transferred to the photographic sound negative (10). (9) Duplicate picture negative combined with (10) photographic foreign sound negative to produce foreign combined print, (11).

mix was made, the preparation of a mixed music/effects track becomes a very straightforward operation. Dialogue on the A/B/C track is excluded and the balance of music/effects remains exactly the same as in the original dubbed track. This foreign version "M and E" track will, of course, have to be augmented as it is being prepared. Those effects which were not salvable from beneath the original language dialogue were specially prepared by the sound effects editor during the effects post-synchronizing session. These tracks have been separately built, ready to be added in during the mixing of the music and effects. Any sound effects "sweeteners", incorporated into the single track dub after the three-track A/B/C was made, should also be included in the foreign version M and E track.

This track, together with the newly post-synchronized foreign dialogue track, will very simply provide the complete new sound negative required for foreign release printing.

Often, several weeks separate the original sound dubbing from foreign version preparation. The M and E track is rarely prepared for shipment until an answer print has been approved on the original version and release printing is about to begin. The sound editor may well have finished his assignment by this time and careful notes should be made at the time of the original sound dub to ensure that all additional foreign effects and augmented sounds are incorporated.

Multi channel foreign versions

The M and E track, as discussed above, is of course a mono track but if multiple channel foreign versions are required then further sound operations are necessary. Suppose, for example, that 70 mm prints with six-track sound, and 35 mm prints with both four-track and mono sound are required for foreign release. The M/E mix must be repeated so that both a six-channel and 4-channel printing master is made, in addition to the monophonic. These, too, must include all added and augmented sound effects.

Six-track problems

Often when 70 mm release prints are involved, all the foreign version release has to be done in the "home" studio, as it calls for specialized equipment. Not only is the printing operation specialized, but both striping and transcribing the six-track sound requires equipment which is not widely available. In this case picture work print and dialogue guide track are shipped to the foreign centres concerned. Translation and post-synchronizing of dialogue takes place and a synchronized foreign dialogue track is returned to the home studio from each centre. A new foreign six-track printing master is made, incorporating this dialogue track with six-track music and effects, panning the dialogue as required for the large screen. The prints and transfer operation are done from the home studio rather than at foreign centres.

With several foreign languages involved, this operation will fully occupy a six-channel dubbing theatre and transfer system for a considerable time. Even though the transfer operation is a matter of routine once the printing master has been made, each print has to be checked through the six-channel theatre system to ensure that the striping and hardening of magnetic oxide has been done correctly and that sound reproduction is in no way distorted.

Dialogue and cutting continuities

These reports are also part of foreign version requirements. They provide a measured and detailed breakdown of the action and dialogue in each cut, reel by reel, and are used to assist foreign translations and local censor requirements.

Should editorial changes be made after they have been prepared, or additional dialogue included in the final original language dubbed sound, replacement continuity pages must be prepared to bring the information up to date.

Title backgrounds

Where main and end, or any other titles, are to be reproduced in a foreign language, any pictorial backgrounds used in the original version must be duplicated so that translation titles can be similarly overlaid.

Known as "textless backgrounds", fine grain duplicating positives have to be made and shipped to foreign centres so that they can overlay their own titles and produce a composite negative for release printing.

Trailers

The production of a trailer is rather like a scaled down film-making operation. Scripts are submitted and approved, a work print is prepared and sound tracks are built so that a dubbed track can be made. The picture negative is cut matching the trailer work print, so that quantity release printing can take place in conjunction with a final sound negative. It is obvious, however, that original picture negative required in the main production must not be cut for trailer use.

Making trailers is a specialist operation—technicians involved are experienced in the reduction and condensation of stories so that an exciting impression of a 2-hr. film can be shown on the screen as a 2-min. sequence. Editors are experts in planning optical tricks and are always searching for an unusual visual effect so that the screen will explode with action when necessary. Many transitions are made, using brief extracts of film. Sound preparation, too, is a specialist part of trailer making. Many sound tracks are used to create an overall impression in a brief space of time, short sections of music being cut and mixed in expert manner.

Picture material can be provided for trailer work print cutting by duping the main production work print, sequences then being already basically assembled for the trailer editor. He will, of course, have to reshape scenes and ruthlessly cut them to fit in with the limited screen time at his disposal.

Working sound tracks can also be provided in the form of a transfer from the editor's sound work print to enable the trailer editor to start an assembly. Eventually he will need a selection of sound effects, music sections, and post-synchronized dialogue where this is involved. But, meanwhile, he prepares a basic working print planning the many visual effects to be used. This is screened for the production company to approve the basic idea. Preparation can then begin for producing a picture negative and a sound track.

Trailer fine grain requirements

After approval, the trailer work print is sent to the production film cutting room so that scenes to be used can be identified, cut by cut, and duplicating fine grain positives ordered from the original negative held at the laboratory. The fine grain prints are assembled to match the trailer work print, allowing extra footage, as necessary, for overlapped dissolves, wipes, or whatever pictorial tricks have been planned. Titles to appear within the content of the trailer are photographed and separately assembled as they are to be overlaid on pictorial scenes. The whole is then amalgamated in one dupe negative, including all visual effects and titles. Making this dupe negative is, naturally, an optical printing operation. It is rather like producing a pictorial montage.

It is an unfortunate fact that trailer work is often one of the forgotten requirements and by the time it has been scripted and approved in work print form, the main production schedule is well advanced. Often, original negative cutting has to take place before trailer fine grain prints can be ordered. In this case there is no alternative but to make fine grain sections for trailer use from reels of production cut negative. This is an operation which, through risk of handling damage, should be avoided wherever possible. It would be safer, although more expensive, to over-order trailer fine grain requirements before the picture negative is cut, even though the final shape of the trailer work print has not yet been settled.

Foreign trailers

Foreign trailer requirements are basically the same as those for the complete production—picture printing facilities which can incorporate foreign language titles, plus a mixed music and effects sound track. All are normally dealt with by trailer department editors, carried out as a separate operation from production editing.

Censorship

Certain censorship requirements are fairly obvious, with basic codes laid down in Britain and the USA as a guide to what is acceptable for public screening. There is however no hard and fast rule and every problem must be viewed and judged in relation to the film as a whole. It is impossible to make different versions for every country. In any case, by the time some of the cuts are known, release printing in bulk has often been completed and there is little choice except to make elimination cuts in combined prints regardless of what happens to the married sound track.

Scripts of delicate subjects are often submitted to censor authorities in advance of filming in order to avoid the more obvious problems or, at least, to obtain guidance as to the direction and editing of a questionable scene. As a result, the director may shoot additional "cover" on such a scene, protecting the possibility of censorship and providing a stand-by alternative.

It is impossible to anticipate every requirement and there are times when censor problems occur in scenes where no such difficulty seemed possible. At some stage, however, the complete picture usually has to be submitted to the appropriate body for screening and approval.

Submitting print for censorship

The problem of censorship screening presents, in many ways, the same difficulty as that which faces the producer at the time of a preview—whether to submit a work print and separate sound track, whether to cut negative and produce a combined answer print. If scenes are known to be doubtful and no additional cover has been provided by the director, it may be thought wise to submit the work print. It is usually a requirement of censorship bodies that the work print be complete with all titles and that a final dubbed sound track accompany it. This is perhaps understandable since sound effects, particularly in scenes of violence, can be as unacceptable as pictorial action.

Censor cuts prior to neg cut

Any agreed changes, in these circumstances, are fairly simple. Picture work print and component sound tracks are recut, a new dubbed sound track is made to cover the alteration, and that is the end of the problem.

If, however, censor cuts are required in a domestic production, but the uncensored version is to be kept for foreign distribution, then two separate versions are needed and a slightly different procedure is called for. Let us suppose that foreign release printing is to be done from a duplicate negative plus a second original sound track negative—it does not really matter if multiple channels are involved because the same principle will apply. The original sequence which is affected must be duplicated before any picture negative cutting and, first, a fine grain duplicating positive is made on all scenes involved in recutting. A dupe negative is then made and, from this, rush prints are provided for cutting purposes.

When received in the cutting room, the rush prints are assembled as a duplicate cut sequence, matching the work print in the film synchronizer. Visual matching of action is necessary since the new prints will carry dupe key numbers. The new work print section is sent to the laboratory so that the dupe negative from which it was made can be cut to match, thus providing a negative section of the original uncensored scene.

The original uncensored work print reel is now used to make a master dubbed sound track of the original version so that a photographic sound negative is available. Censor cuts are then made in the picture and in affected sound components and another master dubbed sound track made to conform with the censored version. The work print picture can then be sent to the laboratory in its censored form so that the negative can be cut for domestic release printing.

The entire cut negative is eventually duplicated to provide foreign printing facilities and the reel which was affected by censor cuts can now be restored to the uncensored version by inserting the small dupe section specially prepared. The dupe positive section is cut into the work print reel and sent to the laboratory as a cutting guide. Two versions are now available. The reel of *original* cut negative conforms to censor requirements and has a matching sound track. The reel of *duplicate* negative incorporates a specially made section which restores the sequence concerned to an uncensored version. It too has its synchronous sound track.

Censor changes after neg cut

When censor cuts are called for *after* negative cutting, and yet two versions are still required, a different method of preserving two versions may be needed. It may be possible to dupe the cut negative in its present form, the dupe being kept as the uncensored version, then make the censor cuts in the original negative to comply with required changes.

If this cannot be done because of the nature of the required change, it may be necessary to make up a small replacement section from unused takes. Picture and track negatives are then prepared for a separate combined printing operation, so that censor requirements can be taken care of by section replacement in combined prints.

Each situation is dealt with in the best way it can, bearing in mind that it is better to leave the original cut negative intact, wherever possible, and use a section of dupe negative to make any censorship changes.

The unexpected censorship problem is unavoidable, but whenever there can be any anticipation it is obviously far better to be ready with properly organized alternatives rather than have to resort to last minute re-cutting.

Film storage

By the time the editorial staff have completed their work there is a large quantity of working film in the cutting room. Similar quantities are in the sound department, apart from unused takes and negative trims held at the laboratory.

All such film must be stored for minimum periods as directed by the production company and kept in groups until disposal instructions are eventually issued. Some of the working film is soon destroyed, other film—sound masters and picture protective masters are kept for an indefinite period.

Film suitable for library

The first consideration should be the preservation of any picture negative, or sound recordings, which may be of future use in the stock film library. Several of the sound effects, at least, specially recorded for the film, may be difficult to repeat and well worth preserving for future use, even though they may not have been used in the final dubbed track. Selected effects can be transferred on to magnetic film, documented with all available detail, and filed in the film library for use in future productions.

Suitable uncut picture negative should also be preserved. Establishing shots made on location, for example, may be expensive pieces of film and there will almost invariably be more than one take, or more than one angle but only one used in the cut version. Background films used for rear projection or for travelling matte shots are generally photographed for a specific purpose but are usually well worth preserving. The laboratory can be asked to separate such negative which they are still holding and this, together with the rush print which is still in the cutting room, can be filed in the picture stock library—again, documented for future use.

Types of material to be stored

All remaining material can now be gathered and stored in film vaults until disposal instructions are given. The following film groups are usually involved:

1. The editor's picture work print.
2. All the unused positive rush prints, picture and sound and all the trims of used material.
3. All component sound tracks which were built for the final sound dubbing operation—dialogue, effects and music tracks, together with dubbing charts.
4. The master magnetic final dubbed track; pre-mixes and three-track magnetic mixes made to produce the single track dub.

5. The master magnetic foreign version music and effects mix.
6. A magnetic transfer of the entire music scored and recorded for the picture, whether or not used in the final version.
7. Original master recordings made at the time of shooting.
8. All picture negative, trims and unused slates. Protective masters of the final edited version.
9. Cutting room records and documents.

Footage returns

Final editorial tasks include preparing information required by the accounts department in order to meet existing regulations and contracts.

If any film, picture or sound, used in the final version was supplied from a stock library source, exact footages have to be given to the accounts department so that contracts can be met and appropriate payment made to the library concerned. Normally, very little picture stock footage is used in a major production but sound effects are almost invariably used, sometimes in large quantities. The sound editor in charge of effects on the production must prepare this information before his assignment finishes.

Music cue sheet

Music used in the film must also be accurately documented whether it has been specially written for the film as an original score, or whether a re-recording has been made of some traditional or copyright work. Details may vary from country to country but the following are usually basic requirements:

1. Title of production. Name of composer, arranger, and where the recordings were made.
2. Copyright details, where these apply.
3. Duration of each music section used in the final version, reel by reel.
4. Whether the recording made on each music section was entirely or partially used, and whether it was visual or non-visual use (i.e. featured or background music).

Final footages

Individual requirements of accounts departments vary but they often have to make returns which give details of the use of foreign labour in a film and the amount of material used when photographing on foreign locations. If this became necessary, the film editor provides a suitable breakdown of the final screen footage, sub-dividing the amount of film made in various circumstances as required by prevailing conditions. A sample would be:

Total footage used in the final version	10,350
Studio interior footage	7,400
Studio exterior footage	1,200
Footage made on domestic locations	850
Footage made on foreign locations	625
Footage obtained from stock library source	25
Titles footage, and where manufactured	250

These figures must be quite accurate, of course, and are prepared from a physical measurement of the final film.

The responsibility for preparing all these documents and returns rest with the editorial department of a large studio organization rather than with the individual film editor.

Conclusion

It is a remarkable fact that, to some of the other departments concerned in film making, an air of mystery seems to surround activity in a film cutting room.

The shooting unit at work on the studio stage, or perhaps thousands of miles away on location is a compact and efficient team which, of course, they have to be. Although very much involved, the editorial crew often seem to be a team which operates apart from the main activity, wherever the shooting unit may be. Editing crews are often unaware of the difficulties and problems which have to be overcome during the shooting activity. This does seem a pity, since all the efforts made by everyone are channelled, day by day, into the small room where the daily rushes are gradually built into the final picture.

Camera assistants, art directors, junior assistant directors, accountants—even producers and directors!—often express a wish to spend a little time in the film cutting room to see what goes on. Directors who have come from the school of the cutting room know that this is unlikely to provide any answer. It is really impossible to spend a *little* time in the cutting room and hope to "see what goes on". One has to spend a *long* time there and, even then, conscious learning will not be obvious amidst the day to day involvement with sometimes dull routines. As with most specialist tasks, the day rarely passes without facing some problem which has never been met before and the best solutions can only be based on experience.

The happiest situation would be for everyone to be reasonably familiar with all the other tasks and problems and this perhaps is possible, to a certain extent, in the documentary field or in feature film making in such countries as the Scandinavian ones where the operation doesn't seem so departmentalized. Even so, it is a rare person indeed who becomes expert in several specialist fields, regardless of time and opportunity.

The techniques used by the film editor when selecting or rejecting sections of film as he makes his assemblies are based on good routines but they are his own, and very individual. No two editors, given the same film, will produce the same result—just as directors and cameramen make their own personal contribution, using set, artist, and camera with a very individual style. As with director and cameraman, the film editor must be completely free to concentrate on his sometimes exacting task knowing that his own small team are operating very necessary routines in a well-organized and efficient way, and ready to deal with whatever quantity of film may be involved.

Editorial staff must always be prepared, particularly when a major film production is involved, for the mass of film which gradually, but with deceptive speed, descends on the cutting room. Those routine log books and records in which daily information is recorded become so important, so quickly, it would be quite impossible to maintain very much order without them. Unless all the information is recorded with care, film filed with intelligence, and each operation performed methodically, chaos will result.

Cutting room assistants must realize the importance of some apparently dull routines; why it is important to record key numbers and roll numbers; why they have to put additional numbers on rush prints; and why each small piece of positive film has to be filed so that it can be found immediately.

Some time ago, on a visit to Norway, it was my privilege to attend a seminar held at the Norwegian Film Institute in Oslo. The main feature was the editing of film and in one of the events, several sets of reprints of a recently photographed sequence were provided and students divided themselves into groups to make their assemblies in whichever way they thought fit. As a matter of interest, the sequence was part of a small feature film, at present in the editing

271

stage, and the director of the film was a member of one of the groups. The assembled results were incredibly different, and the film director, who obviously had some preconceived ideas about the ideal assembly, was probably more surprised than anyone at the screenings. It really was a great lesson to us all, and showed how easily comedy can be inadvertently turned into drama, and vice versa.

Given a few pieces of suitable film almost any inexperienced person will be able to assemble a good pictorial sequence in a very short time. This is just a tiny jigsaw puzzle—the bigger ones have to be built day by day into an ever changing pattern using an ever multiplying number of pieces, only a few of which will be finally used.

The wonderful thing for those who are involved in film editing, day after day, year after year, is its complete lack of mystery, its utter satisfaction as the puzzle begins to take shape and, above all, its never ending excitement.

GLOSSARY

A   **ACADEMY LEADER.** The standard projection leader used at the head of each reel, action and sound, negative and positive. Is marked with picture and sound *Start Frames* and, therefore, can be used in either double-headed or combined print projection. The picture start mark is 12 ft. from the first frame of picture and there are numbers at each footage from 11 to 3 ft. before the picture starts. These numbers enable projectionists to thread up machines making allowance for any difference in their run-up speed.

ACTION. When editing separate picture and sound films the picture reel is often referred to as the "action" reel.

AMBIENT SOUND. That sound which is spread through the auditorium by means of surround speakers and multiple channel release prints.

ANAMORPHIC LENS. Used for CinemaScope photography and projection and causes a deliberate horizontal distortion of the pictorial image. This compression enables a much wider pictorial angle to be "squeezed" on to normal width film. The special projection lens spreads the image so that it is free from distortion.

ANGLE. Strictly speaking, the relationship between the camera and the action, e.g. straight angle, three-quarter angle, close angle, wide angle, etc. The term, "cut to another angle", used in the cutting room, simply means to cut to the same action contained in a different "size" shot.

ANSWER PRINT. The first combined picture and sound print, with picture correctly graded for density and colour and sound correctly synchronized— the first *acceptable* print although several may have been made before the standard was acceptable.

APERTURE. In the camera, the opening in the aperture plate at which point the film is held static as the exposure is made. Full aperture plates allow the film to be framed right to the film perforations at each side. With the academy aperture, the film is masked off slightly on one side so that the pictorial composition allows for the eventual addition of the married sound track. The projection aperture is the opening at which point the film is held static and the frame is projected on to the viewing screen.

ASSEMBLY. The initial piecing together of film in its first, or "rough-cut" form by the editor. It is done with extreme care and the term "rough-cut" is not an indication that the work is done in a haphazard manner.

B   **BALANCE.** One of the aims of final sound mixing of all the various component sound tracks. To correctly balance the volume relationship between dialogue, music and sound effects

BLOOP. A term derived from the noise made in the reproduction of a photographic sound track when an untreated splice passes the sound reproducing head, the noise being caused by the overlapped lines of the join. "Blooping" the join, and thus removing the unwanted noise requires an opaque triangle, or diamond-shaped area, to be painted over the splice lines in a positive print, resulting in a fast fade-in, fade-out effect in sound reproduction. Negative joins have to be punched to produce a similar shape so that the positive print has an opaque triangle or diamond in the sound track area where the splice occurs.

BLUE BACKING SHOT. The foreground component of a travelling matte shot, photographed against a blue background. It is eventually "married" to a photographic background of suitable angle and action, the final shot being known as the composite.

B.P. PLATE. The background film used in rear projection techniques. Sometimes called a back projection "key", or transparency.

273

BUTT SPLICER. Splicing machine which makes a join in two pieces of film without the need to overlap them. The pieces are "butted" together and covered with transparent tape. The method is suitable only for positive splices in a work print.

C   **CELL SIDE.** The reverse side of the film to that which carries the emulsion—be it photographic or magnetic film. Generally it has a more shiny appearance than the emulsion side and is much harder. An abbreviation of cellulose.

CHANGEOVER. The act of changing from one projection machine to another so that reel to reel projection of a film is apparently continuous.

CLAPPER BOARD. A hinged slate board used at the head of each take of each scene. If the shot is with synchronous sound, the hinged clapper produces a visual and audible synchronizing mark on picture and sound films. If the shot is silent, the hinged part of the slate board is kept open as a visual indication that no sound was recorded. It also is chalked with information for the editorial department, e.g. scene and take number, date, interior or exterior, day or night effect. Special instructions for trick work are often written on the back of the slate for laboratory and editorial guidance, e.g. focal length of lens, angle, and camera height. If omitted for some reason from the front of a shot it is photographed at the end, while the cameras are still running at correct speed, but it is then held upside-down as an obvious indication.

CLICK TRACK. A sound track made by the editorial dept., which when reproduced provides a rhythmic "click", or "beat", to guide the conductor during music recording sessions.

CODE NUMBER. The numbers printed on to the editor's working film during production. They not only identify the scene and take number but also provide a synchronizing reference between separate sound and picture for the full length of each take. Hand numbering is still carried out but, in general, is a machine operation.

"COLD LIGHT" PROJECTION. Projection in which the light source is from a lamp rather than from a carbon arc.

COMBINED PRINT. Also known as a composite, or married print. Both picture image and sound track are carried on one piece of film, capable of synchronous projection.

COMPOSITE. A term used in trick work when two or more pieces of film have to be optically "married" to produce a final negative. Travelling matte shots, painted and split matte shots, all involve the manufacture of composite negatives.

CORE. The plastic centre used for a roll of film which is not mounted on a spool, or reel. Wooden cores are sometimes inserted in release prints but in editorial work the centres are invariably the plastic type on which film is wound at the time of manufacture.

COVERAGE. The amount of film, with varying camera angles which the film director shoots on any sequence. Adequate coverage ensures that the film editor has flexibility in assembling the sequences to the best effect.

CURING. When any base film is coated with ferrous oxide for magnetic recording, be it full-coat or striped track, it has to be cured, or hardened, for a minimum period to ensure that a sound signal may be transcribed without any reproduction distortion.

CUTTING COPY. See WORK PRINT.

CUTTING SYNC. Separate sound and picture synchronism where the appropriate sound is kept level with picture in the film synchronizer, in projection and in the editor's viewing machine. Eventually, in the combined print where picture and sound are contained on one piece of film, the sound track is advanced or retarded in relation to picture for the requirements of the film projector (see printing sync.).

D   **DAILY RUSHES.** Called dailies, and rushes. The first prints made from original negative during the production period, usually processed during the night and received each day in the cutting room. Known as uncut dailies, until the editor starts his assembly.

DEGAUSSING. Also known as wiping, or erasing. The act of demagnetizing magnetic sound film so that all sound signals are removed. The film, or tape, is then available for re-use.

DISC. A record, usually of the direct cut variety when specially made for studio playback use.

DISSOLVE. Also known as a mix. Used both for picture and sound, e.g. a picture dissolve and a sound mix. Pictorially, the optical blending of one photographic scene into another.

DOUBLE-HEADED. Viewing and projection involving separate picture and sound films of a synchronous nature. Picture and sound are threaded on to separate, but interlocked, machines in level synchronization.

DOUBLE SIDED RECORDING. Master recording made on 35 mm full width coated magnetic film. Since the sound track area occupies only a small section of the full width, off-set near one set of perforations, two master recordings can be made on one roll—first along one side, and then back along the other. Only possible when cutting is not contemplated.

DUBBING. The process of mixing and balancing many sound tracks into one final sound track. Is also used to describe the post-synchronizing of original and foreign language dialogue. In some countries, dubbing specifically refers to such post-synchronizing and in this case the final sound track mixing is called re-recording.

DUPE. A duplicate, involving a photographic process. A dupe negative is made from the original negative by means of an intermediate positive of suitable fine grain emulsion. A reversal dupe is made direct from the original negative. A work print, or cutting copy, dupe is made from the editor's original so that sound effects and music preparations can be concurrent, each technician having his own dupe if necessary.

E ECHO. The subtle repetition of a sound caused by a single reflection. Many reflections of such a sound will result in reverberation, and the two terms are often confused.

EMULSION. The coated and sensitized side of all film material, whether it be photographic emulsion or magnetic oxide. Usually the side which is dull when compared with the more shiny reverse side of the film. Blank leader film—also known as coated leader film—is sometimes equally shiny in appearance on both surfaces but the emulsion surface can be readily detected by touching each side with the tongue. The tongue will tend to stick to the emulsion and will also leave a faint mark on the surface, whereas it will slide without sticking to the cellulose side.

F FADE. An optical visual effect manufactured on the optical printing machine. A fade-in causes the pictorial image to appear from blackness; a fade-out causes the image to disappear into blackness.

FILL. There may be many shots made without sound during the production, inserts and silent establishing shots, where the correct type of sound is not available immediately. Eventually, the sound editor corrects this situation when final sound dubbing takes place but, in the meantime, the film editor uses "fill" sound track, either the interior or exterior type, which keeps the sound system "open" so that the sound does not go completely dead at these points, as it would if blank film were used. This unmodulated exterior and interior fill sound track is still sometimes called "unmod", or "buzz" track.

FILM STOCK. Raw film, whether positive or negative, which has not yet been exposed and developed.

FINE CUT. The objective in all film editing. Assemblies of sequences, at first isolated, gradually come together in the form of the "rough-cut". This rough cut, containing all the filmed story, is now refined, re-examined, and recut so that the best possible effect is achieved and at the correct "pace" for the story. The "fine cut", is the basis for all music recordings and final sound dubbing.

FINE GRAIN. Any film stock which is manufactured with a fine grain emulsion, generally used in photographic duplicating processes.

FLOP-OVER. To turn the film over so that the lateral direction of the action is reversed, i.e. right to left becomes left to right. In a work print it is simply a matter of joining the section in the wrong way around as a temporary measure, although there will be slight loss in focus when the shot appears on the screen. If required in the final print a flopped-over dupe negative has to be made.

F.P.S. Frames per second.

275

FRAME. The individual picture, one of many in a length of motion picture film. Divided from its neighbours by a narrow line known as the frame line. Although perforated magnetic sound film has no such lines of division its length is also referred to in feet plus frames for convenience, one frame of magnetic sound being the same length as the accompanying picture frame. The term is also used in projection rooms when the image is incorrectly projected with the frame line visible. The projectionist is then asked to "frame" the picture.

G   GATE. The hinged trap through which film passes and is presented at the viewing or projection aperture.

GRADING. The assessment of the amount of light which has to be passed through negative film in order to produce a correct positive print. Also used in colour grading to assess the filter values required to produce correct colour prints.

GUIDE TRACK. A sound track of unavoidable sub-standard quality, made when it is impossible to avoid unwanted sounds. It is used as a guide in the editor's work print and as a guide to future replacement, perhaps by post-synchronization.

H   HEAD. Transducer used to record or reproduce sound waves. Will convert electrical energy via a microphone into magnetic or mechanical impulses. Will reconvert them into sounds via an amplifying and sound speaker system.

HEAD-SET. Headphones, or earphones, held against the ears by a headband.

HORSE (FILM). Heavily weighted piece of editorial equipment on which rolls of film may be suspended on rods, separated by uprights, and free to revolve. Film on the horse can be fed through the film synchronizer or into the viewing machine.

I   INSERTS. Shots containing very close pictorial information, not involving people, e.g. a clock, or newspaper headline. Often photographed in an insert session at the end of a production.

INTERMITTENT MOVEMENT. The interrupted movement of picture film in camera, projector and viewing machines, as it passes through the gate. For 35 mm the movement advances and stops the film, frame by frame 24 times a second.

INTER-POSITIVE. A colour fine grain positive print used in the intermediate stage when making a colour duplicate negative.

INTER-NEGATIVE. A colour dupe negative made from an inter-positive.

J   JUMP CUT. A cut which breaks continuity by the removal of a section of film within the same camera angle. Unintentional jump cuts are, of course, to be avoided but they are often used deliberately to remove surplus footage, e.g. the removal of a long camera pan, using only the front and end of the shot. Perhaps the most obvious example occurs when excess footage is removed and a jump cut is made to an explosion, giving the impression that people who had been seen in the earlier part of the shot were blown up.

K   KEY NUMBER. The number which is printed along the outer edge of negative film stock at the manufacturing stage. They are printed at 1-ft. intervals with an advance of one unit per foot, photographically transferred to the positive print and appear on the outer left edge of the print when the image is held upright and emulsion uppermost. If the numbers appear on the right outer edge they diminish by one unit per foot since the unexposed film negative had been rewound before camera loading. Sometimes known as edge numbers.

L   LEADER. See ACADEMY LEADER. Also manufactured as white coated leader, used by editing staff when making projection leaders for daily rushes and assembled sequences. Used as blank spacing to maintain synchronism between picture and separate intermittent sound effects tracks. When used at the front and end of a reel they are known as head and tail leaders.

LEVEL SYNC. The relationship between separate picture and sound track in all editorial operations. Eventually, in combined printing, the sound track is positioned on the picture film, advanced or retarded in synchronized relationship according to the reproducing system to be used. This is called printing sync.

LIP SYNC. The correct synchronism between picture and sound should result in perfect matching of lip movement to spoken sound in a dialogue scene. One of the important aims in the post-synchronizing of dialogue scenes.

LOCATION. Any area used for photography and sound recording away from the main studio base. If no studio is to be used the production will be referred to as "all location".

LOOP. A length of film joined at its ends to form a continuous band of film. Picture and guide sound loops are made to assist the artist when post-synchronizing dialogue scenes and are known as "work loops". Sound loops, using noises of a continuous nature, i.e. wind, sea, surf, are often made up and used at sound mixing sessions to augment the other synchronized tracks.

LOOPING. See POST-SYNCHRONIZING.

M M AND E TRACK. A mixed single sound track containing all music and sound effects for each reel of a production, minus all original language dialogue. Languages which are foreign to the original dialogue will, of course, be normally included in the M and E track, e.g. isolated lines of German dialogue in an otherwise English language picture.

MAGAZINE. Film magazine which is loaded in the darkroom with unexposed negative film prior to being attached to the camera. A short length emerges between the feed and take-up sections for camera threading. When the film in the magazine has been exposed, it is torn across at this point ready for unloading in the darkroom. Also used for photographic sound recording negative film.

MAGNETIC SOUND. Sound recorded on to a layer of ferrous oxide, either on tape or perforated film. Such recordings can be degaussed, or wiped, and the recording stock used again.

MAG/OPTICAL. The dual sound tracks on some types of release print, capable of being reproduced by magnetic or photographic (optical) sound reproducing systems. Usually to be found on 35 mm CinemaScope release prints which have both four-track magnetic sound and a single optical sound track.

MASTER. The term is used for both picture and sound. In picture use the expression usually refers to a fine grain duplicating positive, or an inter-positive, for visual effects optical work. Also, such a master can be prepared as the means of duplicating the entire film when a production is finished, in this case known as the protective master. Sound masters are all original recordings, right through the production and are almost invariably of the magnetic type, the final master dubbed track being the ultimate goal.

MASTER SCENE. The key angle in any scene and usually the lengthiest. It sets up the geography of the action. Rarely meant to be used in entirety, closer angles being made of the same action for inter-cutting within the scene.

MATRIX. One of three matrices used in the dye-transfer printing process. It is basically a photographic mould which transfers the appropriate colour dye to a blank film.

MATTE. A silhouette, or an opaque area. It is either a film matte, where each frame of a running length of film is opaque in the required area, or a physical matte where a piece of thin card, with correct cut-out shape, is used in front of the camera lens or the optical printer lens.

MIX. See DISSOLVE.

MONAURAL SOUND. Strictly meaning sounds heard with one ear, the term is still commonly used with reference to sounds heard from a single channel, or monophonic sound. Many microphones may be used in making such recordings, several speakers to give reproduction, but the sound is mono if there is only one transmission channel.

MONTAGE. From the French word meaning "mounting", "assembling" and, therefore, refers to all forms of creative film editing. Specifically used with reference to a film sequence in which many shots are used, constantly blending and dissolving, one to the other. Such sequences, for example, can suggest the passing of a period of time, or may be for dramatic impact as in the case of nightmare sequences.

MOVIOLA. The trade name of the editorial viewing machine made by the North Hollywood firm who specialize in this equipment. The machine handles separate picture and sound.

MULTI-CHANNEL SOUND. Sound recordings and reproductions where more than one single sound channel is used. Two, three, four and six-track systems are in use in film production, but in release prints take the form of four-track and six-track recordings for reproduction in multi-speaker systems. Separation of such sound is possible at the screen area and selected sounds can be transmitted to give the effect of surrounding the audience.

MUSIC CUE. Each separate section of music recorded for a film. Choosing the areas to be treated with music is known as cueing the picture.

MUTE. Picture which has been photographed without a synchronous sound track. The word is normally included on the slate board at such times and the clapper (if any) left open.

N   NEGATIVE. Original film stock which is exposed in the camera, be it picture or sound. Image tones are reversed—black becomes white and vice versa.

N/S. Used when referring to a shot which has not been slated with a board. "No Slate".

O   ONE LINE CONTINUITY. A typewritten, reel by reel breakdown of the sequence of events, with a very brief description of "key" action.

OPTICAL. The term involves both picture and sound. A visual effect, such as a dissolve or fade, is also commonly called an optical. Sound recorded on to photographic film is optical sound track.

P   PART TITLE. Titles inserted into negative reel leaders to indicate the title of the production and the "part", or reel number.

PERFORATION. One of a series of punched holes in the film which engage with driving sprockets. Minute adjustments in sync are indicated by so many perforations.

PHOTOGRAPHIC SOUND. Sound recorded and reproduced by an optical process, involving negative and positive film. The sound track is in the form of a narrow band and is visible in a fluctuating pattern.

PICK-UP SHOT. An additional shot made as an afterthought to improve a sequence.

PLATE. A flat disc used on a rewind to support un-spooled film as it is being wound into a roll. Has a "keyed" centre on which a plastic core can be slid.

PLAYBACK. The reproduction of a sound recording. Specifically referred to when artists are miming to a pre-recorded sound track, known as the playback track.

POSITIVE. Print made from a negative so that the image tones are now correct.

POST-SYNCHRONIZING. Also known as looping since it is the loop method of recording new and "clean" sound in studio conditions, maintaining perfect synchronism with picture.

PRE-MIX. An intermediate sound mix made during the sound dubbing operation to reduce the number of separate sound reels to a manageable quantity. Also called a pre-dub.

PREVIEW. Common in America where it is known as the "sneak". The try out of a film, possibly before it is entirely completed, before a public viewing audience.

PRINTING SYNC. As opposed to cutting sync, the advance or retard of the sound track when making a combined print with picture and sound on the same film.

R   RAW STOCK. See FILM STOCK.

RECORDER. Machine by which sound is recorded on to tape or film.

REGISTER. The act of positioning perforated film on to correctly fitting register pins. In the cutting room such pins are to be found on splicing machines to ensure that positive film is cut correctly and evenly along the picture frame line.

REEL. A complete unit of film, edited and carrying changeover cues enabling continuous projection to take place. Unedited film is identified in rolls. Also refers to the metal container on which film is wound, particularly in America, although the term "spool" is generally used in Europe.

RELEASE PRINT. The projection print, or show copy, of a completed film.

REPRINT. A further print from a scene which has already been printed.

RE-RECORDER. A sound reproducing machine. The term is generally used in sound dubbing theatres where there are many such machines to carry and reproduce the many sound tracks which are to be mixed.

RETAKE. To remake a shot, usually because of damage to the original negative or dissatisfaction with the first attempt.

REVERBERATION. The sum of many reflections of a sound as opposed to a single echo.

ROCK AND ROLL. The term used to describe film projection capable of forward and reverse operation. Both viewing theatres and sound dubbing theatres can be fitted with forward and reverse operation facilities for interlocked separate picture and sound.

RUN-UP. The length of film required, or the time taken, from a start mark to the operative picture frame in film projection. Also used in the same sense in sound film recording.

S   SECOND START. Also called a "run-down start". Any start mark, other than the standard leader start mark, made within a reel of film.

SET-UP. The position of the picture camera in relation to the film set and the angle of view. There are, therefore, static set-ups and moving set-ups.

SHUTTER. A rotating fan-shaped blade which prevents light from reaching the film while it is in motion from one frame to the next at the aperture.

SILENT TURNOVER. The expression used in any synchronizing system for separate picture and sound shooting which produces synchronizing start marks without the use of a clapper.

SKIP-FRAME. Also called drop-frame. The printing of every other picture frame to double the speed of the action.

SLATE. The slate, or clapper board, photographed on every take. The shot itself, once in print form in the cutting room is often referred to as a slate.

SOUND EFFECTS. Usually written as FX. All sounds other than dialogue and music.

SPACING. Any film which is used to "space out" sound tracks within a reel to maintain synchronism with picture. White-coated leader film is often referred to simply as spacing.

SPOOL. See REEL.

SPROCKET. The toothed driving mechanism on which perforated film is carried and drawn forward. Often used in the cutting room when, in fact, the reference is to perforations. For example, the removal of two "sprockets" of sound track to improve synchronism in a dialogue post-synchronized shot.

START MARK. The area of one frame marked with a cross as a framing and threading instruction to the projectionist. Synchronous start marks involve picture and one or more synchronized sound tracks.

STEADY TEST. A laboratory film test by which the steadiness of a running length of film is proved, or otherwise. Usually in the form of a reprint with an overlaid static grid, it will show in projection whether any movement of camera or faulty film perforating cause the film to be unsuitable for trick work.

STOCK SHOT. A film library shot, not specifically made for the current production. A duplicate is provided and fees charged for its use vary according to the nature of the shot.

STREAMER. A cue line drawn over a length of picture, ending on an operative picture frame. In projection it will appear to travel from one edge of the screen to the other. Used frequently in post-synchronizing, music recording to picture, and sound dubbing.

STRIPING. The act of coating narrow bands of magnetic recording film. Single strip or multiple stripe.

SYNCHRONIZER. Apparatus used in the film cutting room to enable two or more lengths of film to be wound through while constantly maintaining synchronized relationship. Two drum version for synchronizing daily rushes and matching picture reprints in a work print; four-drum version for editing and building synchronized sound tracks. Used also in a specially made version for matching positive and negative when negative cutting.

SYNC EFFECTS. All sound effects recorded at the time of original synchronized photography, clear of dialogue.

SYNC PLOP. Sometimes called the sync pip. Short sound included in sound leader film, synchronized with a visible mark on the picture leader. Usually of one frame in length, it is a check on the correct threading of picture and sound tracks at the time of sound dubbing and a final check of synchronism when the final mixed track is received in the cutting room.

SYNCHRONOUS SOUND. A sound recording made at the same time as picture is photographed, camera and sound recorder interlocked electronically.

T   TAKE. The single recording of a shot, whether picture or sound. Takes are numbered progressively, take one, take two, and so on, until the result is satisfactory. The next set-up starts again at take one.

TAPE START MARK. Used on master recordings, a short piece of adhesive tape positioned on the cell side of the film, the area of the start frame marked with a cross. Also used when marking second start marks within a reel of picture and sound, e.g. for sound pre-mixing and music recording sessions, so that it is easily seen by the projectionist.

TAPE SPLICER. See BUTT SPLICER.

T/M. Travelling matte.

TONE. Sound of a constant frequency, used often in checking sound equipment. Recorded frequency tone of 1,000 cycles per sec. is used in the cutting room for making click tracks and sync plops, one frame being used for each mark required.

TRACK. Abbreviation of sound track. Also the term used when the camera is transported forward and backward during a shot.

TRACK BUILDING. The "laying" of sound, reel by reel, so that each section of sound synchronizes with the appropriate picture. This involves dialogue, music and sound effects.

TRACK SEARCHING. Pulling the magnetic sound film back and forth in a reader, or a synchronizer fitted with reproducing sound heads, to locate a particular sound.

TRACK STRIPPING. After approval of the fine cut, the single working sound track is "stripped" of all unwanted and unsatisfactory sounds, dialogue and effects, leaving only the usable dialogue.

TRANSFER. A copy sound track made from a master recording.

TRAVELLING MATTE. See also MATTE. The travelling matte is a film matte which constantly changes in size and position with each succeeding picture frame. The matte follows the movement of action, allowing a composite to be made without an effect of superimposition.

TRIMS. The portions of shots removed during the period of editing.

V   VIRGIN LOOP. A recording loop of magnetic film, synchronized with a picture loop, enabling a sound recording to be made with the facility of instantaneous synchronous playback.

VISUAL EFFECTS. Work involving special optical effects, dissolves, matte shots, and all trick work.

W   WILD SOUND. Sound recorded independently of the picture camera, i.e. non-synchronous sound. Also called a wild track.

WORK LOOP. The picture and sound loops made for post-synchronizing.

WORK PRINT. Also known as the cutting copy. The copy assembled by the film editor, used for editing, music recording and final sound recording.

Z   ZERO FRAME. A reference frame in any shot, part of which is level with a key number. This frame, plus or minus additional frames within the area before another key number occurs, is the means of positively and accurately identifying any individual picture frame, essential in laboratory and optical effects work.

280

INDEX

281